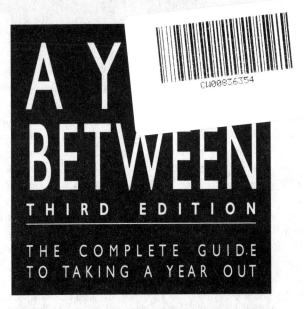

A Y[EAR]
BETWEEN

THIRD EDITION

THE COMPLETE GUIDE
TO TAKING A YEAR OUT

CENTRAL BUREAU
FOR EDUCATIONAL VISITS & EXCHANGES

LONDON   EDINBURGH   BELFAST

Third edition   © Central Bureau for Educational Visits & Exchanges 1997

ISBN 1 898601 13 5

Published by the Central Bureau for Educational Visits & Exchanges
10 Spring Gardens, London SW1A 2BN

Publications Unit
℡ 0171-389 4880
0171-389 4426
books@centralbureau.org.uk

Head of Publications/Editor Thom Sewell
Compiler Lindsey Smith
Researcher Lorraine Gover

Cover illustration: Barton Stabler/Image Bank

Printed and bound in England by Page Bros

This guide is published by the Central Bureau for Educational Visits & Exchanges, the UK national office for the provision of advice and information on all forms of educational visits and exchanges; the development and administration of a wide range of curriculum-related exchange programmes; the linking of educational establishments and local education authorities with counterparts abroad; and the organisation of seminars, workshops and conferences related to professional international experience. Its information and advisory services extend throughout the educational field. Publications cater for the needs of people of all ages seeking information on the various opportunities available for educational contacts and travel abroad. The Central Bureau, incorporating the UK Centre for European Education and Education Partners Overseas, forms part of the British Council. It is funded by the Education Departments of the United Kingdom and is the UK National Agency for many of the European Union education and training programmes. The British Council, registered in England as a charity, number 209131, is the UK's international network for education, culture and development services.

Director Tony Male

10 Spring Gardens
London SW1A 2BN
℡ 0171-389 4004
0171-389 4426
http://www.britcoun.org/cbeve

3 Bruntsfield Crescent
Edinburgh EH10 4HD
℡ 0131-447 8024
0131-452 8569

1 Chlorine Gardens
Belfast BT9 5DJ
℡ (01232) 664418
(01232) 661275

CONTENTS

USING THIS GUIDE

Section I **PRACTICAL OPTIONS**, provides an introduction to those thinking of taking a year between, a personal checklist to evaluate potential, a discussion of the key elements of being a volunteer, plus a section on further resources.

The **INTRODUCTION** covers the pros and cons of a year between and examines the attitudes of all those involved. The personal experiences of students and employers are recounted; further firsthand accounts are given under *Section II* and the individual placement sections.

The personal **CHECKLIST** offers a programmed series of questions to enable all potential participants to evaluate their current assumptions. There is no easy path in coming to a decision as to whether or not to take a year out but this checklist should help a reasoned decision to be more easily arrived at.

Potential volunteers will find vital questions in the **VOLUNTEERING** section: a period of voluntary service requires commitment, it can be emotionally draining and physically exhausting, but the spiritual rewards can be high. To complete this section there are details of organisations who can offer further advice, careers counselling, short courses or other opportunities for those taking a year between. Sources for further reference on paid and voluntary work opportunities, sponsorships, further study and grants, plus details of useful guidebooks for expeditioneers and travellers are also included.

Section II **YEARS OF EXPERIENCE**, is a series of contributions from organisations, giving examples of how they feel their projects benefit both participants and host communities.

The opportunities themselves are detailed under separate sections. An introduction to each section includes comments from participants, after which organisations are listed alphabetically, each entry giving a profile of the organisation and full details on the projects available:

TRAINING/WORK EXPERIENCE
Opportunities to work in industry, administration, tourism and commerce, where participants can gain valuable work experience.

DISCOVERY/LEADERSHIP Exploration, expeditions, adventure programmes and short service commissions in the armed forces offer opportunities for travel and self-development.

CONSERVATION/LAND USE
Opportunities to work in the great outdoors, including agriculture, horticulture, and other work on farms, kibbutzim or moshavim. Opportunities for practical contributions to the environment through conservation projects are also detailed.

TEACHING/INSTRUCTING Teaching English as a foreign language, or acting as a teacher's aide at schools in Britain and abroad.

COMMUNITY & SOCIAL SERVICE
Projects caring for people in need,

such as offering assistance to people with a physical disability, working with the homeless, or helping in a community for those with mental handicaps.

YOUTH WORK/CHILDCARE A range of opportunities to work on projects for children and young adults, some of whom may be disabled or disadvantaged. This section also includes information on au pair work.

CHRISTIAN SERVICE Community, social, evangelical and ecumenical projects based in Britain and abroad. Applicants should have a Christian commitment or at least be thinking seriously about their faith.

STUDY OPTIONS Ideas on short courses and language study, plus opportunities to spend a term or an academic year at a school abroad.

KEY Information on the opportunities in the placement sections has been provided in a set format to aid selection and provide easy comparison:

Name and mail address of the company or placement organisation.

Electronic communications details, including ✆ telephone, ⧙ fax, ✉ e-mail and ✑ World Wide Web site, where applicable. Where no telephone number is given this is at the request of the organisation, where written enquiries are preferred.

Countries/areas Details of where placements may be made. In some cases the destination depends on the projects in operation

in a particular year, or is at the discretion of the organisation.

Profile A general description of the aims and activities of each organisation, together with its status (whether commercial, private, non-profitmaking or charitable) and the main fields of activity.

Opportunities Details of the type of opportunity available, with a general description of what participants will be expected to do. Where possible, details of the annual number of placements made by the organisation are given.

Requirements Age limits for applicants: most organisations cater for school-leavers, but some only accept graduates. Details are also given of the personal qualities, skills, experience and qualifications that participants will require. Any language requirements and nationality restrictions are specified. Where applications from disabled people are considered, this is indicated as follows:

B blind or partially sighted
D deaf or hard of hearing
PH physically handicapped.

Duration Length of the placement, including any minimum and maximum periods. **A Year Between** covers, in general, placements lasting from 3-12 months. Shorter-term opportunities open to those taking a year between are covered by the companion guide **Working Holidays**.

Terms and conditions Details of any cost to participants; hours of work; salary or pocket money provided; any holiday entitlement; type of accommodation; whether travel and insurance costs are covered; and details on fundraising.

Briefing Details of any orientation courses held or any debriefing at the end of placement, plus information on any on-the-job training or supervision, additional training and language courses.

When to apply Applications and requests for information should be made to the organisations direct, and not via the Central Bureau. Early application is always advisable, as owing to the increasing number of students electing to take a year out, many projects may be full to capacity well in advance of the given closing date. When writing to any organisation it is essential to mention **A Year Between** and enclose a stamped addressed envelope or, in the case of an organisation overseas, an addressed envelope and two International Reply Coupons, available from post offices.

Before applying, read carefully all the information given. Pay particular attention to the following:

✓ skills/qualifications/experience needed

✓ length of project/placement

✓ age limits

✓ application deadlines

Note that some organisations will request that their own application forms be completed; others will take applications direct, usually with a minimum outline *cv*. When applying include the following:

✓ your name, address, date of birth, nationality, sex

✓ details of your education to date and future courses, skills, languages, relevant experience

✓ the reason you want to do the project

✓ a passport-size photo, particularly for public contact placements

✓ anything else asked for, eg *cv*

When offered a place on a project, check carefully the offer against your original expectations and if you are going to accept, do so as soon as possible. Even if you have applied to a number of organisations and are awaiting offers, inform recruiters speedily of your decision. If the project is taking place abroad, you will also need to make sure that you have the necessary paperwork, including a valid passport and relevant visas/permits.

Section XI, the final section of this guide, gives practical advice and information on travel and related issues, for example insurance, medical requirements, passports, visas, coping in an emergency. It also contains an index to organisations, a countries index and a report form. Up-to-date reports on organisations offering placements enable us to improve the accuracy and standard of the information in this guide. At the end of your year out we would appreciate the completion and return of the report form to enable us to monitor the work of the organisations, and to enable us to record your experiences.

This guide offers advice, information and details opportunities suitable for those intending to take a year out between school or college and university, whilst still involved in higher education or after graduating and before embarking on a career. The majority of placements listed last 3-12 months.

For those looking for shorter term opportunities in a year out, either because of other commitments, for example to further study, or because the decision to take a year out was made late, possibly not until examination results were known, the Central Bureau's annual guide WORKING HOLIDAYS gives details of over 101,000 seasonal jobs in the UK and 70 countries around the world. Sectors range from archaeology to au pair work, catering to conservation and teaching to tourism.

WORKING HOLIDAYS includes details of both paid and voluntary work suitable for anyone aged 16+ (sometimes younger), with or without experience. Most of the placements listed are for one or two months, although there are options for working holidays lasting from a long weekend to a year. WORKING HOLIDAYS is particularly useful in providing opportunities to acquire some experience before embarking on longer term projects or for those who want to combine a number of jobs to help support travel through several countries.

For those looking for specific opportunities to gain work experience or undertake work placements, rather than generally broaden personal and educational horizons through a year out, WORKPLACE, the complete guide to work experience and work placements, is aimed at pupils and students aged 14 to graduate who are seeking work placements, and teachers or lecturers organising work experience programmes. As well as profiling 120 recruiters offering over 260,000 placements in the UK and abroad, WORKPLACE includes comprehensive practical advice and information, covering issues such as assessment, briefing, funding, health & safety, insurance and resources. Whilst most work experience programmes last an average of two weeks, placements for older students can last anything up to 18 months.

VOLUNTEER WORK is aimed at those seeking voluntary service placements of at least 6 months in the UK and abroad. As well as profiling agencies that recruit volunteers, it offers comprehensive advice and information for those considering volunteering, personal accounts from former volunteers and information resources. Most of the agencies require volunteers with practical skills, professional qualifications or previous experience.

HOME FROM HOME gives details of homestays, exchanges, term stays and home exchanges in 50 countries around the world. A homestay - where you live with a family abroad, usually for a couple of weeks - is an ideal way to improve foreign language skills and get a real taste of the culture of another country.

The Central Bureau also publishes a number of other information guides for those who want to work, study or travel abroad. Further information on the full range is available by sending a stamped addressed envelope to the Publications Unit at the London office (for address see page 2) or ✆ 0171-389 4880, ⊞ 0171-389 4426 or ✉ books@centralbureau.org.uk.

A YEAR BETWEEN

A year between - up to 12 months between school and university, school and work, or higher education and a career - is a rare chance to stand back, assess where your education has brought you so far, and seize the freedom offered to undertake something completely different, possibly on the other side of the world. It gives you the opportunity to develop skills, become more self-reliant and achieve an understanding of your own strengths and weaknesses. But before you make any final decision, it is worth weighing up the pros and cons and asking yourself why you want to take a year between.

Is it simply because you want to see the world? Or do you want to become more mature, responsible, open minded or tolerant? Do you want to earn some money and develop skills before starting academic life? Do you feel that the self-discipline imposed by higher education is something you can't yet cope with? Or are you attempting to delay the moment when you start your working life, concerned you are unprepared?

Discuss your ideas with family and friends, teachers and careers advisers. How will a year out help or hinder your aspirations to higher education or a career? You may want a break from what you see as the conveyor belt of the education system, or from the pressure of exams. But does this mean you will end up having to explain away a gaping hole in your cv to potential employers? The idea of being a year older than your peers when you get into higher education

may appeal, but then again, you may find it more difficult to settle back down to study. Do you wonder if you should grab what may be your last chance to broaden your horizons and experience new cultures, or would you feel more secure getting your education over and done with in one go and embarking upon a career?

There are no wholly right or wrong answers, but as the final decision is down to you, it is vital to be honest with yourself. If you do decide to take time out, the process of examining your reasons and considering the advantages and disadvantages will help you to plan and organise how you intend to fill your year. And when an admissions tutor or future employer asks you about it, you're more likely to have a well thought-out response.

Deferred entry If you intend to go on to higher education after taking a year out you can apply to your chosen institution either before taking your A levels (or equivalent) requesting that the entry be deferred or you can wait and apply during your year out once you know your exam results. To request deferred entry, you simply have to enter a D at 3j on the UCAS application form. Some institutions have a preference for deferred entry; others would rather make unconditional offers based on known exam results. Deferred entry is a sensible idea if you are likely to be on the other side of the world, and therefore unavailable for interview, during your year between. It also means you are able to make your choice of university first and then spend your year out secure in the knowledge that there is a place waiting for you when you return to student life. However, universities have a difficult task allocating hundreds of places conditional on exam results, and because of the numbers involved some faculties can offer only a few deferred places. And once a place has been deferred it may create real problems if you change your mind and decide that, after all, a year out is not for you and you'd rather carry straight on with your studies. It is best to contact the admissions tutor to discuss possibilities; or in some cases the prospectus will provide details on deferred entry.

Universities certainly do not appreciate applicants who are offered a conditional place and then wait until the last minute (usually once they have their results) before asking for their entry to be deferred. They are also wary of applicants who defer for a year then decide not to take up the place. Whilst time to reconsider is obviously of benefit to the applicant, late decisions such as these may deprive other candidates of a place and affect the institution's ability to fill target quotas. The best advice if you opt to take a year out is to state your intentions as soon as possible, and if you do change your mind let the institution know at the earliest opportunity.

After graduating Many students consider taking a break once they have their degree qualification under their belt. You may feel you have earned time to relax after exam pressures and see this point in time as your last opportunity to do something

different before settling down.
Or you may be unsure of your career plans and see a year out as a chance to learn about yourself and the type of work that suits you. However, you should be very wary of going off for a year without having made any plans for what you will do on your return. If you are taking a year out after university, you will be competing against the following year's graduates for jobs when you return, so it is vital that you show that the year was put to good use and that it helped you develop personally, and perhaps professionally, thus giving you the edge over those fresh out of university.

It might be a good idea to finish off your year out with a short course to develop new skills, in which case you should try to arrange it beforehand. Take advantage of employers' visits during your final year to gauge their reactions and opinions about your taking a year out. If you have been offered a position with a company, but you want to take a year out, it may be worth asking the employer if it is possible to delay your start date, although in such a competitive job market this option is uncommon. Or, if you have no fixed career plan, get advice from the careers service to see what type of work interests you, and consider what personal skills and aptitudes you would like to test out in your year between. At this stage it is important to have at least some plans for the future; it could be a big mistake to assume that everything will just fall effortlessly into place once your year out is over.

Attitudes to a year between
Apart from the possible problems of logistics posed by deferred entry,

most universities have no objection to students taking time off before embarking on a course of study, provided it is spent in a worthwhile way. A recent inspectors' report found that 17% of university students fail to complete their courses, and many of the reasons for this stem from faulty expectations, distorted perspectives that a year out can help correct. For courses such as sciences or engineering, a year spent gaining relevant industrial experience is viewed extremely favourably. However, mathematics is often quoted as being a subject requiring continuity of study, and some tutors may view a year's interruption as detrimental. A year between may also be discouraged before long courses such as medicine or architecture. It is best to discuss your plans with the admissions tutor, or at interview.

We asked universities whether students who had taken a year between had problems settling down again to study. Of those who had available information, most stated that they had few or no problems, or that any problems were soon overcome. Things you learn at school don't get forgotten that quickly, but if you're concerned about losing touch, then exercise the grey matter by reading relevant books and periodicals, and do stay in touch with current affairs.

Many institutions agreed that students who had taken a year out before their course showed more maturity and better-defined career aims. Some even went so far as to say they were more likely be better achievers academically. The following quotes are just two examples of the overwhelmingly positive feedback we received.

The consensus in this university is that students who come to us after a year out are more mature, better able to organise their time and better motivated.
Academic Registrar, University of Reading

Most students who return to study after a gap year are extremely committed and well-prepared. In fact, they are some of the very best students.
Noel Morrison, Deputy Registrar (Admissions), South Bank University

As far as employers are concerned, again they are more likely to react positively to a year out if they feel the time has been spent in a relevant and worthwhile way, such as on an industrial placement or working to develop skills and experience.

Many employers are not primarily concerned with degree discipline or at least not for around 40% of jobs advertised. Employers are more interested in other qualities that demonstrate a graduate's employment potential, such as the ability to respond to intellectual and practical challenges, and to communicate orally or on paper.
What Do Graduates Do? 1996
The Association of Graduate Career Advisory Services (AGCAS)

They are perhaps less enthusiastic about a year out taken after higher education; they may have suspicions that you found it difficult to get a job, that you lack drive and ambition, or that you have lost the momentum of your years of study. You must be able to convince them that you have not spent your time drifting or doing nothing, and that your experiences have left you a more mature and capable person. If you can present clear and logical reasons for having taken a year out, and explain how you have benefited from the experience, they will find it easier to view you as a potential employee:

At Ernst & Young we're looking for well-rounded individuals. If you choose to take a year out the aim should be to further your personal development as well as to have fun!
National Recruitment Manager, Ernst & Young, Chartered Accountants

We see any kind of work experience as a plus point in an application, and obviously a year out, if spent constructively, is viewed in a positive light.
Graduate Recruitment Coordinator, Harrods Ltd

Planning and preparation It is most important to plan your year between well ahead of time. Eighteen months may seem rather a long time in advance, but if you start to make plans in the lower sixth, or before the final year of your degree course, you will have a wider range of options open to you and plenty of time to consider them before exams creep up on you. If you leave it late because of indecision or because exam results weren't as expected you may find that many schemes have no places left.

Think about your reasons for taking a year out, and on the basis of these, plan what sort of things you want to do. If you want to see the world consider whether you want to travel independently, work or volunteer overseas, or join an expedition. Will you need to raise money to pay travel costs? You may have to spend some

time trying to earn it or raising sponsorship. Many people follow a period of voluntary service by a stint of paid work; this gives a good mix of experiences, projects and countries, and helps to balance limited finances. Would you rather gain work experience where you can use your A level qualifications or see how a particular type of employment will suit you? Many of the opportunities in the **TRAINING/WORK EXPERIENCE** section are for those with good results in science-based subjects, but there are also placements for students of any subject.

Remember that future employers will want to know how your year was spent, and what you gained from it overall. If you spend a whole year doing nothing in particular or working in a mundane job then potential employers are unlikely to be convinced by your ability to assume the responsibilities and take the initiatives involved in working for them. If you plan things well in advance instead of in a last-minute rush then your year between has a better chance of being worthwhile.

Do it yourself! One thing we would like to stress is the importance of doing things for yourself. It can be very easy to rely on your parents to do all the groundwork for you, especially if you feel you've got other, more pressing commitments. However, one of the main principles behind taking a year between is to become more independent. This is incorporated into the philosophies of many placement agencies, who are looking primarily for applicants who can demonstrate self-reliance and maturity. So it is worth starting now, at the planning stage. If you can't rely on your own capabilities to plan your year between, how will you cope when you are far from home, or in an alien environment, or when crucial decisions have to be made? Of course you should seek advice from parents or teachers, and discuss your ideas with them, but try to ensure that the majority of the initiatives and planning comes from *you*, and that *you're* the one making the final decision - this is all part of the challenge.

When writing to any organisation you should mention where you found out about them (for example, in **A YEAR BETWEEN**). Introduce yourself, explain briefly when you will be available to take up a placement, why you are interested in their opportunities in particular, and in what way you feel you are a suitable candidate. **Enclose a large stamped addressed envelope, especially if you are writing to a voluntary or charitable organisation.** Don't go into too much detail at this initial stage; in all probability they will send you an application form where you can enthuse at length about your qualifications, interests, experience and suitability for the placement. Keep a copy of all your correspondence and application forms, as these will probably be referred to during interviews - or may even get lost in the post. Make sure you apply well within any deadlines; some placements have an element of first come, first served, so the earlier you apply, the better.

Depending on the organisation, candidates are selected firstly from the information given in their application forms, then on the basis of their performance at interview or on a selection weekend. Such weekends usually consist of a series of challenges set to test aspects such as decision-making skills, ability to work in a team, physical stamina, motivation, determination and commitment, and may include items like assault courses, outdoor pursuits and group discussions. Before attending an interview or selection weekend spend some time thinking over your reasons for applying to this particular organisation. Read through any literature they have supplied; consider how your skills, qualifications, experience and personality fit you for a placement and what you hope to gain in the long-term.

If you are selected, you may also be asked to attend further training. These training sessions are invaluable, not just in preparing you for the work you will be doing, but also by allowing you to meet your future colleagues, find out more about the organisation itself, and discuss the project in detail. You owe it to yourself, the organisation and the people with whom you will be working to ensure that you are well-informed before beginning the placement, so do your best to find out as much as you can. Talk to people who have previously worked with the organisation and who can give you information based on personal experience. Read any field, project or expedition reports that are available.

If you are going on a placement abroad, read up about the country. The relevant embassy or tourist office may be able to provide some information, but it is also worth investing in a good guidebook, such as those published by Lonely Planet or in the Rough Guides series. The organisation arranging your placement should be able to provide help and advice on visas, work permits, medical precautions, travel and insurance, but it is down to you to make sure that these aspects are settled well in advance to avoid any last-minute panics. Remember that in some cases medical protection can take the form of a course of injections over several weeks, so allow plenty of time.

Finally, try to prepare yourself mentally for the experience. You will be meeting new people, attempting new tasks, perhaps finding out about new cultures. Expect the unexpected, and keep an open mind.

Fundraising Many organisations arranging placements or expeditions overseas require you not only to pay your return fare, but also to contribute towards administration and organisation costs. This figure may end up in the thousands, so you will need to think of ways to raise funds. Getting a job which will earn you enough money to pay the whole amount would be ideal, but it may take you a while to save up the sum required, so you may still need to organise other kinds of fundraising activities.

If you want to try tapping alternative sources then start by publicising yourself. If you make enough of a splash locally people will have heard of you when it comes to asking them to give their support. Tell your local newspaper all about your plans, where you will be going and the work you will be doing. Make it sound exciting and worthwhile. Keep them informed throughout your fundraising campaign; it will encourage others to contribute when they see you have a target to reach. If you can, offer to send regular bulletins once you've begun your placement. Keep copies of any press articles featuring your project to use during your campaign.

Publicise yourself at school, at university, at church, at your parents' social club or work. The bigger the network, the more likely you are to find someone who can help, if not financially then with advice, further contacts or equipment. Organise sponsored events; the more imaginative they are, the more likely they are to hit the headlines, but don't attempt anything too dangerous or time-consuming! Try harnessing your creative talents to design jewellery, paintings or T shirts; grow houseplants; make cakes; walk dogs; organise fundraising events such as car boot sales or barn dances. Whatever you do, remember to explain the point of the exercise, and tell people what the proceeds are going towards.

Find out if there are any grants available from your local authority or from businesses and trusts. The reference library should have a copy of the *Directory of Grant-Making Trusts*. Published by the Charities Aid Foundation, it lists voluntary grant-making bodies in England and Wales covering all fields of voluntary activities. Also try contacting local companies; they may be interested in the publicity afforded by a goodwill gesture to a local young person.

When writing to organisations such as companies or trusts, remember that a personal letter is likely to get more attention than a photocopied circular. Keep it fairly brief: tell them about your project, ask for their support, and explain how the project is relevant to that particular organisation. For example, will it enhance the company's green or caring image; does it fit in with the aims of the trust?

During the project, try and drop your sponsor a line, telling them how you are getting on and describing your new experiences while they are fresh in your mind. A colourful postcard will not only give them a flavour of the country, but will also brighten up their office!
Two months into her trip to Peru with Quest Overseas, Polly-Anne Scambler wrote to her sponsors; here are some extracts:

Once again thank you very much for your sponsorship, it has been worth every centavo and more. I have spent time on the coast, in Lima city, in the mountains, on Lake Titicaca, and tomorrow I head off into the Amazon jungle.

After a week of acclimatising we began our work in the orphanages. The five I worked in were dramatically different from one another. I spent two weeks at a home run by Christian missionaries, living with 20 children from the jungle whose families had been the victims of terrorism. Although short of funds, the home ensured that there was no lack of attention, personal possessions or fun.

My last two weeks were spent in an orphanage in a shanty town of Lima, where the children had no facilities or fresh air since the street in front was a no-go area. Nevertheless the girls were occupied in pottery, jewellery-

making and motherhood at the age of 16. Again I found the children enchanting and I learnt a lot about them as we kept each other amused conversing in Spanish. Saying goodbye was very difficult and I wish them all the luck in the world.

There is more to come and I am looking forward to our trip down the Apurimac river (sacred to the Incas), followed by further Amazon expeditions from Atalaya to the lower reaches of the Madre de Dios river. More of this in the future.

Everything that has happened to me has given me an understanding and deep respect for Peruvian culture and its people. Shortly after my return to England in May, I hope to deliver to you a copy of a review I shall compile. My personal diary has been maintained and I am also keen to show you some of the photos which capture the essence of this trip and will emphasise just how worthwhile it has all been.

Once you return, it is important to write to your sponsors, thanking them for their support and help with the project. This will show them how valuable their contribution was in enabling you to do something worthwhile during your year out and will hopefully encourage them to sponsor other gap year students in the future. Your letter could include details of the tasks you undertook, the impressions you got of the country and the people you were working with, and how you think you benefited from the experience. You could also offer to write an article for the company magazine, give a presentation or publicise their contribution in the local newspaper - all of which will raise the company's profile either to employees or in the local community.

Raising money can be very hard work, but if you summon all your reserves of imagination and determination your target can be achieved. You can generally count on help and advice from the organisation who will be placing you; they will already have plenty of fundraising experience. Lots of other people have managed to fund themselves - so can you!

Other people's experiences

If you're dithering about making the final decision to take a year between, how to plan it, what to do, when, and where to get the finance, then have a read through the following accounts, collected from young people we contacted in the course of preparing this third edition of **A YEAR BETWEEN**.

Steve Blake went on an expedition with Trekforce Expeditions and says that for him, taking a year out was of tremendous benefit:

I decided to go on an expedition after attending an introduction weekend where we found ourselves building shelters, attending talks on jungle survival, medical hints, tips for travellers to the tropics and slide shows about expeditions to Belize, Indonesia and Kenya. Later we walked cross-country by night and the next morning became thoroughly soaked during a raft race across a small lake.

A talk on fundraising at the weekend helped us plan how to raise our financial contribution and that in itself was an enormous challenge. It felt great to have raised the funds

ourselves and feel that without our contribution the project we were to work on would not have been possible.

With a great feeling of excitement we met up with everyone at Gatwick airport. There were 25 of us including doctors, nurses and members of staff. Amazingly, just one week later we had flown to, and explored, backpackers' land in Jakarta, completed 4 days jungle training, flown out to Kalimantan and caught a boat up river to a proboscis monkey research centre.

Here the real project work started. We were to build a 12m x 10m laboratory, sink an 18m deep well, help the scientists with monkey counts, identify flora adjacent to the monkeys' habitation and, finally, cut paths through the jungle. As we worked away at these tasks other members of the expedition were busy constructing a 65m extension to a swamp walkway. It was the hardest few weeks of my life but tremendous fun and a massive learning experience.

Lera Miles didn't venture as far afield as Steve, but she used the time she had available to test out many different opportunities:

My year out didn't really start until March. Before that I stayed in my home town frantically composing letters to various organisations offering my services in exchange for board and lodging. I made the most of my time by learning to type and doing some voluntary work locally. I had not planned to take a year out at all, but once I had inadvertently entered into one, I was determined to try plenty of things.

INTRODUCTION 20 INTRODUCTION

I spent time as a voluntary assistant warden at a bird sanctuary, helped with the lambing on a friend's hill farm, worked as a childcare assistant at a seaside holiday home, volunteered at the Monkey Sanctuary in Cornwall and on a children's camp in Dumfriesshire.

I returned to Scotland with a friend to finish my year with a youth hostelling trip. Taking a year out has given me some much-needed confidence, some new practical skills (decorating, axing wood, improved bareback riding, tea-making, preparation of monkey food ...), social skills, a good cv, new friends and a sprinkling of self-knowledge. I now know for sure that I'd much rather work with adults or animals than with children. I also know that I'm capable of doing a much wider range of jobs than I'd thought. I've been converted - I would recommend a year out to anyone.

Before starting at Reading University, Tim Smyth spent six months in Israel working as a volunteer for the Church's Ministry Amongst Jewish People:

I was sometimes working nine consecutive days hard labouring, but the work was character-building and strengthened my faith. I was given much opportunity to travel and took it. I have grown immeasurably, both spiritually and mentally. I find it easier to talk to minority races in this country as I know how they feel.
I was in Israel during the Gulf Crisis and was only evacuated after 3 hours' notice, 2 days before the war began. This tested me and my family to the limit and taught me a great deal about God, myself, my family and friends ... imagine being prepared to stay in a country, away from your family, during a war. In Israel this meant preparing a sealed room, collecting supplies, receiving gas masks and feeling what an entire country feels and fears. Then to be suddenly evacuated is a tremendous shock, with all the feelings of betrayal of the Israeli friends you've left behind.

I can honestly say that the 6 months I spent in the Israeli culture weren't enough. I think I learnt so much about the way I am and react that has only gone to help me in the way I study. I am more eager and keen to learn than if I'd come here straight from school, plus the added benefit of being a year older than my counterparts. One problem is that I've forgotten how to do calculus at the moment!

Fiona Hatchell considers that deciding to take a year out was one of the most important decisions she's ever made. Looking back she feels that the year changed her attitudes, expectations and perspectives on life:

I spent 7 weeks working as a volunteer in an outdoor centre, then worked in an office for 4 months to raise some money. From January to April I worked as a physical science and maths teacher at a secondary school in Malawi. Teaching at a school with just one other expatriate taught me volumes about the African way of life and living alone in this different environment taught me much about myself and the peculiarities of our Western life. The remaining four months I spent with BSES Expeditions on an expedition in Svalbard, an archipelago just 700 miles from the North Pole. My year out was entirely self-funded and I consider this as *important as the places and people I visited. Had I not had to work hard to raise the money the experiences would not have been quite as satisfying.*

Henry Morris worked for Shell Research Ltd for 11 months and spent most of his placement working on a feasibility study into the automated inspection of recycled oil drums:

This was meaningful and relevant work to the company, not a spurious exercise, and was valuable experience for someone about to start a degree in engineering and management. I felt that there was an element of luck about student placements. How repetitive or interesting the work was depended on which department the student joined. I had my own project, and to a large extent was my own boss. Other students spent more of their time working as assistants to senior workers or carrying out routine tasks. However, it must be stressed that all placements are as interesting/ stimulating as you want them to be.

All in all, I think my year was successful. I became a member of the PFUE organisation and through them I was introduced to the Young Engineer for Britain competition, where I reached the regional final and won my age group. The speech to 150 people at the Manchester Museum of Science and Technology at the end of the year must be preparation for any public speaking I will do as an engineer!

Chris Collins spent her year out working as a Community Service Volunteer and as a voluntary helper at Churchtown Farm where she cared for people with disabilities and organised outdoor pursuits. She is now doing a course in occupational therapy, and feels her experiences have helped her considerably:

Taking a year out was one of the best things I've done. I learnt a lot about myself, other people, and life in general. I grew up a lot in that year. I feel it made a great difference to the way I've coped on my course. If I had started training straight from school I wouldn't have got this far.

Jo Barron took her year out after graduating, and worked for 3 months on a placement with Health Projects Abroad in Tanzania. She was involved in two projects, helping to supply a district hospital with a water and drainage system, and building a medical dispensary:

I didn't make a conscious decision to have a year off after graduating, but now, in retrospect, I am really pleased that I did. I didn't have a job when I graduated and an advert asking for volunteers for Tanzania immediately caught my eye. I had always been interested in Africa and was keen to get first-hand experience of life in a rural, developing country, although I never really thought it would be possible. The selection process was quite tough and involved a weekend in the Peak District with all kinds of group tasks designed to allow everyone to demonstrate their strengths and weaknesses. Eighteen volunteers were then chosen and we were informed of the decision within a week. From start to finish HPA were very friendly, efficient and organised. They kept in touch by letter before the project and organised two training weekends prior to leaving the UK which not only helped us with fundraising but fully prepared us for going away from home and living in rural Africa.

The Volunteer Coordinators in Tanzania had researched and organised everything for our arrival, so that we could start work straight away. The experience was definitely beneficial: working in a team with people that I didn't really know before, working with African villagers and getting first-hand experience of life in a developing country. I learned Swahili, saw the problems and way of life in rural Africa and came back with a greater awareness and self-confidence than I had 3 months earlier.

Elizabeth Hemingway spent much of her year out in Europe, working in hotels on placements organised for her by Jobs In The Alps. Here's how her year went:

June: A levels.
July-September: Worked as a catering assistant in London to earn money.
September-end October: Worked in Bavaria as a general assistant in a hotel. Hard work, but the plus side was worth it. I got a trip to the Oktoberfest paid for by the hotel and also went on a trip to Venice.
November-mid December: Back home. Visited some friends and passed my driving test (at last!)
Mid December-mid April: Hotel work in Switzerland. Probably the best part of my year off. Hard work (often boring) but I learnt how to ski (even with a somewhat unique style!) and did a little travelling. Best of all, I made some really good friends and met lots of different people.
Mid April-mid May: Went Inter-Railing with two friends, seeing a total of 10 countries.

May: Went to Canada for two weeks, visiting relatives (using the money I'd earned).
June-September: Worked as a waitress in a hotel in France.
September: Went to Ireland for two weeks to visit friends.
October: Started at Bradford University.

I would certainly recommend taking a year out to anyone. Given the choice I would do it all again. It financed itself completely, giving me money to do some travelling I would otherwise have not been able to do. I'd recommend Jobs In The Alps; jobs are very difficult to arrange for yourself in hotel work. However, places are limited so make sure you have backup plans.

Miranda Hayman took a year out before studying Spanish at university:

I would definitely recommend taking a year out, but only if you utilise your time well. There are so many opportunities to take that it is worth doing them now, before you go to university or whatever. The experience of a well-organised year and seeing other cultures stands you in good stead for the future. The principal concern against having a year out seems to be that it is difficult to return to studies. I do not think that this is necessarily the case. University work is different to A levels, and I think that so far I have done just as well, if not better in my work. Having had a year out and been outside the educational system has only made me more determined to do well and benefit from university life.

Dan Harlow started planning his year out in the lower sixth, and saw it as the ideal opportunity to experience other parts of the world while taking an academic break:

I was keen to travel, as well as to do something constructive. After looking at several organisations offering placements abroad, I had an interview and secured a place with Africa Venture. We were required to cover the cost of the airfare, insurance, orientation course, allowances and a week's safari. Prior to leaving I spent four months working in a hospital and some time grovelling for funds!

My six months in Africa were fantastic. Four months were spent teaching in Kenya, a unique opportunity to work in a 1,000-strong all-boys school. While the first weeks were difficult, trying to fit into the school and adapting to a very foreign environment, we soon settled in. I taught history and geography to classes of over 50, which was a real challenge. Sport also became part of our timetable, and while we trained their football team, rugby was surprisingly popular, along with athletics. At the end we visited the tropical coast and game parks and then travelled on safari to the fascinating Lake Turkana area. From May I travelled down to South Africa through Tanzania, Malawi, Zambia and Zimbabwe using the local buses and trains.

If you are considering a year out it is crucial you decide as early as possible how you intend to spend your time. Be realistic, you have to want to work to raise funds to make it worthwhile, and the belief that you have the application to make a success of whatever you may do. I have no regrets just amazing memories of a great experience.

What next? As you will have gathered from these accounts, after spending a constructive year between, your outlook and attitudes are liable to have changed somewhat. You may have had to learn how to cope in difficult situations, how to get along with people from a wide range of backgrounds, how to stand up and talk to a group of complete strangers, how to handle responsibility and make decisions. You will probably have come out of the experience a more mature and confident person.
You may also find that academic or working life now appears a bit tame compared to the challenges that you have just faced.

It is understandable if you feel a bit unsettled when you first return. If the challenges you face now don't seem so crucial they are still important ones, and the experiences of the past year will probably help you to meet them with more maturity. If you are anxious not to lose the momentum and enthusiasm you have built up over the year, then look around for other projects you can help with in your spare time or during vacations. The organisation that placed you may arrange meetings or weekends for returners, who can thus share experiences, evaluate the work they've done, keep in touch, even plan new projects together. You may also be able to help them with fundraising, public awareness or briefing meetings for new recruits. We too would like you to share your experiences with us by filling in the Report Form at the back of this guide. Completed forms help us to improve the information and advice we offer, and allow you to share your experiences with others.

Above all, enjoy your year out.

CHECKLIST

This checklist is for those who from the outset have known they are destined for a year between; for those who haven't a clue what to do at the end of their sixth form or degree course; for those with some idea of what a year out would achieve, but are still firmly on the fence; for those who are determined to slog on with their formal education, come what may; for those who have over a year to carefully plan and prepare for a year between; and for those who, either through lack of foresight and preparation or through indifferent exam results are having to face a last-minute crisis. In short, for all for whom the considerations of a year between are vital. There is no easy path to coming to a decision as to whether to take a year out or not; what this section aims to do is to force self-analysis, cover most of the pros, cons and options, and in so doing allow individuals to arrive at their own reasoned decision.

For those who have always planned to take a year between, this programmed series of questions should radically evaluate your current assumptions:

Have you really made the right decision in taking a year out?

Have you been totally honest in your motives?

Is what you have chosen to do really the right project for you and your future area of study?

Wouldn't something more relevant/ totally different be more valuable in terms of educational content/personal development?

Those undecided as to whether a year between will really be of benefit should read of others' experiences in the **INTRODUCTION** and **YEARS OF EXPERIENCE** sections first, then follow through with this section. The questions here should then evaluate individual potential and sharpen your focus. The year between is a time to try out new experiences and test your independence; if you are undecided about your year between then these personal areas probably need closer examination:

What is the longest period you have been away from home on your own?

How much do you rely on your tutors, parents and friends for support?

How well thought through is your future area of study/eventual career?

Has your education to date really tested you?

Do you know how far you can stretch your physical and mental limits?

If you are against even considering a year between carefully read this section first:

Why are you in such a hurry to get on with the next stage of formal education?

Have you got a thirst for knowledge or are you simply looking to get away from parental ties as soon as possible?

How wide are your educational horizons?

Can you hold a decent conversation in anything other than your chosen subjects and your immediate environment?

For those with little time left and who are now having to face a year between with little advance preparation, don't panic. Yes, many of the opportunities on offer will have already gone to those better organised. Yes, with some forethought you probably would have got a lot more out of a year between. But no, all is not lost, and much can be salvaged, even at a very late stage. Read through this section carefully, check your options, make a shortlist of what appeals to you, and don't be rushed into choosing/accepting the first opportunity on offer.

FOR & AGAINST

You have decided to take a year between
Check the **FOR** boxes below which have formed part of your decision. If you have additional reasons, list them. In the **AGAINST** section check those boxes you agree with. On balance, is taking a year out still a valid option? If so, proceed. If not, exactly what has tipped the balance against your original decision? Carefully examine your initial decision and how you arrived at a different decision, then re-read the **INTRODUCTION** section. Then start again here.

You are undecided about taking a year out
You should have read the **INTRODUCTION** section; if not read it now. Then go through the **FOR** and **AGAINST** lists, checking those options you agree with.

Do you come to a positive conclusion? Have you any reasons of your own to add to either list? Continue on to the next part.

Still on the fence? Read the **YEARS OF EXPERIENCE** section. You should then at least be on one side of the fence or the other. Depending on which side, follow through the choices here before going on to the next section.

Positive that a year out is not for you? Talk it through with friends, tutors and parents; you may be right.

You don't feel a year between is for you
Go down the **AGAINST** list, checking all the options you agree with. If you have an additional case to make, list those reasons. Then go through the **FOR** list, checking the options you are willing to consider. Now do you want to re-evaluate your decision for discounting the idea of a year between? If not, read the **YEARS OF EXPERIENCE** section. If you are still convinced that a year out is not for you, then your are probably right. If there is even an element of doubt, carry on!

FOR	AGAINST
☐ Opportunity to broaden horizons	☐ It will be difficult to return to formal education
☐ A break from years of continuous education	☐ Out of step with friends not taking a year out
☐ Time to evaluate options	☐ University/family against deferred entry
☐ Opportunity for independence	☐ Difficult to give up home comforts
☐ Time to earn some real money	☐ Course of study long enough without an extra year
☐ Rare chance to travel at length	☐ Not yet ready to grasp opportunity for independence
☐ Opportunity to give rather than take	☐ Can't think of a positive alternative to current plans
☐ Time for self-development	☐ Offered a suitable job now
☐ Opportunity to widen contacts with other people	☐ Appears as an unexplainable blank on the cv
☐ Time to evaluate chosen career or course	☐ May not be available for college/ job interviews
☐ Opportunity to try something new	☐ Not yet mature enough
☐ Will improve chances on degree course	☑ Other reasons (list below)
☐ Time to examine other cultures and lifestyles	
☐ University/family are in favour of deferred entry	
☑ Other reasons (list below)	

Options

Look at the list below and select the one option that you feel offers the most value in your terms for taking a year between:

☐ Travelling overseas, discovering the way of life in other countries, evaluating other cultures

☐ Working, doing almost anything to earn money, to finance future studies and the opportunity to travel, or to buy that longed-for cd player or new clothes

☐ Acquiring work experience/ training related to future areas of study/career, possibly through graduate sponsorship

☐ Undertaking something seemingly unrelated to past/ future education patterns, but something quite selfless like a community or social service project

☐ Doing something possibly quite self-centred, a personal development programme for example

☐ Continuing education under your own steam, reading as much as you can about your future subject, learning a new language, finding yourself through philosophy, maybe

Let's now analyse your choice. As we said before, there aren't necessarily *right* and *wrong* answers. What *is* important is that you realise that these questions need answers.

✔ You opted for work experience or training

Why? The year between is a time to experiment, to make use of an element of freedom you may never have again. Why do you want to tie yourself closely to what you are going to be doing in the near future anyway? Up to 40% of the job opportunities open to graduates are for those of any discipline. What will give you the edge in a job application over a similarly qualified colleague is your personality and your wide-ranging experience. Your potential employer will want to know whether you can get on with people, work as a team, communicate well. Will you be able to take positive decisions then carry them out? Do you know anything about the wider world of work, or are you only familiar with the corridors of *academia*? What you have actually achieved beyond academic qualifications will make you stand out from scores of other applicants, and the opportunities for such achievement may only be available to you in those precious twelve months of a year between.

You opted for a year of travel

Fine, but how much of another way of life will you be discovering? You speak the language and have a background to their culture? If you have to finance at least part of your travels by working, how much character-building experience are you gaining washing dishes in some international hotel? Will some future employer misconstrue your travels as simply a skive as you bum around the beaches of the Mediterranean? Maybe you will write the definitive travel guide, discover a tribe who have never seen an American Express card, but unless your travels are well structured, apart from contributing to the ills of irresponsible tourism you will gain little more worthwhile than a tan on your jaunts. Yes, plan a period of travel during your year between but don't let it become the be all and end all of your programme.

☑ **You need the money and will do almost anything legal to get it** Fine, this entrepreneurial streak will impress academics and employers alike! What did you do to earn the money? And more importantly, what did you do with it then? You may have achieved little beyond informing the world of your self-centred nature. And the relevance of labouring on a building site to your future study/career? Some positive benefit if it is civil engineering or architecture, practical materials handling is always useful, but wouldn't that time have been better spent developing more of your personal and technical skills through building an orphanage in an underdeveloped country, for example?

☑ **You opted for a period of adventure to develop your personal qualities** A period of testing and self-development is no bad thing in a year between, but make it part of the scheme of things. Relate it to future environmental studies or a science-based career, for example. Make sure there are other goals in sight, or it will turn out as a purely selfish exercise. You may come out of it as a true leader, but then again you may have gone into it rather smug in the first place. You're not planning to be a politician are you? Be careful that this course of action doesn't give the wrong signals of your intentions and limit your options later on.

☑ **A period spent acquiring skills in the community** A period of personal growth and maturity? You saw yourself helping others less fortunate than yourself? A little too altruistic perhaps? Have you read the **VOLUNTEERING** section? Be careful you are not justifying a period in a far-flung country, with elements of conscience-salving community work.

☑ **A period of study related to the future or something different** After something like thirteen years of continuous formal education you want more? Or even more if you've just completed higher education. Sooner or later you're going out there to get a job. You'll need more than just academic qualifications; isn't this the time to broaden your educational horizons? If you are committed to further study, explore beyond your own subjects.

Having made your initial choice and then read the comments above, do you want to re-evaluate your options? At this stage we are simplifying things by only examining one option at a time; a year between may very well consist of two or more complementary but distinctly different projects. Having re-evaluated your first choice and either having stuck with it or gone for a second choice, check your option below. If you have come to the conclusion that a year between is not for you then it is still worthwhile looking at the personal experiences throughout this guide. The writers of these accounts are the sort of people you will be competing against on your degree course and in the interview room. You should think carefully about acquiring the fully-rounded education that they possess. Your future employer will be asking some serious questions if you haven't.

☑ Travelling overseas

On its own this is probably one of the most expensive options, particularly in relation to the perceived benefits. However, relatives, family friends and parents' business networks can all be used to help you find places to stay. They may also help you find temporary jobs to help you pay your way. Check the statements below that you agree with, then see on balance whether you are still committed to this option:

- ☐ Probably the only time in my life I'll have this length of time to travel

- ☐ The cost, in time and money, is too high

- ☐ My foreign language ability will improve tremendously

- ☐ Travel broadens the mind

- ☐ Not very good at coping in foreign situations, a poor linguist at best

- ☐ The experience will mature me and help me cope on my own

- ☐ Only ever been on package holidays, unsure whether I could handle this

- ☐ The resourcefulness and independent attitude will look good on the cv

- ☐ Not very good at meeting people, or coping with new situations

- ☐ Months of travel could look self-indulgent to a future employer

In a recent survey STA asked 10,000 students what they would do if they were given an extra £2,000. 50% said, without hesitation, that they would take time out and buy a round-the-world ticket. Although you may want a flexible itinerary, some forward planning is essential. Passports, visas, work permits, residence permits, inoculations, vaccinations, medical precautions, insurance requirements - the basic checklist is seemingly endless. See *Section XI* for further information, but be prepared for considerable work on your own behalf. The **RESOURCES** section, pages 42-50 also lists useful contacts and publications for further advice and information.

☑ Earning money

There are a thousand and one ways of doing this, but care must be taken to ensure that there are rewards other than financial. For real benefits to be gained the work must either be related to future study/career, or the value of doing something completely different is intrinsic in the activity. For example, work on a building site or on the shop floor can give you experience of life and working conditions that you might otherwise never have to face. Even fairly routine jobs in the travel and tourism fields can be of direct educational benefit where foreign language fluency, for example, can be utilised and improved. Certain elements of the business world, such as marketing, can be explored by those with a flair for people contact. In the right context, and for a defined period of time only, sales jobs in publishing, financial services and the domestic installation markets, such as double glazing, central heating or insulation, could be constructive.

Much of the readily available work is seasonal, and you need to think carefully about the periods of possible inactivity. Tackled in the right way, even a series of manual jobs could contribute much to a degree course in the university of life. Is this still the option for you? See whether you are still committed by checking the statements below that you agree with:

☐ The money will come in useful for holidays and at university

☐ Bit hard going, working for a living, I've just left school

☐ I've had enough of education, let's see the real world

☐ All my friends are earning now

☐ The experience looks good on the cv

☐ I'm not sure what relevance grape picking has to my studies/career

☐ I can be independent, and leave home

☐ I'd spend all the money I earn, so what's the point?

☐ The company may give me a permanent job later on

☐ The company offers me a permanent job now. What do I do?

☐ It'll be hard to give up a wage for a student grant and loan

☐ My parents are well-off so I don't need to earn the money

☑ **Acquiring work experience**

You may feel the most important factor in taking this option is its relevance to your future course or career. However, the elements of work offered to you as a school leaver or recent graduate may be quite different from that of a qualified postholder. A high percentage of administration work may be involved, and some of it fairly basic. Make this a positive element; it is useful to get experience of all areas of a particular business or service. The networking available will provide employable skills, a vast amount of information, and useful contacts for the future. It may be just the beginning of work on a project that can continue through study and into vacations.

In any case, a valid period of work experience can be as short as 2 or 3 weeks - a full year out allows you to do more than this. **WORKPLACE**, a complete guide to work experience and work placements, has thousands of short-term opportunities in the UK and abroad. See page 11 for further details. A period of work experience, therefore, can be just one element in the overall picture of a year out.

Allow yourself therefore the widest options in acquiring knowledge and developing skills that the company can offer. Check the statements you agree with below so that you're sure this is the option for you:

☐ The work will help me relate better to my course/future career

☐ It will give me the option to see if this is the career for me

☐ It will help me gain sponsorship

☐ I'll become more mature/
responsible

☐ All my friends are on holiday while
I'm still working

☐ I'll be independent, show my
parents what I'm capable of

☐ The company I work for could
offer me a job later

☐ It'll make me realise I'd be wasted
going on to higher education

☐ I'm not getting wide enough
experience of life/other work

☑ Community or social work projects

It is sometimes difficult to separate out the demands and differences of a voluntary placement as opposed to a paid job. In the **VOLUNTEERING** section the exact nature of the commitments that voluntary service entails are discussed; the section also helps you to check whether this is the option for you. In itself community involvement is satisfying; in the wider context the opportunities to learn specific skills, to work with a wide variety of people from different backgrounds, nations and creeds, and to give something to others can contribute greatly to the experiences of a year between. There are few openings that can offer the wide range of emotions, challenges, demands and rewards that a period of community service does.

☑ The study option

The obvious reason for taking a further course of study is to prepare for the next step, whether it be a degree course or a job. The options available, and the reasons for taking them, go far beyond this. A short course could provide a taster of what a degree course entails, and go some way to making up your mind if you're currently wavering. You could use the time to develop your international outlook, either in language study or by acquiring work experience in another country. The European Union throws up all sorts of pressing reasons for adding a European or international dimension to your skills. The study option in the year between may also give you the opportunity to acquire keyboarding and other computer skills, test out some vocational options, particularly if your degree course is not immediately vocational in nature, or to continue with a subject you may have had to relinquish in order to concentrate on A levels, for example. However, you should ensure that a short course does not deflect you from your chosen path, nor involve you in the heavy burden of financing your own study. Check these statements:

☐ A study course will be expensive

☐ It'll show my study commitment

☐ It will only be part-time; what do I
do with the remaining time?

☐ I'll be adding practical educational
skills to my cv

☐ Offers little in the way of personal
development

VOLUNTEERING

Voluntary service is a popular option for those taking a year out. This section is to help you, as a potential volunteer, consider your motivation and commitment, think carefully about what is meant by development, and gain some insight into the type of person the volunteer-sending agencies are looking for. It sets out to force self-analysis of just what volunteering can achieve, for the volunteer as well as the host community, to challenge any myths and stereotypes that exist, and to cover most of the pros, cons and options. We hope that by reading this, potential volunteers will arrive at their own reasoned decision for volunteering, and become more aware of what they ultimately hope to achieve. To begin with, much of this advice is aimed at those thinking about volunteering overseas, on a development project in a Third World country, for example. Towards the end of this section there is information about volunteering closer to home. However, do read it all, because much of this advice is relevant to both situations.

Motivation Your reasons for thinking about voluntary service may be many and varied, but they are definitely worth analysing. It is very important that you get at least some understanding of your motivation before deciding whether or not to volunteer, either at home or abroad. You must be absolutely clear, positive and honest with yourself about your reasons for even thinking about voluntary service. All volunteers will share a certain amount of idealism, but a realistic expectation of what can be accomplished through voluntary service, and what you will return with in exchange, needs to be set down from the outset. Which, if any, of the following apply to you?

- [ ] I feel voluntary work will give me valuable experience and improve my career prospects

- [ ] I want to get away from problems at home, at work or at college

- [ ] I did consider volunteering in my home country, but going abroad is more exciting

- [ ] I have a political commitment to the struggle of exploited people

- [ ] I have felt a call from God

- [ ] I'm fed up of this country, I'm heading for the sunshine

- [ ] I honestly haven't really though about why I want to volunteer

Considering the importance of the answer, the question of why one is volunteering is often passed over by both volunteer and sending agency alike. You may find difficulty in answering; there may not even be a clear-cut answer, but the process of thinking about your motivation is a vital one.

If you're considering undertaking a project in the Third World, for example, your understanding of why those countries are viewed as *underdeveloped* also needs careful examination:

Why are there people in need who have to rely on other people's voluntary help?

How do the people of such countries come to be so poor, badly housed and underfed, and what are the industrialised nations doing to help?

What about disadvantaged people in your own country - couldn't you volunteer to work with them?

One thing is clear: time spent in voluntary service is far too valuable to waste. For such an investment of time and energy it is essential that there is a clear understanding of what volunteers expect and what is expected of them. Read through the following ten reasons for volunteering abroad - some may strike a chord. You may not be prepared for the responses, but these are aimed at provoking you into really thinking about your commitment.

I want to help the less fortunate A perhaps well-meaning but rather patronising attitude. Have you given any thought as to how and why these people you want to help actually are less fortunate? What sort of help do they need, and how are you in a position to give it? In what way do you consider yourself *more* fortunate? Better off, better educated, more intelligent, in some way superior? Are these people less fortunate in a cultural sense? Third World countries are no longer colonies. Perhaps you need to acquire some understanding of international citizenship and development issues. Perhaps a change of attitude is required.

I'm sure they'd benefit from my skills and expertise But are these appropriate to the conditions existing in the country where you will be working? The idea that the developed West can solve all the Third World's problems is a dangerous one. Hi-tech methods are not invariably the best ones, and may disrupt perfectly adequate systems that have been in use for generations. Will you be taking a course in the local language? Do you think you'll be able to communicate well enough to transfer your skills to the people that matter? Is the introduction of your skills and expertise going to have a material benefit in their day-to-day lives? Has it occurred to you that you will perhaps learn more than you teach?

I want to show solidarity with the poor and oppressed And presumably you want to work to put an end to poverty and oppression. Do some research. Is the agency you have in mind really working to change things, or is it just treating the symptoms, rather than the causes of poverty? Will the project you will be working on really benefit those who need it, or just help the elite and perpetuate an oppressive system? What kind of government does the country have, and what sort of Human Rights record? Couldn't you work for change far more effectively from your home country? What about the poor and oppressed in the *developed* world; aren't they also in need of solidarity, or are you really just looking for the thrill of foreign travel?

✔ **My life's going nowhere, I want a change, a break from the pressures of school or work** Volunteering abroad will certainly be a change, but it won't solve your problems for you. If the rat race is getting you down now, will it be any easier after a year abroad? Running away from problems won't necessarily make them disappear. Nor should you consider volunteering to be an easy way out. And how do you feel you're in a position to help anyone, when you're in no position to sort out your own problems effectively?

✔ **I want to do something worthwhile**
Define *worthwhile*. What is it that you want to give or gain? If you expect to get immediate good feelings about setting the world to rights you may be disappointed. Volunteers usually take time to settle in and find out what is required of them. It may even take several months before they feel they're making any progress. Many volunteers return home feeling that they actually contributed very little to changing the world or helping others, and that it is they themselves who have gained most from the experience.

✔ **I've just left school/college and I'm having difficulty finding suitable work here**
Unfortunately, applying for voluntary work abroad is not the answer. The majority of volunteer-sending agencies tend to take on employed people with professional qualifications, and are not likely to be able to offer you a placement unless you have considerable work experience and appropriate skills. Those agencies who do recruit less experienced people will expect them to raise quite a bit of money to contribute to the cost of the placement. There are, however, many opportunities for voluntary work in Britain, which will help in giving you experience and proving to potential employers that you are a responsible and caring person. But remember, you need commitment to volunteer. It's not some sort of easy alternative to work; indeed it requires all the skills and expertise of permanent employment, plus more.

✔ **I want to experience the culture and way of life of a far away country** Very honest! Is a period as a volunteer the best way to do this? How much have you experienced the culture and way of life of another area or country whilst on holiday? Getting to know the people and what makes the country tick takes time and effort. Will you be living in the community or in an expatriate compound which will remove you from the daily lives of local people? Even as a volunteer you may be considered to be in a position of power and authority - is this what you want? How will it affect your working and social relationships? How much do you know about the country already? Can you speak the local language fluently? How much chance do you think you'll get to become involved in the way of life and the culture whilst working? You'll be working, not on some extended holiday. Do you have to go abroad to experience another culture and way of life? What about getting to know members of other cultures in your home country, including working to improve their lot in life?

✓ **I'd benefit from the challenge and experience of working abroad** You might benefit, but who else will? You may enjoy being thrown in at the deep end, but wouldn't you be of more service if you already had experience of voluntary work and development issues? Perhaps you could consider working as a volunteer in Britain, or campaigning for a development organisation before trying an overseas placement.

✓ **My western lifestyle has been very privileged and I would like to do something in return** It might also be considered a privilege to take a year out to travel to a far off country and work in the sunshine every day - not everyone can afford to do this. And watch out: this idea of privilege also has a patronising *West is best* air about it! Just how privileged is the lifestyle of other members of *your* community? Virtually all countries have extremes of wealth and poverty, bad housing, illiteracy, high unemployment and immigrant or minority populations discriminated against on many levels. What do you do on a regular basis to help improve their condition? If you do consider yourself fortunate, there are lots of ways to give a little back, and volunteering abroad may not necessarily be the best one, especially if you lack the skills to contribute. Working for fundraising, campaigning or development networks at home can also bring results.

✓ **The situation out there is so desperate, I've just got to do something** Hold on a minute. First of all, what sort of skills have you got that can help? Sympathy and compassion are all very well but they alone can't change things. In cases of famine and disaster for example, the need may be more for cash than people, so your energies would be better channelled into fundraising and working for change from home. How much do you actually know about this crisis that's arisen? Isn't the help you can offer only very short-term? What can you do on a long-term basis that would be more effective? And in the long-term, shouldn't people be given the chance to solve their own problems instead of being told what to do by well-meaning foreigners? Do we really have all the answers?

As you can see, working out your motivation and expectations may prove to be complicated, but it is nonetheless important to try sorting out in your own mind both what you expect to give and to gain from volunteering and whether these are realistic expectations. The most useful projects may come about as a result of the needs and initiatives of people at the grassroots, where volunteers help those people develop *themselves*.

Qualifications and experience
The days of agencies sending unskilled school leavers to work in the Third World are long gone. As well as the fact that these countries may themselves already have large numbers of unskilled, unemployed young people, it is also the case that most volunteer-sending agencies need to recruit people who can put

specialist skills and experience into practice. Even recent graduates will find it difficult to be placed as volunteers if they lack work experience. This is understandable: someone who has made the transition from being a student to working within the structured discipline of an office or work environment will have gained valuable management and organisational skills and will be better placed to organise their work in a new situation overseas.

If you lack experience and still want to volunteer overseas then, rather than applying to the larger, more well-known development agencies, you would be far better advised to contact the organisations listed in **A YEAR BETWEEN**. They will generally expect you to raise quite a large sum of money to cover the placement fee, travel and living costs, viewing the placement not simply as a period of service, but also as an educational and cultural experience. You could also consider doing a voluntary placement in your home country, and postpone volunteering overseas until you have more experience under your belt. This has the advantage of giving you more time to consider the options, find out what specific skills are needed and get yourself properly prepared. The following tips may help you better plan any period of preparation for voluntary service:

Pick up some basic skills Learn to drive - in some areas this is an essential skill, as is a knowledge of vehicle maintenance. Take evening classes in office skills such as book-keeping or typing, or practical subjects such as bricklaying or plumbing. The ability to turn your hand to a variety of tasks will always

be worthwhile on a development project.

Go for breadth of experience At village level there is likely to be a need for generalists rather than specialists, so if you can get a job which moves you around departments, take advantage of this to get as broad a training as you can. The more adaptable you can be, the better.

Go for hands-on experience Look out for any chance to get real practical experience, find out how and why jobs are done in a certain way, find out how to do-it-yourself. The more hands-on experience you get in doing tasks, the better able you will be to do them overseas, even if materials are not ideal and tools are missing. A knowledge of simple, practical jobs is likely to be most useful to you in the field.

Get experience of teaching Most agencies expect volunteers to transfer their skills to those around them, so start now by learning to be a communicator. You could perhaps help to run a youth group, volunteer to teach basic English, literacy or maths, or take a Sunday school class. Anything involving the sharing of skills and ideas is bound to stand you in good stead.

Learn about the issues There are many different organisations and charities involved in development issues that can offer a variety of resources. It is also worth reading up about development work in your own particular field, be it health, agriculture, technology or teaching. Getting involved in campaigning or fundraising will also be an excellent way of learning about the problems facing Third World countries and the means that exist to solve them.

Personal qualities Qualifications and experience are no good unless a volunteer has the right personal qualities. To begin with, if you can't communicate your skills to, and learn from, other people, then you are unlikely to be of much use to any development project. The ability to make friends and get on with all kinds of people is vital. Volunteers also need to be able to show sensitivity and tolerance towards cultures different from their own, as well as enough flexibility, patience and humour to enable them to work with people who may be used to doing things in a different way and perhaps have a different sense of priorities. You may well find yourself in a more responsible position than you have been used to, with people coming to you for advice and treating you as an expert, so a considerable amount of initiative, confidence, self-reliance and decision-making ability will be required.

Prospective volunteers should think carefully about what it takes in terms of personal skills to make the most out of a placement. How many of the following can *you* check positively:

☐ I can get on with people

☐ I can work independently and show initiative

☐ I am prepared to learn from the community I will be working in

☐ I can work as part of a team

☐ I can bridge the gap between what the project expects of me and what I am

☐ I can work the way others want me to work (I don't *have* to do things *my* way)

☐ I could learn the language

☐ I am adaptable and flexible

☐ I am tolerant and sensitive to other cultures

☐ I have got good communication skills

☐ I am patient and tactful

☐ I am independent and self-disciplined

☐ I have a sense of humour

☐ I have a desire to seek challenges

Aside from the working environment, you may also have to deal with your own feelings of isolation and homesickness, not to mention strange food, the heat, weird insects, and a lack of basic amenities. In addition, local people will be understandably curious about you, a stranger; they will want to visit you and talk to you, and may not comprehend your occasional need for privacy.

Coming to terms with cultural differences constitutes a major aspect of living and working in a new environment. If you've grown up with a certain set of beliefs, viewpoints and ways of working you may take it for granted that these are *right*, especially if they have never seriously been challenged before. Everyone has their own preconceptions or prejudices, usually determined by their upbringing and the social attitudes of the culture to which they are accustomed. In order to break down barriers it is therefore important for you to be able to see where your own assumptions come from and to try and understand and live with the way other people see things. It would be inappropriate for you to impose what may be a western, urbanised outlook on a completely different, rural community. Be open to differences, even if you think they are *wrong*. They have been developed over generations, are probably well-adapted to the surrounding environment and may teach you a lot about your own beliefs and attitudes. The following comments from a volunteer who worked in Zimbabwe are a good illustration of this:

Coming to Zimbabwe has shown me many things about my own cultural assumptions and habits of thinking and behaving. Things I used to regard as generally valid I now see, in the light of a quite different rural and communal way of life, as specialised and even odd social traits ...

I came out with typical criticism of my project, like there's no system to working, everyone spends too much time talking together in the office, or they come to decisions in such a roundabout way. It was just that I often didn't understand what was being said, or the significance of it, the relationships between people and the importance of showing hospitality. People joked about me always being busy, unable to spend time with them.

In agricultural work one day we were shifting earth from one place to another where trees were to be planted. All project members were working. The bucket chain broke down after a little while and everyone began to carry the buckets of earth from A to B in pairs or groups. I started to

argue about inefficiency - the first time I'd expressed frustration I'd experienced in other situations, but of course I spoke up on work I thought any fool could organise (more fool me). Some workers just smiled, others were hurt and humiliated by my condemnation. One woman spoke up: We are not machines, she said. We are people. And the work continued.

The best way to gain an understanding of another society's customs and values is through personal contact. If you know which country you will be going to, try to get the chance to talk to a native of the country before you leave. There may, for example, be an immigrant community near where you live, or a refugee group. The cultural section of the relevant embassy may organise social events or put you in touch with a society for promoting understanding between Britain and that particular country. People are usually happy to talk about the way things are back home and you may learn a lot more from them than from reading books.

Volunteering nearer home
As you can see, if you lack special qualifications, skills or experience, then opportunities to work on a development project in the Third World may be fairly limited. However, you don't have to travel far afield to find out about other cultures. Britain's population, for example, is made up of many cultures and many faiths, and there are plenty of opportunities to work with them. You could also volunteer in another European country or in North America. Working to overcome the problems caused by disability, poverty, bad housing, illiteracy, unemployment or discrimination against an immigrant

population presents a very worthwhile challenge. Or if you are motivated by a desire to work for world development you can do this in your own country. Many charitable organisations need volunteers to help with fundraising, campaigning or administration. Voluntary experience such as this can make it easier to be accepted as a volunteer overseas, quite apart from the contribution you can make to the welfare of the community with which you will be working.

Jonathan Allat, a former volunteer with The Missions to Seamen, found that he could work for the improvement in education, conditions and welfare of people from all over the world without leaving the UK:

I had hoped to spend a year abroad, so I was disappointed when I was posted to Southampton, but the multinational, multi-cultural clientele at the Mission meant the world came to me. I spoke to British seafarers in transit to and from the Gulf War, Indians at the time of Gandhi's assassination, and Yugoslavians when their civil war started.

If you've never done any voluntary work before and feel a little daunted by the prospect of committing yourself on a long-term residential basis there are still countless opportunities to volunteer in your home area. In its Survey of Voluntary Activity in the UK the Volunteer Centre UK defined voluntary work as *any activity which involves spending time, unpaid, doing something which aims to benefit someone (individuals or groups) other than or in addition to close relatives, or to benefit the environment.*

A very broad definition, which can encompass an enormous variety of opportunities. Put like this, even helping someone across the road can be classed as volunteering! It has been estimated that in the UK between one third and one half of the population devotes some spare time to organised voluntary work. So you don't have to be an extra special person with proven skills - *anyone* can volunteer.

Faced with such a wide variety of opportunities, the first thing you need to do is decide what sort of voluntary work is right for you. Your motivation might be political, environmental, humanitarian or religious; perhaps you have a desire to help other people, look after children, campaign for change, stop pollution, reduce poverty and need, care for animals or offer help in emergencies. Discover what it is that you really care about, and look for an organisation that has this issue at its heart.

You should also be aware of what it is you are good at and what sort of work you enjoy doing. There's no point volunteering to do practical work if you don't know one end of a screwdriver from the other. If you like talking to people then you might not be very happy stuck in an office doing the filing. On the other hand, if you're neat and methodical you may quite enjoy the administrative side of things. Everybody has their strong and weak points, and all types of people are needed to keep a voluntary organisation going: campaigners and lobbyers; people to offer support and friendship; practical people who like to be where the action is; counsellors, advisors and problem-solvers; clerical workers, administrators, secretaries, organisers and managers.

Ask around your local area to find out about voluntary organisations; check in your local library; consult the phone book, *Yellow Pages* or *Thomson's Directory*; or contact your local volunteer bureau. Once you've found a voluntary organisation you would like to work for, ask to speak to the volunteer organiser, who will be able to tell you what sort of work is available. You will probably have to fill in an application form and attend an interview - this will help them to place you in work to which you are most suited. You may be asked to provide references, either from a past employer, teacher, tutor, or just someone who knows you well, simply to confirm that you are who you say you are and that you'll be able to do the work. If you are going to be working with children, you may also be asked to disclose any police record. The interview is also an opportunity for you to find out all you can about the organisation and where volunteers fit into the structure, so don't be afraid to ask lots of questions.

As a volunteer, even though you may feel you are working fairly informally for no financial reward you still have rights and should not just be treated as an extra pair of hands or someone to do the dirty work. Volunteering is a matter of free choice, and your willingness should not be exploited, so don't feel pressurised into doing something you really don't want to do. Your hours of work should be agreed and put in writing - you have other demands on your time, and therefore should not commit yourself to giving more time than you can afford. You

should have some kind of verbal or written description of the job you will be doing, and if the job is likely to change it is only fair that you should be consulted. Make sure you know who is supervising your work and whom you can approach to talk through any problems. If your work is likely to incur any expenses, find out how to claim these back; if any special clothing or equipment are needed then these should be supplied by the organisation, not by you.

You should be adequately insured by the organisation whilst at work, and as with all employees, you should not be expected to work in unsafe or unhealthy conditions. Above all, make sure that the work you are doing is genuinely voluntary - you should not be putting someone out of a job by doing work which was previously paid.

Volunteering should give you a chance to enhance the skills you already have and learn new ones, either on-the-job or in some cases through a training course. As your skills develop, so should your work, and like any job it should be reviewed at regular intervals. If you find the work tedious and unsatisfying, then make your voice heard and ask if you can do something that is more demanding or entails more responsibility. Remember, it's in everyone's interest for you to feel fulfilled and happy in your work, because then you're much more likely to carry on with it!

If you are claiming benefits such as the Jobseekers Allowance you must inform your Jobcentre if you are doing any voluntary work. Payment of benefits will not usually be affected as long as you are still available for and actively seeking work. This means that you must be willing to give up your voluntary work at short notice to attend an interview or take up a job, and that you must be able to show for each week you claim benefit that you have taken reasonable steps to find a job. Your local Social Security office or Jobcentre should be able to give you advice and supply you with a leaflet which discusses the issue in more detail. If you incur any out-of-pocket expenses whilst undertaking voluntary work (such as travel expenses, for example) the reimbursement of such costs should not affect the payment of benefits.

Obviously, residential voluntary projects will require more of a full-time commitment from volunteers than more informal voluntary work, and because of this you may not qualify for benefits as you will not be able to say you are actively seeking work. However, you will not be entirely without resources as most residential projects provide board and lodging and will supply volunteers with pocket money to cover basic personal expenses.

Jane Manning now works as a salaried worker on a housing project in Bedford but on her year out worked for Cambridge Cyrenians as part of a team living at a direct access hostel for nine homeless people:

I see my time as a volunteer worker as one where I used my abilities to assist people to improve aspects of their lives or to accept them. As a live-in volunteer the project had an aspect of family community that many residents had not experienced for many years. This made the residents feel more at ease talking to me and I was viewed less as an outsider.

In the six months I was at the project I found myself in an environment that was often challenging and frequently confronted with new situations. However I feel that what I put into the work was a fraction of what I received back from it. I forged and maintain many friendships with the residents and in the local homeless population.

I would recommend voluntary work as a way of discovering parts of your own expectations in life and realising the hidden problems that exist in our society.

RESOURCES

ORGANISATIONS

Career Analysts Ltd 90 Gloucester Place, London W1H 4BL © 0171-935 5452 was established 30 years ago to help people of all ages discover the education, training and career opportunities best suited to their needs. They specialise in the 15-24 age range, concentrating on post-A level courses and careers. Consultants are chartered psychologists who combine expert assessment of aptitudes, interests and personality test results with a personal counselling approach to help each applicant plan their career and make the best possible educational and career choices.

Careers and Occupational Information Centre Room E405, Moorfoot, Sheffield S1 4PQ © 0114-259 4569. For catalogues and orders: PO Box 298A, Thames Ditton, Surrey KT7 0ZS © 0181-957 5030. Produces a wide range of publications, videos and materials dealing with careers, education and training.

Cavendish Educational Consultants Clarendon House, 16 Brooklands Avenue, Cambridge CB2 2BB © Cambridge (01223) 369483 ☎ (01223) 464707. Offers a wide range of educational services including advice on courses for those taking a year between, on university entrance including Oxbridge, on re-take courses, interview technique and cvs.

Christians Abroad 1 Stockwell Green, London SW9 9HP © 0171-737 7811 ☐ wse@cabroad.u-net.com

http://www.u-net.com/~cabroad/wse. An ecumenical body funded by aid and mission agencies, providing an information and advisory service on work abroad to help volunteers discover opportunities related to their skills, age, aims and circumstances. World Service Enquiry, an activity of Christians Abroad, provides free information on voluntary and paid opportunities, short- or long-term in aid, development and mission agencies. Updated annually, it is geared towards unskilled people without professional experience.

Expedition Advisory Centre of the Royal Geographical Society 1 Kensington Gore, London SW7 2AR © 0171-591 3030 ☎ 0171-591 3031 ☐ eac@rgs.org. Offers information and training for those planning an expedition overseas. A range of publications and training seminars provide a service primarily to scientific and youth expeditions, but the Centre also helps adventure projects, those wishing to join an expedition or travel independently.

Gabbitas Educational Consultants Carrington House, 126-130 Regent Street, London W1R 6EE © 0171-734 0161 offers expert, independent advice to parents and students on the choice of independent schools, colleges and courses; planning and preparing for higher education; career guidance and options for a year out.

Local education authorities will be able to provide information on grants available for various types of courses. Listed in the phone book under the name of the county, borough or metropolitan council.

National Association of Volunteer Bureaux New Oxford House, Waterloo Street, Birmingham B2 5UG ✆ 0121-633 4043 ✉ 0121-633 4043 was set up to serve and represent Britain's volunteer bureaux and to promote volunteering in general. Does not recruit volunteers but can put enquirers in touch with their local volunteer bureau, who will be able to advise them of the entire range of voluntary work available locally.

National Youth Agency 17-23 Albion Street, Leicester LE1 6GD ✆ 0116-285 6789 ✉ nya@nyainfo.demon.co.uk ✎ http://www.foobar.co.uk/nya. Houses a comprehensive collection of resources on work with young people and the issues that affect them. Can provide information on community involvement and youth volunteer organisations in England and Wales.

Odyssey International 21 Cambridge Road, Waterbeach, Cambridge CB5 9NJ ✆ Cambridge (01223) 861079 is a travel club which aims to match like-minded travelling partners. An advice line is run by members who have just returned from abroad giving details of visa problems, vaccination requirements and employment prospects. Publishes a biannual newsletter detailing travel offers. Annual membership £25.

Ormonde Advisory Service 2 Market Square, Petworth, West Sussex GU28 0AH ✆ Petworth (01798) 344123. Run by a group of senior businessmen, teachers and military officers who have a wide experience of helping sixth form students due to go to university or before starting a job, to spend their year out sensibly and profitably. They provide a lecture service for schools and colleges, advising on taking a year out. Also produce a range of leaflets, distributed at these conventions.

Returned Volunteer Action 1 Amwell Street, London EC1R 1UL Produces a newsletter and a range of training resources for those considering working overseas, and publishes *Thinking About Volunteering* and *Volunteering and Overseas Development: A Guide to Opportunities.* Available jointly, £3.05 + 38p SAE.

Scottish Community Education Council (SCEC) Rosebery House, 9 Haymarket Terrace, Edinburgh EH12 5EZ ✆ 0131-313 2488 promotes community involvement and service by young people in Scotland. Although it does not recruit volunteers or find places for them, it provides an information sheet giving details of volunteer projects in Scotland, including conservation work, workcamps, community projects, playschemes and some opportunities for long-term volunteers.

Taking Off PO Box 104, Newton Highlands, Massachusetts 02161, United States ✆ Boston (00 1 617) 630 1606 ✉ (00 1 617) 630 1605 ✉ glr44@aol.com offers a consultation service which helps students all over the world develop their plans for taking time off from traditional education, identifying interests, evaluating priorities and securing opportunities tailored to their needs. The company holds a database containing several thousand opportunities in a wide range of areas, including media and journalism, marine biology and wildlife, community service, manual labour, arts, women's issues, the environment, worldwide travel and special education. Initial phone consultation is free of charge, then hourly fee is $150 and flat fee is $895.

Universities and Colleges Admissions Service (UCAS) PO Box 67, Cheltenham, Gloucestershire GL50 3SF ℗ Cheltenham (01242) 227788 deals with applications for full-time and sandwich first degree, DipHE and HND courses at all UK universities (except the Open University) and most colleges of higher education. *UCAS Handbook* lists courses in the scheme and is distributed to schools and colleges with the application form in May/June; if you are not at school or college it is available from the above address or local careers offices.

Youth for Britain Higher Orchard, Sandford Orcas, Sherborne, Dorset DT9 4RP ℗/℡ Corton Denham (01963) 220036 is a registered charity, set up in 1994, which offers a computer-based guidance system specifically developed for young people, aged 16-25, who wish to embark on a period of voluntary service. A database, listing over 250,000 placements in 211 countries worldwide, matches volunteers' requirements against those of over 700 volunteer organisations. Information is given on type, length and location of projects; activities involved; start date, when and how to apply; financial details and qualifications needed. The database is available to schools and careers services, price £95 which includes initial disk and an update after six

months. Also offers a postal enquiry service for individuals, price £15; write to above address for a questionnaire.

YouthNet UK Beaumont House, Avonmore Road, Kensington Village, London W14 8TS ℗ 0171-605 1693 ℡ 0171-605 1694 ✉ youthnet@ thesite.org.uk ⬡ http://www. thesite.org.uk. A small registered charity, launched in 1995, which gives advice, help and information on agencies, groups, clubs and publications of interest to young people aged 12-30. It is currently developing a Web site called The Site which will act as a signpost to the opportunities available to young people. There are also proposals for CD-Rom and paper versions in the future. Those wanting further information are encouraged to visit The Site or to contact YouthNet via e-mail.

PUBLICATIONS

Taking a year between *A Year Off ... A Year On?* £7.99 is a guide to temporary jobs, voluntary service, vacation jobs, study courses, scholarships, travel and expeditions. Author: Suzanne Straw; available from Biblios, Star Road, Partridge Green, West Sussex RH13 8LD ℗ Partridge Green (01403) 710851.

The Alternative Guide to the Sixth Form £5.95 helps students recognise all their options and plan effectively for the future. Includes information on sponsorship, taking a year out, jobs and money. Available from Trotman & Co Ltd, 12 Hill Rise, Richmond, Surrey TW10 6UA ℗ 0181-332 2132 ℡ 0181-332 0860.

The Gap Year Book £4 contains informative articles and details of a wide range of organisations for those planning a year out. Also includes a section on tutorial and sixth form colleges who offer retake and revision courses. Published annually by Cavendish Educational Consultants, Clarendon House, 16 Brooklands Avenue, Cambridge CB2 2BB ℂ Cambridge (01223) 369483 ℼ (01223) 464707.

Go For It! £8.99, produced annually, is a guide aimed at young people in their late teens and early twenties. It profiles organisations and companies offering opportunities across a wide range of categories, including volunteering, expeditions, arts and crafts, sport and leisure and working holidays. It also gives information on how to apply for jobs and details of organisations offering help and advice to young people. Author: Martyn Lewis. Available from Lennard Books, Windmill Cottage, Mackerye End, Harpenden, Hertfordshire AL5 5DR ℂ Harpenden (01582) 715866 ℼ (01582) 715121.

Opportunities in the GAP Year £3.95 looks at what is available to sixth-formers wishing to take a break between school and university or college. It weighs up the pros and cons of a year between and gives hints on how to make the best of a once-in-a-lifetime opportunity. Edited by Anna Alston; published by the Independent Schools Careers Organisation, 12a-18a Princess Way, Camberley, Surrey GU15 3SP ℂ Camberley (01276) 21188 ℼ (01276) 691833.

Spending a Year Abroad £8.99 sets out the numerous options available and contains practical information on short-term opportunities and travelling, supplemented by many personal accounts from those who have spent a year abroad. Author: Nick Vandome; published by How To Books, Plymbridge House, Estover Road, Plymouth PL6 7PZ ℂ Plymouth (01752) 202301 ℼ (01752) 202331.

Taking A Year Off £8.99 takes a new look at the option of taking a year off before, during or after higher education or during employment, encouraging the reader to identify his or her own needs by placing emphasis on case studies, group discussions and interviews, letters, a quiz, checklists, and the experiences of young people who have taken time out. Author: Val Butcher; published by Trotman and Co Ltd, see above. Also available on video, £25 + VAT.

Paid and voluntary work

Working Holidays £9.99 is an annual guide to over 101,000 paid and voluntary seasonal work opportunities in 70 countries. Full information is given on the jobs available together with details on work/residence permits, travel, insurance, accommodation and further sources of information. Published by the Central Bureau for Educational Visits & Exchanges, see below.

Workplace £9.99 is a guide to work experience and work placements. As well as profiling over 120 companies and organisations offering work experience in the UK and abroad, it gives comprehensive advice and information on planning, delivering and evaluating work experience programmes, covering issues such as assessment, briefing, funding, health and safety, insurance and resources.

It also includes case studies and insights from companies, placement organisers, teachers, pupils and students, and provides information on work-related projects and graduate traineeships. Published by the Central Bureau for Educational Visits & Exchanges, see below.

Volunteer Work £8.99 is a comprehensive guide to medium and long-term voluntary service with details on some 80 organisations recruiting volunteers. The guide covers projects lasting 3-36 months in Britain and 120 countries worldwide, and also offers practical advice. Published by the Central Bureau for Educational Visits & Exchanges, 10 Spring Gardens, London SW1A 2BN ✆ 0171-389 4880 ✉ books@central bureau.org.uk.

International Directory of Voluntary Work £9.99 is a guide to short and long-term volunteer opportunities in Britain and abroad. Edited by Victoria Pybus; published by Vacation Work, 9 Park End Street, Oxford OX1 1HJ ✆ Oxford (01865) 241978.

Directory of Work & Study in Developing Countries £8.99 is a guide to employment, voluntary work and academic opportunities in the Third World for those who wish to experience life there not just as a tourist. Published by Vacation Work, see above.

Directory of Summer Jobs Abroad £7.99 including UK postage is an annual publication detailing vacancies in over 40 countries, including information on jobs offered, wages given and addresses of employees. Edited by David Woodworth; published by Vacation Work, see above.

Directory of Summer Jobs in Britain £7.99 lists opportunities all over Britain with details of wages and hours, conditions of work and qualifications required. Edited by David Woodworth; published by Vacation Work, see above.

Summer Jobs USA £10.99 gives details of thousands of summer jobs for students in the US and Canada. Includes a section giving advice on legal requirements and visa procedure for non-US citizens. Published by Peterson's Guides and available in the UK through Vacation Work, see above.

Internships USA £15.99 lists career-oriented positions enabling students and graduates to train through a period of work with an established employer. Published by Peterson's Guides and available in the UK through Vacation Work, see above.

Working in Another Country of the European Union, free, is a leaflet produced by the European Commission as part of its Citizens First information campaign. It gives information on looking for work abroad, employees' rights and advice for self-employed people.
Other leaflets in the series are: Studying, Training and Doing Research in Another Country, which includes information on students' rights in other EU countries and details of the relevant funding programmes; and Living in Another Country, which covers the rights of residence and gives information on eligibility, how to vote and practical considerations like moving personal property and sorting out taxes. All three booklets have accompanying factsheets and are available by calling ✆ 0800 581591 or ➲ http://citizens. eu.int.

The Overseas Placing Unit has produced a series of guides on working in each European Union country. The guides are aimed at professionals with several years' experience but include some information, such as details of accommodation agencies, which would be of interest to younger people seeking short-term work. Local Jobcentres will hold reference copies.

Working in the European Union £15 is the European Commission's official guide to job opportunities in member states of the EU. It contains a starting-out guide for employers and job-seekers and has a chapter on each country giving details of postgraduate study, the structure of institutions and their courses, the timing of recruitment, and guidance and placement services. Authors: W H Archer and A J Raban. Available from HMSO, PO Box 276, London SW8 5DT ✆ 0171-873 9090 ⚏ 0171-873 8200.

Directory of Volunteering & Employment Opportunities £9.95 is a comprehensive guide to the opportunities for both volunteer and paid work in over 650 of the UK's major charities and voluntary organisations. Edited by Jan Brownfoot and Frances Wilks; published by the Directory of Social Change, 24 Stephenson Way, London NW1 2DP ✆ 0171-209 5151 ✉ info@d-s-c.demon.co.uk.

The Third World Directory 1997 £12.95 covers over 200 organisations working for overseas development, with information on possibilities for volunteering. Edited by Lucy Stubbs; published by the Directory of Social Change, see above.

The Voluntary Agencies Directory £24 is a comprehensive listing of voluntary agencies in the UK, compiled by the National Council for Voluntary Organisations. It lists nearly 2,000 agencies ranging from small, specialist self-help groups to established national charities. An invaluable source of reference for anyone thinking about doing volunteer work in the UK. Available from Hamilton House Mailings, 17 Staveley Way, Brixworth Industrial Park, Northampton NN6 7EX ✆ Brixworth (01604) 881889.

Sponsorship
Engineering Opportunities for Students & Graduates, free, details sponsorship and training offered to 6th form or college students applying for university engineering degree courses and for final year engineering degree students seeking a graduate training post. Published annually in July and available from the Institution of Mechanical Engineers, Schools' Liaison Service, Northgate Avenue, Bury St Edmunds, Suffolk IP32 6BN ✆ Bury St Edmunds (01284) 763277 ✉ schools@imeche.org.uk.

Sponsorship for Students £9.50, is an annual publication listing sponsorship offered to students by employers and professional bodies for first degrees, BTEC and SCOTVEC higher awards or comparable courses. It also looks at the range of options available to students about to enter further and higher education and seeking to raise funding for study. Available from the Careers and Occupational Information Centre, PO Box 298A, Thames Ditton, Surrey KT7 0ZS ✆ 0181-957 5030. Orders can also be placed through Biblios PSD Ltd ✆ (01403) 710851.

Further study

Home From Home £8.99 is an authoritative guide to over 120 organisations arranging homestays, exchanges, home exchanges, farm stays and term stays in more than 50 countries. At a time when travellers are turning away from the alienation of mass tourism, the guide offers a wide selection of responsible alternatives. Published by the Central Bureau for Educational Visits & Exchanges, 10 Spring Gardens, London SW1A 2BN ✆ 0171-389 4880.

How To Study Abroad £8.99 brings together advice and reference information including what to study, entrance requirements, grants and scholarships, useful contacts and a country-by-country guide. Author: Teresa Tinsley; published by How To Books, Plymbridge House, Estover Road, Plymouth PL6 7PZ ✆ Plymouth (01752) 202301 ≡ (01752) 202331.

Directory of Further Education £66.50 contains details of over 65,000 further education courses available in the UK, including those of a vocational and practical nature. All courses show the award, course duration, mode of study and levels of attainment. Edited by Cath Laing; published by Hobsons Publishing plc, Bateman Street, Cambridge CB2 1LZ ✆ Cambridge (01223) 464334 and available for consultation at careers offices and libraries.

Directory of Independent Further Education £6.80 contains basic information on over 2,500 colleges and training establishments. Colleges are grouped in nine sections, from those offering tutorial courses through to those offering more specialist courses. Published by the Independent Schools Careers Organisation, 12a-18a Princess Way, Camberley, Surrey GU15 3SP ✆ Camberley (01276) 21188 ≡ (01276) 691833.

Second Chances £27.95 is a popular reference book on education and training sources and opportunities for anyone aged 16 and over. Available from the Careers and Occupational Information Centre, PO Box 298A, Thames Ditton, Surrey KT7 0ZS ✆ 0181-957 5030.

Time To Learn £4.95 including postage is a directory of adult education courses in the UK. There are 2 editions each year, covering the periods October-March and April-September. Published by the National Institute for Adult & Continuing Education, 21B De Montfort Street, Leicester LE1 7GE ✆ 0116-204 4200.

Grants and financial aid

Charities Digest £19.95 including postage. A useful publication listing details and addresses of some 1,200 national and regional charities in the UK, including a number of educational charities. Published by Waterlow Information Services, Paulton House, 8 Shepherdess Walk, London N1 7LB ✆ 0171-490 0049.

Directory of Grant-Making Trusts £69.95. A list of voluntary grant-making bodies in England and Wales covering all fields of voluntary activities including medicine and health, welfare, education, the sciences and humanities, religion and the environment. Published by Charities Aid Foundation, Kings Hill, West Malling, Kent ME9 4YA ✆ Tonbridge (01732) 520000.

The Educational Grants Directory 1996/ 97 £16.95 is a comprehensive listing of educational charities which support children and students in need. Covers over 260 national and general sources of help, giving a total of £32 million per year in education grants to individuals. Published by the Directory of Social Change, 24 Stephenson Way, London NW1 2DP © 0171-209 5151 ❏ info@d-s-c.demon.co.uk.

The Grants Register is a guide to educational grants worldwide, and covers scholarships, fellowships and research grants; exchange opportunities, vacation study awards and travel grants; grants for artistic or scientific projects; competitions, prizes, honoraria; professional and vocational awards, and awards for refugees, minority groups and students in unexpected financial difficulties. Published by Macmillan Reference Ltd, 25 Eccleston Place, London SW1W 9NF and available for consultation in libraries.

Student Grants & Loans - A Brief Guide for Higher Education Students, free, explains higher education grants available from LEAs. It details what the grant covers, who is eligible, how to apply, and is available from local education authorities or from the Department for Education & Employment.

Student Money Matters £7.95 is a guide to help students and their parents face the challenges of a university or college career without the constant worry of financial pressure. It gives information on students' costs, sources of finance for undergraduates and postgraduates, sponsorship, scholarships, bursaries and budgeting.

Author: Gwenda Thomas; published by Trotman & Co Ltd, 12 Hill Rise, Richmond, Surrey TW10 6UA © 0181-332 2132 ☎ 0181-332 0860. Also available on video, £25+VAT.

Study Abroad 1996/97 £14.95. Lists over 200,000 scholarships, fellowships, assistantships and travel grants at university level throughout the world. Published by UNESCO and obtainable in the UK from HMSO © 0171-873 9090.

Expeditions and travel
Expedition Planners' Handbook and Directory £12.95 is the best and most comprehensive guide to all aspects of expedition planning with articles by over forty specialists from the world of science and exploration. Includes sections on research, adventure, charity, community and youth projects; planning, logistics and techniques; plus directories of reference sources, grant-giving bodies and equipment suppliers. Several of the chapters are available for sale (price £2.50) as individual booklets, including *Fundraising for Expeditions, Insurance for Expeditions, Reference Sources for Expeditions*, and *Guide to Writing Reports*. Edited by S Winser and N McWilliam; published by the Expedition Advisory Centre, 1 Kensington Gore, London SW7 2AR © 0171-591 3030 ☎ 0171-591 3031 ❏ eac@rgs.org.

Fundraising to Join an Expedition £2.50, a guide for those raising funds to join ventures such as Raleigh International. Author: Catherine Lucas; published by the Expedition Advisory Centre, see above.

Joining an Expedition £5 details how to take advantage of the expedition opportunities offered by over fifty UK-based organisations, with fundraising advice. Edited by Shane Winser; published by the Expedition Advisory Centre, see above.

Sources of Information for Independent and Overland Travellers £5 is a reference guide giving details on where to get the best information about travel, maps, health, equipment, visas, insurance etc. Edited by Shane Winser; published by the Expedition Advisory Centre, see above.

The Travellers' Handbook is a reference and source book for the independent traveller, with chapters on travel, camping and backpacking, hitch-hiking, health, clothing, where to stay, dealing with people when things go wrong, photography, choosing maps, passports, visas, permits, insurance, currency and Customs. Also includes special chapters for students, single women and people with a disability. Published by the independent travel club WEXAS International, 45-49 Brompton Road, London SW3 1DE ℗ 0171-589 3315, price £14.95 (£7.95 to members).

The YMCA World Directory £5.50 including UK postage, lists over 2,500 YMCAs in 120 countries offering accommodation for both sexes. Available from YMCA Supplies, National Council of YMCAs, 640 Forest Road, London E17 3DZ ℗ 0181-520 5599.

International Youth Hostel Handbook Vol 1 £6.99, gives addresses and brief details of hostels in Europe. Available from YHA Adventure Shops plc, 14 Southampton Row, London WC2E 7HY ℗ 0171-836 8541.

Travellers' Health - How to Stay Healthy Abroad £8.99 is considered the definitive guide to all aspects of health abroad, and offers comprehensive health advice for those planning journeys anywhere in the world. Author: Dr Richard Dawood; published by Oxford University Press and available from most good bookshops and long-haul travel shops.

Lonely Planet's *Travel Survival Kits* and *Shoestring* guides are detailed travel handbooks to countries in Africa, Asia, Australasia, Europe and the Americas, giving background on the country, advice on places to visit, information on where to stay, what to eat, how to get there and ways to travel around. Also produce a range of useful phrasebooks containing essential words and phrases for effective communication with local people. Available in most good bookshops and long-haul travel chains. Prices range from £1.95 for some of the smaller phrasebooks through to £16.95 for the bigger travel guides.

Rough Guides is a series of practical handbooks to most countries in Europe and some areas of Asia, Africa, South America and the United States, giving full details on cities, towns and places of interest, plus a wealth of practical information on places to stay and how to get around. The range also includes *More Women Travel*, a guide for women travellers; also *Nothing Ventured: Disabled People Travel the World* containing first-hand accounts of disabled people's travel experiences and practical advice on planning a trip. Available in most good bookshops and long-haul travel chains; prices range from £6.99-£11.99.

Throughout this guide, in the sections on practical information and advice and in the individual sections on placements, there are accounts from students and employing and placing organisations alike. As wide-ranging as the experiences are, the underlying message is that for those concerned a year between gave a positive impetus to their personal development, future studies and eventual careers.

In this section we asked six quite different organisations, GAP Activity Projects, The Missions to Seamen, Raleigh International, The Project Trust, The Year In Industry and AFS/Intercultural Education Programmes, to recount the values they place in a year between and to highlight some of the experiences of students they place.

Also included in this section are personal accounts from gap year students in which they discuss their expectations, the activities they undertook and the learning outcomes.

Francine Barley on her year between at the Waldorf Kindergarten, Berlin, placed through GAP Activity Projects

From the invaluable recognition of a British engineering company to being accepted as a fully-fledged member of a Brazilian community, from having an insight into New York criminal activity to working in the orphanages of Peru, from helping disabled people in Kent live independently to teaching Christmas carols to children in Thailand, these reports are vital testaments for all those considering taking a year between.

EXPANDING YOUR HORIZONS

GAP Activity Projects explain how a mixed bag of work and travel can lead to self-discovery and greater maturity. GAP is an educational charity, founded in 1972 to give those with a year between leaving school and going on to higher education or vocational training the opportunity to travel to another country and live and work among its people.

A recent survey indicated that already at least 25% of those currently entering higher education have had a break of varying duration between school and college. Those who have grown weary of A level or equivalent examination pressures and the attendant problems of university entrance may see a year out as a chance to recharge the batteries before the final challenge of a degree/ diploma course. At a time of economic recession some find it necessary to raise funds to help them through their student years. Others have a burning ambition to broaden their vision by undertaking challenging work in some distant part of the world where lifestyles are different and a culture shock can be a stimulus to new thinking. Whatever individual motives may be, the year between, if carefully planned and constructively used, can be an excellent foundation for gaining a more balanced approach to higher education and thereby reaping greater benefit from it.

At one time universities and colleges were a shade cautious about welcoming the newly emerging phenomenon of a year out with open arms. There was still an old guard who favoured an unbroken progression from school to college and the argument was often put forward that those who opted for an intervening year were in danger of losing touch with the process of learning and might even forget much of what they had learned at school. However in the world of higher education there is now little support among lecturers and teachers for this view. In a few areas of study - mathematics and music are sometimes quoted - the importance of continuity is still mentioned but the prevailing opinion now is that the advantages of a constructive year out considerably outweigh the disadvantages.

Increasingly, international influences are an everyday part of our existence. Food, television, theatre and films all serve to open our eyes to faraway places. It's hardly surprising therefore, that when considering the options open to them for a year out from education, young people are keen to pursue adventure overseas. It's worth stopping to consider, however, whether travel alone is the best way of exploring a different culture.

Choosing to do voluntary work in another country can give you the best chance to become assimilated into a totally new way of life. By offering the chance to live and work with a different people, voluntary work enables you to form friendships and experience their life in a way that would not be easily accessible to a passing traveller. Having the time and energy to devote yourself to doing something for the benefit of others can also be viewed as a luxury. In later years the desire might be there, invariably the time and freedom to do so will not. The intense, personal satisfaction of contributing to a community which has welcomed you into its midst should not be underestimated.

Gap Activity Projects has a wide range of projects which enable year between students to experience life in another culture, allowing them to use their skills with people who require them.

Whether you are lending your native language skills to someone learning English, or a hand around a farm in the Falklands, you know you will be in a community who needs you.

If planning to defer entry to university then approval from admission tutors could depend on your explanation of what you expect to gain from your planned year out. The benefits of doing a structured project within your time overseas may well be easier to sell than the ubiquitous phrase *going travelling*! The majority of university admission offices that we have spoken to support the idea of a year out, provided you do something positive with it. Not only does this time out result in increased maturity and a wider perspective on life, but in most cases students are refreshed by this break in their education and, on their return, are ready to take up the challenge of learning once more.

Increasingly companies are seeking to recruit employees who have developed an international awareness in some way. Through programmes such as GAP you can gain experience that will provide a distinct advantage when seeking future employment with any company that is globally aware. Not only have you proven that you have the drive and commitment needed to be selected for an overseas voluntary project, but you have had an invaluable exposure to working within a different culture.

Maia Lawson at Freshfields, an international law firm, emphasises the credibility given to those who have chosen to spend their time working on voluntary projects overseas:

We have built our business through

striving for excellence in meeting clients' needs... We recruit law and non-law graduates as trainee solicitors. As well as high intellectual calibre, we are looking for people with a rounded resourceful personality with a sense of humour - qualities which we believe are nurtured by the experience that a year out placement can offer.

Remember, the decision to undertake a year out project will not necessarily deprive you of the opportunity to travel, see glorious sunsets and visit beaches, glaciers or rainforests. Projects last, on average, 6-9 months so you will still have plenty of time for expeditions across foreign lands and, of course, enough time to work in order to fund this incredible journey.

As a volunteer your accommodation and food will be provided by your host. In most cases, where the host can afford it, you will also receive some pocket money, to help with day-to-day expenses. The total costs for your placement will depend however on the location of your project. Apart from any interview and placement fees, you will usually need to raise the money for your flight and your insurance; again, both are dependent on the location and duration of your project. Some projects will also involve medical and visa costs. If you are assisting in the Teaching of English as a Foreign Language (TEFL) you may also have to attend a training course, arranged with an accredited language school. Courses start from approximately £110, and are designed to give you the confidence to plan your own lessons and work with children in what can be a very different environment to schools in the UK.

These costs can appear incredibly daunting when you first calculate the amount required. It is however, possible to work on a project whose total costs will not exceed £800. You don't have to raise thousands to do something truly remarkable!

There is no archetypal gap year volunteer, because there is no typical project. Organisations such as GAP are looking for people who have a sense of commitment to go alongside their flair for adventure, who will cope with being in a strange culture, and who are determined to complete their project, even through adverse circumstances. Can you improvise solutions to problems, communicate with a wide range of people and retain a sense of humour and fun above all else?

Life skills matter far more to GAP than academic capability, but, if you enjoy the classroom environment, then GAP has teaching placements worldwide that you could be ideal for. If you are a practical person with an aptitude for mucking in and physically demanding work, then projects such as practical conservation and land management placements might make the most of your skills. Community-based social projects require volunteers who enjoy working with people of mixed abilities, with patience and a caring attitude. These can be some of the most rewarding projects that are on offer.

Regardless of where you would like to go, and the kind of project you would like to do, the most important thing to do is apply, and the earlier the better. GAP welcomes applications from September onwards, and the stage at which you can apply has a direct consequence on the number and range of projects that will be available to you. Many organisations can accept applications up until the start of the projects in the following September but at that stage the vacancies will be limited.

Thousands of GAP volunteers have seen the benefits of applying. Izzie Johnston wrote to GAP after working on a practical conservation project in Australia, just before going travelling around New Zealand:

It is hard to express my appreciation of an organisation that has given me a new set of eyes, to see things I wouldn't normally see. My year out has left me with many adventures and a knowledge that will last a lifetime.

Another volunteer was placed in Israel to work on a kibbutz near Nazareth. She worked in the bakery, often late at night:

When I decided to go to the kibbutz I considered that it would be a means of seeing the Holy Land but the kibbutz itself turned out to be the main focus of my time in Israel. I have no regrets at having taken time off between school and university to do something different.

Looking back, many returned volunteers can see with clarity the experience that they have gained. Rebecca Carter taught in Namibia:

I feel now that I learnt more from the children at St Michael's Mission School that I could ever have taught them. My whole perspective on life has changed . . . I often pine for Namibia and the children I grew to love.

Two volunteers who worked at a Cheshire Home in Malaysia, caring for the handicapped residents, commented on their experiences:

The residents are fantastic people. They are all so individual and have great personalities. We love working with them as they have so much to offer.

A penetrating thought came from a volunteer who worked in a preparatory school. She summarised the effect of her year out as follows:

I not only gained in experience but grew mentally, becoming more independent and learning about myself. Being away from family and friends broadens your mind - you find out who you are and what you would like to become. I now feel I have the confidence to make decisions for myself and by myself.

Rachel Hobcroft was placed as a volunteer school's assistant in Canada. She wrote expressing her belief in the value of a constructive year out before university:

It is so true that the more you learn about the world, the more you realise how little you know - a valuable lesson. By living abroad you are immersed in and learn firsthand about new, different and exciting cultures . . Living away from home in a new environment and looking after yourself results in a more mature, independent, self-reliant, self-confident and responsible young person. These are excellent qualities to have under your belt when starting university and for entering employment.

It is difficult to summarise the benefits

Rebecca Carter and Katherine White on their year out, helping out at St Michael's Mission School, Namibia

you can gain from doing a year out placement because of the range of experiences to be had by such a diverse group of people. It is true to say however, that you have to be prepared to put in a substantial amount of effort into your project - but what you receive in return is far, far more valuable that anything you can give.

When the final balance sheet is drawn up, it would seem that those who benefit fall into three groups: Universities gain from the added input of students who have been out there in the real world and have educated themselves in the school of life. They will have greater motivation for their studies and will be less likely to pull out during or after the first year. It is not uncommon for universities and colleges to have problems with younger and less mature students, who have doubts and misgivings about their choice of course. Some research has been done on the eventual attainments of those who have taken a year away from formal training, and the conclusion is that such people do better both in academic results and in the likelihood of completing the course than the mass of their contemporaries. Employers, too, can fairly claim to be beneficiaries of the year between. They are frequently to be heard stressing the importance of work experience and several captains of industry have publicly stressed the relevance of a constructive in-between year. The ability to relate to other people and to show initiative in dealing with practical problems is much valued by prospective employers. In this country the curriculum for potential graduates is often both shorter and narrower than elsewhere and this makes it even more desirable for young people to seize every opportunity of gaining wider experience in the outside world.

A YEAR OF CHALLENGE

Jan Burbery, from The Missions to Seamen, describes how a placement as a Mission chaplain's assistant in the year between offers the challenge of practical Christian service. The Missions to Seamen is the Anglican Church's ministry to seafarers, founded in 1856, caring for the spiritual and material welfare of seafarers around the globe. The Mission helps to combat isolation, exploitation and the dangers of the sea, working for improvements in conditions, education and welfare, offering a ministry of word, sacrament, counselling care and Christian welcome.

When I first heard I was being sent to Japan with The Missions to Seamen, it seemed like a dream come true - and I was not to be disappointed.

The writer, Jill Sheldon, went to Kobe, some 400 miles south of Tokyo, to assist the port chaplain, after being accepted for The Missions to Seamen's voluntary service scheme which offers 21-26 year olds the opportunity to become involved in practical Christian service within the shipping industry.

The scheme provides chaplains at the Mission's Flying Angel centres in 20 of the world's busier ports with much needed extra help, and gives those chosen to assist the chance to learn about and help others in an environment with a truly international flavour. Assistants help chaplains in most aspects of the work and they have to be prepared to do anything from visiting seafarers on board ship, welcoming them at the club, helping them make phone calls home, changing money, running the shop and, not least, providing a sympathetic ear and helping with a problem.

Jill loved the work and the variety of experiences it offered. Daily ship visiting meant she met people from all over the world, and the friendships formed in one case led to a 3 day trip on a regular voyage between Japan and South Korea when Jill got to try most jobs, including steering the ship.

As a chaplain's assistant, you get to see all aspects of life at sea - the best and the worst. I dined on the QEII and on ships where food rations were as little as a dollar a day. I often met crews having to live in horrendous conditions who were on contracts up to a year long, but they didn't complain because so many others want their jobs.

Chaplains' assistants also have to be prepared to go anywhere. It could be to the heat and dust of the far flung Australian mining community in Dampier or the tropical lushness of Mombasa. It could be across the Channel to Rotterdam or Dunkerque, or across the Atlantic to New Orleans. On the other hand, it might be to comparatively familiar surroundings in a UK port.

I had hoped to spend my year abroad, so I was disappointed when I was posted to Southampton, said former volunteer Jonathan Allatt. *But the multinational, multi-cultural clientele at the Mission meant the world came to me.*

Meeting and talking with seafarers is a large part of the work, and this often takes place during a visit aboard ship - a job which can be daunting when first undertaken.

Visiting ships proved quite a challenge and at first I found it a little nerve-wracking having no idea who I would meet at the top of the gangway! wrote Kirsty Fraser. *But as it became much more familiar, I felt that my approach improved with my self-confidence.*

You diced with danger walking up dodgy gangplanks, wrote another volunteer, *prayed that the ship wouldn't sail while you were on board, struggled to explain in pidgin English where the centre was. The reception* would vary from disinterest to being the centre of attention in an excited crowd clamouring for leaflets.

Working with people from so many different countries and cultures is one of the experiences volunteers find most valuable. The comments made by this chaplain's assistant after his year with the Mission are echoed by many: *On a personal level I feel I have grown up considerably. I have seen, and have some understanding of, situations that I never knew existed. I feel more aware of myself, my weaknesses and my strong points, and I am more able to talk with anyone.*

Certainly, as a chaplain's assistant with the Mission you have to be prepared to cope with a huge variety of new experiences. You may be far from home, living in a different culture and you will have to come to terms with the fast-moving modern shipping industry and its international personnel. But these experiences help chaplains' assistants understand the problems and experiences of the seafarers themselves. When they are at sea, seafarers are completely isolated from the community ashore. When in port - for periods of time made ever briefer by more efficient cargo handling techniques - they often find themselves in places where they feel alienated by language and culture.

When Sophie Gregory was sent out to Brisbane she had times when she missed her home and family and as a result she really appreciated how seafarers would miss theirs:
The difference was that for me it was only a year, for them it's a way of life. And at least my family was at the end of a phone.

On a more practical level, Aiden Kennedy wrote from Fremantle: *I had to learn to run up and down Japanese tuna boats without knocking my head off, drive into town to find lost seafarers and do airport runs in the middle of the night, as well as learn the ropes as centre duty officer which meant handling foreign money, book keeping, cooking meals for seafarers and so on. But if I thought I was thrown in at the deep end when I started this job, imagine how seafarers feel arriving in Fremantle speaking no English, with no clue where they are - strangers in a strange country. They are in at the deep end, not me.*

An important part of the job is being open to seafarers' needs. You may get very specific requests, such as being asked to arrange a football match for a crew or to help in a justice case such as non-payment of wages. But more often it is a question of offering friendship and spending time talking and listening. It may not seem very much, but to seafarers far from home, it can mean a great deal that someone cares enough to spend time with them.

Another assistant wrote:
Simply giving an hour of my time and listening, no matter how mundane the conversation, seemed to be a way of affirming their value as individuals. I also became aware of the reciprocal nature of many exchanges with seafarers. Far from me giving something to the seamen, it was more a question of vice-versa, for often, in the warm welcome of a group of badly treated men, I experienced glimpses of God's joy.

For others, self-development came with taking on more responsibility than they had dreamed of before they left home. In one centre, the two assistants were to run the centre in the chaplain's two-week absence ... and then one broke his leg.

It suddenly dawned on me that I would be running the centre alone, said the other later. *A mixture of fear and excitement followed. The first week was the busiest since I had started work and I didn't get home before 23.00 any evening. But the second was a complete contrast and the enemy was loneliness. During that time I learned a lot about myself. Unsure at first, I found myself capable of more than I expected.*

Almost without exception, returning chaplains' assistants talk of the benefits of learning a lot about themselves, usually as a result of the demands of the job, and gaining self-confidence as a result. Many of them feel that they have gained as much, if not more, than the people they have been sent out to help. Mike Morris and Patrick Puddle who worked together in Singapore often managed to go out with seafarers, especially if they were regular callers, or if their ship was in dry dock for repairs. They valued being regarded as friends and felt it an important part of their role.

We also did a lot of hospital visiting, which was an equally valuable part of our work. Apart from often being the only people seafarers saw outside hospital staff, we also acted as translators, were in touch with their families and provided them with clothing. One Burmese seaman spent five months in hospital after he had a serious fall on his ship. We became great friends and this at least helped brighten his otherwise exasperating and painful life.

THE EXPEDITION EXPERIENCE

Raleigh International here profile the opportunities that an expedition can offer, to the volunteers themselves, from whatever background, and to the communities they help along the route. Raleigh aims to provide a unique opportunity for young people of many nations to develop their self-confidence and leadership skills by stretching themselves mentally and physically in the service of others.

Raleigh International is a youth development charity which aims to help young people develop by giving them the opportunity to work on demanding environmental and community projects during 10-week long expeditions around the world. It provides not only lasting benefits for the communities in the host countries, in terms of conservation, scientific research, and medical and social help, but also presents a unique opportunity for personal achievement and advancement for the young people involved.

Anyone aged 17-25, able to understand English and swim is eligible. Candidates are assessed on selection weekends throughout the year in the UK and overseas. Applicants are able to judge whether Raleigh is right for them through the demanding problem-solving and team-working challenges encountered. The aim is not to select an elite, but to discover who will benefit most from, and contribute to, the exciting and worthwhile projects carried out.

To support Raleigh's work at home and abroad, all Venturers, as volunteers are called once they have been selected, have to raise funds before going on an expedition. The sum varies according to the applicant's background. Venturers are very resourceful and raise funds in a variety of ways: sponsorship, car boot sales, bike rides and so on. Raleigh's head office and the Venturer Support Groups (past Venturers) help with ideas and initiatives.

Ten expeditions are planned each year to countries as diverse as Belize, Namibia, Uganda and Chile, with about 100 Venturers taking part on each. Living conditions are very basic: tents, open fires, simple food, and the work is very hard, but ultimately, rewarding as Venturers discover the values and cultures of communities with very different ways of life. The Venturers take part in a mixture of environmental and community projects, as well as getting a real taste of adventure. They may find themselves involved in working on sight-restoring programmes, building schools or clinics, carrying out wildlife surveys or trekking to glaciers in southern Chile to monitor their movements.

Jo Hirst from West Yorkshire is going to Leicester University:

After speaking to a careers advisor, I decided to apply for an assessment weekend. I then went to Hebden Bridge in West Yorkshire and was selected three weeks later. After being selected to go to Chile, I then had to raise £2,995 for Raleigh International before going on the expedition. This involved writing to companies and charitable trusts, organising a sponsored event and running jumble sales and boot fairs. Now I'm here in Chile, all my hard work has been really worthwhile.

Raleigh carries out projects on its own, with other non-governmental aid organisations, such as SEE (Surgical Eye Expedition) and Save the Children Fund, and provides support for geologists, biologists, glaciologists and other natural scientists. Some year between students get the opportunity to work as support in similar disciplines as the ones they may go on to study at university, whilst still taking part in other ventures which test them physically as well as intellectually.

Sally Dalton from East Sussex is studying biology at Imperial College, London:

Raleigh International has certainly been an experience. I have found it challenging but have acquired new skills, been to unusual places, made some great friends and some even better doughnuts!

Jonathan Pope from Winchester joined an expedition to Guyana before going on to read geography at Cambridge:

After attending a Venturer post-expedition talk, I soon found myself writing to numerous local businesses in order to finance my own Raleigh expedition. I have since found it a great opportunity for personal development and leadership skills. It's the experience of a lifetime.

In Guyana, volunteers were involved in a variety of projects, including vaccination and malarial smear programmes, nutritional surveys, the building of two schools, the preservation of an 18th century Dutch fort, the refurbishment of a leprosy hospital and the protection of a forestry reserve. Raleigh has reached some of the most remote settlements, vaccinating young children and babies against tuberculosis, diphtheria and whooping cough. Malaria is an ongoing problem in the country and the volunteers worked with local medics dealing with the cases found as the groups visited

each community. Diagnosis was followed by treatment on the spot.

The aim of Raleigh is to develop a higher degree of self-knowledge and self-reliance, as well as enhance interpersonal skills, through a tough and rigorous testing experience. Travelling between project sites alone presents the volunteers with major challenges, with many spending up to ten days walking and canoeing through difficult jungle terrain, testing physical and tolerance levels to the fullest.

Alison Englefield from Cheshire went on to study languages at Oxford Brookes University:

At first I found the thought of going on a Raleigh expedition rather daunting. But after being here for six weeks I have adapted well to the work and camp lifestyle. I've become much more tolerant of many different types of people in my group and made many strong, lifelong friendships. Being one of the youngest in the group isn't a bad thing - everyone treats each other

Amanda Salmon worked alongside locals building a house at the SOS orphanage in Dudhial, Pakistan

with equal respect and that has given me confidence in my approach with other people. Each person has their own strengths and weaknesses. I found all the adventure and challenge I was looking for in the project assigned to me.

From climbing mountains, trekking through jungles and being set almost impossible tasks such as building a research station for scientists in the middle of the rainforest in Belize, it has been hard work but lots of fun.

The most rewarding challenge, however, has been within myself, giving everything to the friendly and hospitable people of Belize. I would strongly recommend any student thinking of taking a year off to try to get on a Raleigh expedition both for themselves and for developing communities around the world.

A Venturer undertakes a health and nutritional survey in the Northwest Region, Guyana

Venturers returning from expedition bring with them a clearer perspective and broadened horizons, as well as a great deal of motivation and enthusiasm to channel into their lives and chosen careers. Both college tutors and companies sending employees on expeditions find that, on return, the volunteers have heightened leadership qualities and improved general knowledge, in addition to better team-working skills, making this type of investment extremely worthwhile.

Venturers also return with a heightened awareness of their environment and of the needs of others. For many this means putting back into their communities some of the skills and experience gained from expedition. Venturer Support Groups exist around the world; apart from promoting the aims and ideals of Raleigh and assisting new Venturers with their fundraising efforts, the Groups organise a variety of community and environmental projects. In Britain each year some 200 projects and over 50,000 man-hours of work are completed. Overseas, the Support Group has adopted a school in a deprived area of Santiago, Chile; organised a fundraising event in aid of earthquake relief for the people of Kobe, Japan; and Support Group members in Siberia have put together and carried out their own conservation projects.

In addition, many returning Venturers find other ways of putting their new-found skills and experience to good use, by working for international aid agencies or giving much of their spare time to helping local voluntary organisations, or perhaps embarking on formal study of areas of scientific and social interest initially prompted by an expedition project. Venturers return from expedition enriched by what they have learnt, and in turn enrich their own communities.

A YEAR OF ADVENTURE

Project Trust sends young people from all over Britain overseas for twelve months. It offers placements in twenty four countries, all outside Europe. It recruits from those students who wish to spend their gap year doing something worthwhile for a full year before they go on to university. The work they undertake includes giving English conversation lessons in schools in Thailand.

Louise Histon from Stratton-on-the-Foss in Dorset was at school at St Antony's, Leweston, and applied to go overseas with Project Trust in the November. She was selected to go to Thailand and flew out to Bangkok, with nine others, the following September. She wrote a long letter to her sponsors in the December, part of which is reproduced here. Louise plans to return at the beginning of September to go to university to read either an arts course or medicine.

My Thailand experience began on 2 September in the teeming metropolis of Bangkok. After a long and exhausting flight, all ten Project Trust volunteers arrived to be greeted by the suffocating humidity and general chaos of this place. My first glimpses of Bangkok were through the dirty windows of a city bus. Through sleepy, disorientated eyes I caught only fleeting snapshots of the city as we sped along the highway, weaving crazily through the horrendous queues of traffic.

I remember being struck by the haphazard character of the city: a curious conglomeration of old and new, East and West, the exotic and the commonplace, serenity and chaos, all thrown together to give Bangkok its fascinating and unique flavour. Glittering skyscrapers tower majestically above warrens of corrugated iron squatter settlements, intervened by luxurious shopping plazas, continuing on and sprawling out in this disorderly manner.

We spent only one night in Bangkok before making the four hour train journey up to Nakhon Sawan, my home for the year. My partner, Ceri, and I were met at the train station by some members of the English department and also our host families. We were given such a warm welcome and made to feel at home immediately. I stayed with my host family for two weeks and was instantly included in the family. I was invited to refer to my host parents as mother and father and have also acquired two brothers and a sister. Amidst the warmth and security of my new family I began the long and slow process of adjusting to a new and dramatically different culture.

Those first few days in Nakhon Sawan were some of the strangest I have ever had. Everything around me was so foreign - it was all quite overwhelming. Having lived in the country for so long it was strange to be dropped in the centre of a humid, noisy and dusty city. The centre is typically commercial, choked with department stores, shops, offices, banks and other consumer amenities similar to those found in any city worldwide. However if you slip down one of the *sois* (side streets) off the main road you encounter a uniquely Thai scene. Bright and colourful markets line the streets, boasting an enormous variety of fruits, vegetables, flowers, forming a kaleidoscope of variety, colour and taste. All of this is canopied under rainbow-coloured umbrellas, shielding the produce from the unrelenting sun.

Nakhon Sawan is anything but a tourist spot: in fact after almost four months here I have seen all of about six other white faces. As a result, the people of Nakhon Sawan are somewhat sceptical about *farangs* (foreigners). Thus Ceri and I are a great source of interest and amusement. The continual shouts and curious stares are somewhat unnerving and are a constant reminder of how different we are. However, gradually people are getting use to us. It's the smallest signs of recognition that mean so much: a welcome smile from the old lady at the local market; becoming regulars at our local street restaurants and exchanging morning greetings with the street vendors at the end of our lane, on the way to school. All of these small gestures contribute to a greater feeling of belonging and acceptance into our new community.

Those first few days also saw the beginning of my present career as a teacher at Nakhon Sawan school. The school is a large, mixed government-run secondary school, and has the prestigious reputation of being the best school in the province. There are close to 5,000 students and a correspondingly large team of staff. The school covers a large area, comprising seven subject specific buildings, although in spite of its size it is overcrowded. The average class size is fifty five students packed into orderly wooden desk rows in hot and very basic classrooms. I began teaching almost immediately and will never forget walking into my first class and being totally overwhelmed by the huge number of smiley faces beaming out at me.

I teach first and second years, ages 11/12 and 12/13, respectively. Due to the number of students in the class, there is a wide range of both ability and motivation. Although very demanding and sometimes frustrating, I really love my work. The students are just fantastic, every class is completely unique, each comprising a different cocktail of characters, imparting their own distinctive flavour. They all share a common trait, however, as with all Thai people, an infectious appetite for life, a warm and friendly disposition and a genuine consideration for others. This is recognisable right through Thai society, and unique to Thailand, aptly nicknamed The Land of Smiles. Most of my classes are based on conversation and everyday English, my prime aim being to get the students talking and using the language, and also I try to inject a little bit of British culture.

I only taught for three weeks in September before the school broke up for their holidays in October. During this holiday all ten Project Trust volunteers travelled north to Chiang Mai for a three week intensive Thai language course. It was an excellent course and gave us a solid foundation on which to build and develop our language skills. The course also gave us the opportunity to explore and get to know Thailand's second largest city. This seven hundred year old, once remote and isolated settlement is yet another victim of time and progress, as tourism has taken the city by storm. Impressive hotels, high-rise condominiums, luxury shopping plazas and a whole range of cosmopolitan amenities have transformed the city into a tourist's paradise.

However, underlying all this modernisation lies the real Chiang Mai. It remains a complete contrast and refreshing alternative to the pollution and chaos of Bangkok. The city is dominated by the green mountain of Doi Suthep, crowned with the ornately beautiful temple, Wat Phra Doi Suthep. Geographically it can be divided into two sections, the old city and the new city. The former is enclosed by a moat and four wells, around which has grown up the latter, newer addition. As well as visiting some of Chiang Mai's stunning temples and historic monuments we also got down to some serious shopping at the infamous Chiang Mai night bazaar - an endless stretch of

clothes, arts and crafts, jewellery and many other such wallet-lightening opportunities.

We returned to Nakhon Sawan for the second semester. My timetable has been increasing steadily over the last few weeks and now I am really busy. I teach nineteen timetabled lessons a week and also English conversation groups, every day after school between four and five o'clock. Also I am teaching two adult conversation classes a week and have Thai language lessons once a week.

In the New Year I am beginning work at the city hospital, organised as an extra by myself, which should be really interesting. I am currently coaching a little choir of twenty five of my students to sing some carols for assembly on Christmas Day and have also persuaded one of my colleagues to dress up as Santa and arrive in the middle of assembly with a big sack of sweets for all the students. Ceri and I are going to give a short presentation about Christmas also, so it should be really good fun. It's really good to be busy especially at this time of the year when the mind wanders to thoughts of home, family and friends.

I hope this letter has gone some way to describe my new life style and I am sure you can sense my growing affection for the people and country of Thailand.

A HEAD START

The Year in Industry scheme, now in its tenth year, has placed almost 3,000 students with industrial partners. It aims to attract young people into industry and make sure they return after graduation. The scheme typically places 18 and 19 year olds with employers for a year before they begin university, offering them the chance to acquire valuable experience, to earn some money and the opportunity to find themselves in exciting and challenging situations. On past experience, those taking a year out in this way end up with a better degree than they would have by going straight from school to university and are certainly more employable as a graduate.

Over 300 young people beginning engineering degrees at universities around the country at the start of the next academic year will have a clear head start on their fellow students - a year of solid work experience under their belt.

Many of them have had a lasting impact on the companies where they worked under the Year in Industry scheme. Cost savings, new products, innovative development work and new working practices are just some of the legacies left behind.

Rebecca Billau tackled some serious shopfloor issues at West Midlands-based Firth Cleveland Engineering, the UK's largest supplier of safety toecaps. Rebecca had a wide and potentially daunting brief, to look at any areas where cost reduction and efficiency improvements could be had. She was given a free hand to consult with suppliers, customers and staff, from shopfloor workers to company directors.

Her performance won her the top award in a scheme run by the Engineering Employers' Federation to reward the students who made the best contribution to their host businesses. Her achievements were significant and have had a lasting impact on the small company.

Firth Cleveland's manufacturing process involves pressing, degreasing, heat treatment, powder coating, inspection and packing toe caps and is complemented by the company's toolroom and maintenance facilities.

YEARS OF EXPERIENCE 69 YEARS OF EXPERIENCE

Poor paint adhesion to some toe caps meant that the company imposed a 48 hour quarantine between coating and packing. Research trials on the chemical properties of various degreasing agents and rust preventatives allowed Rebecca to solve the intermittent quality problem. Her work also meant that toe caps could be packed directly from the coating plant, significantly reducing despatch times.

Her work helped Firth Cleveland to reduce the cost of its view-and-pack operation by 16%, reduce labour costs in the press shop by 29% and reduce the time from final production to despatch by up to 48 hours.

A major factor in accomplishing all Rebecca did was her ability to think clearly, act decisively and obtain the cooperation of customers, suppliers and staff says Maurice Cox, technical director.

At Nortel Technology in Harlow, student Alex Meehan made an impact on several of the company's telecommunications research projects. His work centred on the development of optical fibre devices. The most sophisticated project involved a new idea for designing array transmitters - devices in which light is coupled from the optical source, a semiconductor laser, into an optical fibre cable.

Alex picked up an idea initiated by senior research staff but which had not been tried and tested. It involved developing a method for coupling light from an array of 10 lasers into a corresponding array of 10 fibres via micro lenses formed directly on the fibre ends. These lensed fibres make a transmitter five times more efficient.

Alex researched what shape to make the lens, designed and made equipment so that lenses could be fabricated and developed a suitable production technique.

Alex took a relatively crude laboratory process and developed it into a form suitable for transfer to production says Nortel senior research engineer Terry Bricheno.

The technique has been used in three types of array transmitter designed by Nortel in the past year. The new method is three times more accurate than other methods. It takes only 5% of the time to make the lenses and Nortel's initial saving is £30,000 a year. Once the transmitters go into full production, potential savings will be closer to £200,000 a year.

The technique is so accurate and cheap that it now is used for single fibres as well. It is considered the best way to launch light into a fibre says Alex.

An improved process for fixing lights to the glass of cars' rear windows was Lucy-Marie Sharpe's contribution to Triplex Safety Glass during her work experience. Triplex is the UK division of Pilkington Automotive and one of its newer responsibilities is to bond studs to glass supplied for rear car windows so that a third brake light can be attached.

Triplex was using long cycle time, low productivity technology to bond the studs to the glass. Lucy-Marie's brief was to develop a high productivity process, while improving process control and quality. Her solution was a new assembly system with an automated application of the studs.

But the most important development was using a heat cure tape instead of glue to fix the studs in place. Cycle times have been reduced from three days to several minutes.

Glass processors now have to develop assembly capabilities. Lucy-Marie's work will make a significant contribution says Pilkington Automotive's glazing projects manager.

The assembly system cost £7,000 to make and saves around 50 pence on every glass produced. Over the next two to three years the process will lead to savings of £35,000 a year for Triplex.

Over 250 companies regularly take part in the Year in Industry programme - blue chip multinationals and small/medium-sized enterprises alike - spanning a wide range of different industries and technologies. There is a clear payback both for the students and the employers. For students, it gives some appreciation of what industry is really about. For industrialists, it allows them to benefit from some of the best innovative young brains in the country.

Rachel Poole spent her year at engineering consultants William Halcrow and Associates. She was involved in projects as diverse as motorways, weir gates, pumping stations and flood warning schemes. Rachel says:

The Year in Industry is one of the best things I have done. Before I started my placement I was unsure about fitting in. This was my first job! I knew very little about engineering consultants or the business world. Despite this, I have thoroughly enjoyed the experience. This placement has reinforced my aspirations to become an engineer. I have a place to study electro-mechanical engineering at Southampton University in October, and hope my work at Halcrow will help me relate to the coursework. I can recommend the Year in Industry to any student about to start university. You meet lots of people, learn a great deal and, best of all, have fun!

On the evidence to date, the Year in Industry scheme helps produce more mature, more committed undergraduates better equipped to achieve on their degree courses and in their careers.

Past students have gone on to achieve exceptional degree results - so far 24% have got Firsts and 43% Upper Seconds - well above the national average. Looking back on their experience, Year in Industry graduates typically say that it helped them develop the people skills which employers seek in addition to the technical competence provided by a degree course, that is the ability to work in a team, leadership and personal initiative, business awareness, communication and problem-solving skills.

What's more, with 70% of Year in Industry graduates finding permanent employment within 6 months of graduating (compared to just 44% of all graduates), it also appears to have given them a head start in the graduate job market.

COMMUNITY EXPERIENCE

AFS Intercultural Education Programmes aims to provide young people with an insider's understanding of another culture, and an awareness of global issues, through the challenge of doing volunteer work on a social project in a community in Latin America, Africa or Asia. Adrian Sellers from AFS profiles the opportunities the Community Service Programme offers, and the recent experiences of young people. AFS is an international, voluntary, non-profit organisation that operates in 55 countries around the world. It is the world's second largest volunteer organisation. AFS has over 50 years of experience of running programmes for the world's youth, and has been awarded a citation by the United Nations for its work.

Those on a Community Service Programme go to work on projects run by local people, rather than by AFS, developed in response to the needs of their community. The projects deal with issues such as health, education, the environment, agriculture, women's issues, drug rehabilitation, human rights, community development, and working with underprivileged children, people with disabilities and the elderly. How they will spend their time working with these issues will vary from project to project.

Their work on the project, and the contributions to the local community that they make, are not just valuable in themselves, but a way to become involved in the local community. Ben Lawton went with AFS to Brazil to work on a social project linked to a school for underprivileged children, teaching life skills and arts and crafts:

Working on the project was amazing. Through the project I got to know so many people. There were 150 kids at the school and whenever I walked around the town I would get kids waving and yelling, Hey, Uncle Ben! I would go home with them to have dinner and meet their families. With these people I got a real insight into the other side of Brazilian culture, which is where the real differences in culture are.

AFS do not send people to impose British culture on these countries, but to learn about the social problems, and to help with the solutions that the local people are putting forward.

Participants may have skills and experience to share, but the main part of the experience will be learning rather than teaching. Skills and personal qualities will be developed through the experiences that can be used in the rest of their life.

Catherine Blackham went to Brazil with AFS:

My experience over the six months was truly amazing. It was sometimes very hard but I had so many opportunities that just would not have been possible had I stayed in the UK. I have come back happier, more confident and secure, and prepared to face the challenge of university.

One cannot change the world in six months, but you can touch the lives of a few people in another community across the world, and share your own culture and knowledge of the UK, so that those people become more aware of life outside their own community and country. As your eyes are opened to a wider world, so are those of the people with whom you come into contact.

Ben says of his work on the project:

Just being there was important. This was a frontier town on the edge of the rainforest. It was like the Wild West! All these kids knew was that the UK was very very far away, near New York. They would ask me How come you came all this way to see us? And I would tell them Because you're special.

Catherine went to work with children in a small village in the centre of Brazil. She spent her time playing with the children, and teaching them drama, ballet and English. She says of leaving her project:

Though there was much more that I felt could be done, I was reminded by a friend that every waterfall begins with just one drop. I was sad to leave the girls, who also cried as I left and my hope is that they will remember that I was able to help them in some way, and that I care for them.

Whilst they are in that community participants live with a volunteer host family, not as a guest in the home but as a part of that family. This is an important part of the experience. Catherine says of her family:

I lived with my two year old 'sister' Rafaela, my 'mother' Marilene and 'grandmother' Zina, all of whom I became close to during the six months. Family is generally more important in Brazil than in Britain, and relatives usually live closer. This meant that I became part of an extended family as aunts, uncles and cousins were often in the house.

It is essential that volunteers learn the language through the course of the programme, and most people return fluent. Intensive language training is provided in the first month, which Catherine found helpful:

None of my family spoke English and I spoke no Portuguese when I arrived, which made the first few weeks very hard. I started Portuguese lessons straight away, and picked the language up quickly because I had to speak it to be able to communicate with most people!

Gaining fluency in the language means that participants can mix with any people in the community, not just those that speak English.

Robert Greenoak found that by the end of his six months working at a school for deaf children in a small town in the south of Brazil, he had really established himself in the community:

In Brazil, when you are saying goodbye to people you give them a kiss. Well, when I left to go to the little airport outside town, 170 people came with me to see me off. The airport staff were pretty alarmed at first! They had to hold the plane while all my family and friends lined up for their kiss goodbye!

This programme is an opportunity for a year between for those going on to work or further study. It is also open to older people for an experience after university before settling into a career, or even incorporated into a university course as part of a year of work experience abroad, an increasingly common element in many courses.

AFS do not require that applicants have professional qualifications relating to the kind of work done on the project. In fact, this is an opportunity to try out work in a field that participants are interested in pursuing as a future career. They can find out now whether this kind of work feels right for them, and if so then go into a course with valuable practical experience of the subject.

If they decide this field is not for them, they have saved themselves from spending years of study and training before finding out, and will have developed a much better idea of what it is they really want to do with their life.

Ben, Catherine and Robert attended a group selection event, and needed to fundraise towards the cost of the programme with advice and support from volunteers in the UK. Before departing on the programme, they attended orientation courses to help prepare them for the experience and to give them the chance to discuss the challenges of the experience with people who have returned from the programme. They also attended orientations at regular points through the six months to assess how they were progressing, and had a debriefing when they returned.

The local AFS volunteers who arrange for young people to come to their community provide support for them, and there is a 24 hour emergency backup service for major problems, so participants are not alone whilst they are away.

Whether they are in Brazil, Colombia, Honduras, Peru, South Africa, Malaysia or any of the other countries on offer, they will develop an understanding of what life in that country is really like, through living it. As Ben Lawton said on his return:

To me before I went, Brazil was like Mars. I had heard of both of them, and seen pictures, but how was I to know what they were really like?

You could take a holiday in Brazil and see some incredible sights but you would miss the best part of the show, the people - their struggles, their attitudes and their strength. Now Brazil is no longer like Mars. It's as real to me as the UK.

Together with the immediate benefits of participating in an AFS programme - the opportunity to learn a foreign language, to get to know a different culture, to develop practical skills and to meet new friends - students return home having developed vital life skills. Studies have shown that AFS students develop their emotional maturity - the ability to recognise the causes of stress and work out ways of handling them with minimum disruption to themselves and others - by up to 10 times more than their counterparts who have stayed at home.

That means that, after participating on one of the programmes, students aged 17 or 18 have a maturity closer to that expected of a 26 year old. By having to adjust to an unfamiliar environment, students develop a very important extra capacity for handling future stress maturely and are able to take the knocks of life in their stride.

Catherine Blackham became integrated into the local community when she worked on a Community Service Programme in Pirenopolis, Brazil

CHALLENGES & CONFIDENCES

To give an idea of the rewards and challenges offered by a year between, and of the range of activities available, the following accounts have been contributed by recent students. They include comments from those who have taken time out between school or college and university, and from those who decided to take a gap year after graduating.

Here, the students explain why they took a year out and discuss their expectations, how they chose activities, any problems they encountered and how they dealt with them, and how their time out has helped them in their further studies and careers.

Matthew was placed as an agricultural trainee on a 1,400 acre cropping farm on the Alberta/Saskatchewan border in Canada through a programme run by the International Agricultural Exchange Association (IAEA). His duties included feeding stock, greasing machines ready for the fieldwork, working in the workshop, hauling grain to the elevator, digging up potatoes and swathing and cultivating the stubble for harvest:

As well as providing me with a wealth of experience and the opportunity to live life in a different culture, I can also thank the IAEA for a somewhat swelled address book. From participating in the programme, I now have friends all over the world from as near as Denmark, to as far away as Australia and New Zealand and this doesn't even include the multitude of Canadian friends I made! The best advice I can give as a past trainee is try it: to live as a member of a completely different family and to be able to work in a totally strange environment, taking the rough with the smooth and the good times with the bad, is all part of the challenge.

Julie also went to Canada with IAEA. Her time was divided between working in the home, helping to care for the host family's three small children, and working outside with the 300 head herd of single sucklers, feeding out hay, administering drugs to sick calves, branding and de-horning:

The area I was in was extremely beautiful with mountain trees and lakes all around. There was plenty of fishing, hunting and water and snow sports to participate in. I enjoyed a most wonderful experience and would thoroughly recommend going and working in another country.

Emilie spent her gap year before going to Edinburgh University with SPW teaching English and science at a rural secondary school in Zimbabwe. She also worked on development projects within the local community for which she raised funds in the UK before her departure:

At first I was shocked by the basic living conditions but when I was thrown into teaching I did not have time to worry about it anymore! Through working together on projects with the local people I feel I was given a unique insight into their lives and formed great friends. The fundraising was hard work but it all paid off when the pupils had a new sports ground at their school.

Simon joined the SPW environment programme in Nepal after finishing a degree in geography. He thought it was really important to get practical experience and wanted to take the opportunity to travel before starting work:

Learning from our Nepali colleagues and using my knowledge gained at university, I helped feed new ideas into rural communities. The most rewarding part of the whole programme was eating a meal cooked on a new smokeless stove which we had shown the local people how to construct. I learnt so much extra by being out of the lecture room and I now feel that I have many more practical skills to build on in the future.

Camilla Byk left school with A levels in French, German, economics and art and decided to take a year out to make some decisions:

First I learnt to type and drive a motorbike, then found a job at a pizza restaurant, but I still had to decide where I wanted to go to university and what I wanted to study. Someone told me it was easy to get into Oxford for Chinese, but I chickened out and chose Italian and French. I had to at least visit Italy before trying to persuade tutors that I'd be any good - a four week crash course in Sienna solved that problem and got the university hurdle out of the way.

I then happened to meet some YMCA volunteers who were taking supplies to orphanages, so I wrote to a Romanian headmaster and offered my services as an English teacher. Two weeks later I arrived in Transylvania with another language to learn. Being faced with a class of 18 year olds when you are only 18 yourself is a shock but, through teaching them and kids as young as six, I quickly entered the culture. I realised that I was fascinated by teaching and they were all fascinated by me as the only westerner ever to have lived in the village.

After 4 months I came back to England with plenty of waitressing money left over so I sped off to Guatemala and Belize on my own so that I could spend time painting and writing. I had some wild experiences like having my bus stopped by violent guerrillas and an attempted mugging at the banana stall, but I came home healthy, happy and ready to dive into university life.

Eastern Europe and Italy now play a huge part in my life - something which I would never have known without that year. I also now know that I can teach, travel alone, learn languages on the spot and smile sweetly at a guerrilla's gun barrel!

Leo Smith went to Peru with Quest Overseas and spent part of his time working in local orphanages:

I certainly took pride in looking after the children, but it wasn't easy. Children have irrepressible reserves of energy, and they often showed us a thing or two; many a time did we suffer a humiliating defeat by 10 year-olds in football! I know that our group made their lives a little happier for the short time that we were there, and that was certainly proven by the rapturous reception we got on return to Camino de Vida and Casa Hogar. In their holiday time we were their friends, to look after them, play with them and give them love.

Afterwards, Leo and his colleagues had a chance to explore the country:

The strength of our loyalty to each other was certainly put to the test on the expedition. On the first day of my leadership training I had the prospect of climbing the first pass of the Inca Trail. I really gained in confidence and the deep-rooted knowledge that I really could ask people to follow me was brought out by the instructors. I learnt a lot from the talks on leadership skills and I know that I will never lose my motivation again, as I had perhaps done at school.

In climbing the steps of the ruins on the Inca trail, learning about the strategy and planning involved in

building them, and hearing about the mythology that enshrouded it all, we really felt we got to grips with Peru's past. As a Catholic, I particularly enjoyed exploring the convent of Santa Catolina and the beautiful churches in Cuzco too.

The expedition wasn't just about teamwork and leadership, it was also about having fun. Trekking through the thick jungle vegetation, wading through bogs and crossing log bridges to catch a glimpse of caymans, otters, monkeys and macaws certainly fulfilled all the Indiana Jones fantasies I had as a child!

Peru will always retain its mysticism, but because of the friends we made out there it will never be inaccessible. I'm just glad that I have the opportunity to go out there again, so that I can say hello to everyone I met. The last three months were the best of my life and it was a privilege to be given the opportunity to live and work in such a fascinating country, in a culture unlike any I had experienced before.

Alastair Cairns stayed a little closer to home, working for the charity L'Arche in a community house in Kent for people with learning disabilities. He explains how his experience changed his perspective on life and the disabled:

I liked the simple aims of L'Arche but suspected that the daily life might prove anything but. And so it has. Most of our tasks are very ordinary, boring even, but if the life of L'Arche is truly entered into there is no such thing as an ordinary day. People with learning disabilities call us constantly into relationships, often in a disquieting way. So many seem fundamentally fired by a need to relate and when this is mixed with the fear and memory of rejection, these relationships can prove even more demanding. We are being asked to relate not so much intellectually as with our whole bodies and realise that we are not so different after all from those we live with, just better at explaining or processing things.

Some people take more than one year out. Stacey Hunter had been working for two years before she decided to return to full-time education:

During my time working, I decided what I wanted to study, as opposed to what my school assumed I would do well in. In retrospect, this was the first step in taking control of my life - the year between working and starting university gave me the confidence to take the next steps.

Initially I took a job working as an au pair in Switzerland. I studied French, spent most weekends visiting different parts of Switzerland and made new friends from many nationalities. This was a safe way to leave home for the first time, but after five months I was ready to move on and found the perfect job as a holiday courier on a French campsite.

Essentially I was a cleaner, but there were additional responsibilities: I coordinated arrivals and departures, arranged on-site entertainment for adults and children, reported regularly to senior management and acted as a personal tourist information centre for campers. I had to know everything and everyone! On arrival at the site I was confronted with a series of problems: double beds still in storage,

caravans that required plumbing to the mains water supply, even a five-man tent that had to be assembled, no easy task for an experienced montage team, let alone one inexperienced courier and a camper with nothing else to do that day! Problems continued to arise throughout the season - they didn't get any less challenging, experience just made them easier to solve. I relished the initiative, independence and responsibility the job required and appreciated the role of a courier in the making of someone's holiday.

You learn so much more about a country and the people by living there, not just passing through. I would recommend a year abroad to anybody who is even just a little curious. I gained experience in life and skills that aren't taught - I learnt a great deal about human nature, improved my social skills and gained confidence. The plumbing and electrical skills I learnt were an added bonus!

Having left college with few vocational qualifications and no clear career direction in mind, Rebecca saw working in a youth hostel as an opportunity to broaden her practical experience, learn new skills and develop her career aims:

I knew I had to go out and gain some vocational experience and working as a seasonal assistant warden with the YHA allowed me to do this whilst at the same time broadening my career options and providing me with new challenges. What I gained most from this position were practical skills I could use elsewhere. I am still working for the YHA but I am now working in the recruitment department where I am further developing the customer service skills I gained at the hostel and hoping to join the NVQ programme. The YHA's commitment to training has allowed me to develop my skills and career further.

Another option is to take a gap year after graduating, like Tony Edwards did:

When I finished my degree I knew that I wanted to do a Masters degree but felt that it would be good to do something different before continuing with my studies. The idea of living abroad had always appealed to me and I looked into ways of doing that. Teaching English seemed one of the best ways, so armed with nothing much more than a degree and a reasonable grasp of the English language I set about replying to advertisements in The Guardian *and* The Times Higher Education Supplement. *There were some jobs that required a TEFL qualification which I couldn't apply for, but many that did not, and within a month I had landed myself a job in Portugal to start immediately.*

It was quite daunting when I arrived: I had no Portuguese and had never taught before. But after the first few weeks I really began to enjoy it. The work was mainly in the afternoons and evenings so I had most of the day free - as I lived by the beach this was just fine! Living in a different culture was a real learning experience for me and I made friends with local people who I still keep in touch with. In fact, I enjoyed the year so much I opted to stay for a second year, doing the RSA/UCLES TEFL Certificate during the summer at the school's expense. I managed to drag myself back to Britain at the end of the second year

to do the Masters and have since gone into lecturing.

I would recommend TEFL as an excellent way of spending a year or two between a degree and whatever comes next; it gave me knowledge of a very different culture, teaching experience, a language and a decent suntan!

While teaching English on the Japan Exchange and Teaching (JET) programme, Paul Sands was lauded as a cultural ambassador by his Japanese peers. Upon a somewhat nervous departure from the UK, Paul notes he was weighed down by false preconceptions:

The Japanese I knew were always formal: they were obsessed with intricate codes of politeness, they 'thought differently' from Westerners and, trusting in the biggest cliché of them all, I was even prepared to find them all 'inscrutable'.

However, after two years of working as an assistant language teacher in high schools in Yokohama City, Paul's notion of typical Japanese life was a far cry from what it had been:

My students were colourful, thoughtful, responsive and sometimes hilariously funny individuals. When the time comes after one, two or three years to leave the programme, many JETs find it very hard to leave the people they have found to be every bit as warm and approachable as the folks back home.

Law graduate Chris Sharp participated in the Council on International Educational Exchange's Internship USA Programme to experience the world of New York criminal activity. He worked as a legal aide for the Criminal Prosecutions Bureau, becoming involved in a plethora of legal procedures up to and including criminal investigation:

I learnt an incredible amount about the US criminal procedure system, despite having to work at a very fast pace to catch up with the American interns. I was involved in legal research, learnt about the loopholes available to plea-bargaining defendants and attended legal strategy sessions. Weighing the disparity between the British and American criminal systems really helped me understand the deficiencies and advantages of our way of dealing with things.

Martin LeTissier had two months before the start of his accountancy training contract so, harbouring a long-standing desire to learn French, he decided to enrol in a short course at the university in Grenoble:

In the interests of improving my conversational French by freeing myself of my inhibitions, I went out more often than I have done at any time since I was last at university. Getting to know my classmates and making friends at my residence and on the various social events organised by the university not only helped open my eyes to the world around me, but also helped improve my French language skills.

Reene spent two terms at Culver Girls' Academy in Indiana, through the scholarship scheme offered by the English-Speaking Union, and also found that her learning extended beyond the confines of the classroom.

When I first left England the full implications of time spent abroad did not occur to me. What I gained at Culver was far different from anything I had imagined and highly educational. This year has become a turning point in every part of my life and it has strengthened my character.

Tom spent three terms at St Michael's University School in British Columbia, and enjoyed the wealth of different courses offered by North American high schools such as bio-ethics, espionage novel studies and space studies:

I valued the opportunity of studying a much broader range of subjects than the restricting A level system allows. It is not only the memories of my wonderful year that I will live on, but also the experiences, insights, independence, maturity and friendships I am so grateful to have gained.

TRAINING/WORK EXPERIENCE

This section covers opportunities to undertake paid work, either as a study or career-related training placement or more simply as a period of work experience. Placements include opportunities overseas through agencies based in this country; training/work experience programmes with companies in Britain, in some cases as part of a sponsorship scheme; and work experience including jobs with travel companies as a courier or representative.

In compiling this third edition of **A YEAR BETWEEN** we contacted hundreds of companies in order to identify opportunities for placement schemes for post-A level (or equivalent) students and undergraduates. Those who offer suitable schemes have been included; in addition over 250 companies offer placements under the Year in Industry scheme (see pages 68-70 and 113) and therefore are not listed here individually. Other companies have no nationwide policy of placements; they may offer a limited number of placements but not a sufficient number, nor on a continuing basis, to be included here. In many cases such international or national companies prefer those interested to apply to their nearest regional branch, who may have specific links with local educational establishments and offer places accordingly.

There are also companies who in the past have offered placements but are currently unable to do so. However, their policy may change depending on market circumstances, and it is worth approaching major companies on an individual basis to enquire about any current possibilities. Your school careers teacher, local careers office or Jobcentre should be able to help you identify opportunities locally.

WORKPLACE is a guide focusing specifically on work experience and placements, listing over 120 companies and organisations which offer opportunities, as well as advice for those planning work experience programmes including information on issues such as health and safety, insurance and funding. It also includes case studies of students who have undertaken placements and insights from companies offering work experience programmes. It is available through good bookshops or direct from the Central Bureau © 0171-389 4880.

For many, a period of training during a year between provides an invaluable transition from years of school, where they are isolated from commercial realities, to the wider world of business. Working in an office, a laboratory, or on the shop floor, you will no longer be surrounded by people who are the same age as you, at the same ability level and studying the same things. Rather, you will mix with many different types of people, from a variety of backgrounds, age groups and intellectual abilities, specialising in different fields, but all working together to solve real problems and complete a common project in the time available.

One of the major benefits of any period of work experience is the placement of educational studies within the greater context of the industrial or commercial world. If you do a sponsored degree in engineering, for example, the work experience will enable you to put into practice what you are learning, helping you to understand complex theories by putting them to practical use. In addition to this contextual benefit, an industrial placement benefits students by giving them an opportunity to find out about business life before committing themselves to a career. For some companies it is standard practice to encourage students to take a year out, as in their view it provides an opportunity to gain valuable industrial experience. The placement also benefits the companies by giving them the equivalent of an extended interview period.

Many major companies commit large resources to their sponsorship programmes, including opportunities in the pre-university year, confident in the knowledge that such a programme has and will continue to provide them with senior managers. The placement also provides the students with the opportunity to assess a future in that particular job/industry, and the potential benefits of the individual employer. With so much at stake, employers will go to great lengths to ensure that the industrial placement is well organised and meaningful. Many will organise specific courses to develop interpersonal, decision-making and team-building skills in addition to the period spent at the workface itself. A well-rounded placement will also include stints in other commercial areas of the organisation, such as finance, personnel, sales and marketing. Many of the industrial training opportunities should also be open to those who decide to go straight into higher education after A levels or equivalents, following either a thick or thin sandwich course.

The Year in Industry is a charity specialising in industrial placements in the year between. Now in its 10th year of operation, some 3,000 students have benefited from the programme so far. It currently places around 700 students annually in a range of industries nationwide. The

organisation believes the combination of real challenging work in a company backed by structured off-the-job training helps develop students' personal skills - communication, problem-solving ability, teamworking and business awareness - leading to better degree results and a competitive edge in the graduate employment market. This view is supported by analysis of past Year in Industry students: 24% have graduated with First Class Honours degrees and 44% have graduated with Upper Seconds; 88% returned to industry, almost all finding employment within a few months of graduating.

Sponsorship is where an employer provides financial help during a degree course in the form of a bursary or a salary, in return for certain commitments on the part of the student. The employer may require the student to work for them during their pre-university year, and during vacations or industrial placement periods; they may even require them to attend a specific degree course at a certain university. There is often no legal obligation for the student to work for the employer once the course is completed, but in many cases a good working relationship has built up that both employer and student are happy to continue. Most opportunities for sponsorship exist in those areas where employers find it difficult to recruit enough high-calibre staff. This means that about 60% of all sponsorships are for science or engineering students. However, sponsorships also exist in the fields of finance, retail, business studies, mathematics, computing/IT, building and surveying. Sponsorships vary widely in the degree of obligation placed upon the student and the amount of financial help they offer. In a few cases, students are treated as employees during the whole of their degree course, and are paid a salary. More usually, you are paid a lump sum, termly or annually, or you may receive an allowance to pay for books or other items. During periods of work experience, such as a pre-university year, vacation work, or the industrial training part of a sandwich course, you will probably be paid a full-time salary, and given some help with finding accommodation. You may be asked to work on one specific project; alternatively you may be moved around to gain breadth of experience. There will often be a major training element, perhaps involving short study courses or team-building exercises.

If you want to be sponsored throughout your degree, and do a year's pre-university training, then you should think about the possibilities of sponsorship at the same time as you are considering applying for a degree course. University admissions tutors should be able to tell you whether any firms sponsor students on their courses; some firms may insist on you attending a particular course. Your school or college careers adviser will also be able to help. When completing sponsorship application forms, remember that although academic achievement and the potential for good grades are important factors, the employers are looking in particular for students who will make good managers. So make the most of any extracurricular activities or other ways in which you can show that you have initiative, organisational skills and leadership ability. Competition for sponsorships is high; be prepared for a fairly demanding selection procedure involving interviews and assessments. Sponsorship is a contract between student and employer, and you should

make sure you know what sort of agreement you are entering into before signing it. You may be required to work for your sponsor for a specified number of weeks each year. If you don't pass your end of year exams or if you fail to make good progress in your studies, then the company may withdraw their support. You are not usually obliged to take up a post within the company once the sponsorship is complete, but then, neither is the company obliged to offer you one. Your local education authority will take your sponsorship into account when assessing grant entitlement. If sponsorship exceeds your course fees and maintenance, no grant will be paid and you will be expected to meet all costs relating to your study. In exceptional circumstances you may qualify for an allowance, in which case a proportion of the sponsorship will be disregarded in the calculation of a grant.

One of the main reasons for sponsoring students is so that the company can attract high-calibre personnel, especially in fields of technology and engineering where they may have problems recruiting. Over periods of work experience a company can train students to their particular methods of working and give them a good grounding in the company's aims and philosophy, so that students can eventually become managers within the company. It enables both student and employer to establish a good working relationship, find out each other's good and bad points, and decide whether this relationship is worth continuing in the future. Sponsorship will mean you are better off financially whilst a student, because not only will you benefit from the extra cash provided by a sponsorship bursary, but you will also be able to earn money through periods of work experience before and during your studies. It does mean, however, that you have to make a definite career commitment at the age of 17 or 18, rather than waiting until you graduate. You may also find working through your vacations a real pain, especially if all your friends are holidaying in the sunshine. However, sponsorship does allow you to put what you learn in lectures into practice in the workplace and find out what life is like in the real world of work. You will also be at an advantage when you graduate: you will not need to worry about choosing a career as your choice has already been made; if you join your sponsoring company the initial salary is likely to be higher than that of other graduates; and even if you decide against being employed by your sponsor, your work experience and training will make you more attractive to other companies in terms of recruitment.

Sanjay was accepted onto the Arthur Andersen scholarship programme, which offers the opportunity to gain insight into chartered accountancy, business and finance, starting with a pre-university year. He feels he had a tremendous head start over his contemporaries:

Some of my friends have had to stack supermarket shelves in order to finance their pre-university travels. Others managed to gain professional experience but without the benefit of a travel grant or the encouragement to take time off before university. I had the best of both worlds.

Susan was also attracted to join the Andersen scholarship programme before going on to read accountancy and finance at Warwick University. She had already decided to do an accountancy degree, but felt it would be useful to gain some practical experience beforehand:

To begin with the work seemed very daunting, but the training I received gave me the confidence I needed. It has been very challenging, but I have been given plenty of feedback and support. I have learnt a lot about my own capabilities and limitations.

Both Sanjay and Susan have now joined the firm as trainee chartered accountants. Their experience gained on the scholarship programme enabled them to start their career a year ahead of other graduates, and of course, this is reflected in their salary.

Other types of work Many thinking of taking a year out may feel it is still too early to commit themselves to a particular career or sphere of business. They feel that a period of work is necessary to give themselves an educational break, and the placement is seen as a way of testing the waters of business and commerce, generating some income for further years of study or offering the opportunity to put gained educational skills, such as foreign languages or mathematics, into practice. Interspeak specialises in finding *stages* for year out students. They lay particular emphasis on the linguistic, cultural and social experience. Interspeak consider that a year out can lead to greater social mobility and a better understanding of different ways of life. However, they warn that generally the foreign language competence of British students taking a year between is far below their mainland European counterparts, and this will limit the greater benefits to be achieved from a placement in another country.

If you are uncertain about the long-term commitment of a work placement or sponsorship, or are unable to be accepted on a particular scheme, then you may be able to find short-term paid work. Sometimes local councils offer suitable temporary employment for students or school leavers. Supermarkets also take on short-term staff, and department stores often recruit for busy sales periods (usually Christmas, January and July). The Central Bureau's annual information guide **WORKING HOLIDAYS** lists thousands of short-term paid work opportunities, ranging in length from a few weeks to several months, in over 70 countries including Britain. However you should bear in mind that time spent stacking shelves or grape picking, for example, is unlikely to improve your own self-esteem or impress future employers reading your cv, unless the job is to be used as a means to finance a more challenging project, such as an expedition or a period of community service on the other side of the world.

If your year between is to be of real benefit you should concentrate on opportunities that will stretch your capabilities and give you new skills along with a greater sense of responsibility to society as a whole. However, don't necessarily assume that only a training placement or a period of work experience in the area of industry or business in which you plan to study or finally work in will be the only option of any relevance. Think laterally, use the opportunity of a year between to broaden your horizons; undertaking a work placement complementary to your future course of study can be a greater challenge and, in the long term, of greater value.

Andersen Consulting
Arthur Andersen
Australia Work & Travel Programme
Binnie Black & Veatch Consulting Engineers
British Steel
British Universities North America Club
Caledonia Language Courses
Canvas Holidays
Carisma Holidays
Club Med
Data Connection Ltd
Direct Training Services
Equity Total Travel
Eurocamp
Ford Motor Company Ltd
GAP Challenge
GEC-Marconi Research Centre
GEC-Marconi Sensors
Greek Dances Theatre
Hoogewerf & Co
Horizon HPL
Hoverspeed Ltd
Internship Canada Programme
Internship USA Programme
Interspeak Ltd
Jobs in the Alps Agency
John Laing plc
KPMG
Lishman Sidwell Campbell & Price
Local Government Student Sponsorship
Mentor Language Training
Pfizer Ltd (Central Research)
PGL Travel Ltd
ProEuropa
Shell Research Ltd
Smallpeice Trust
Solaire Holidays
Superchoice
UK/US Career Development Programme
UK/US Hospitality & Tourism Exchange
The Year in Industry
Youth Hostels Association

ANDERSEN CONSULTING

Andersen Consulting, 2 Arundel Street, London WC2R 3LT

℡ 0171-438 5000 🖅 0171-438 5745

Throughout the UK

A world-leading business and technology consulting firm with clients in all areas of business and industry. Develops strategies for change that take account of every aspect of the client's organisation using information technology to implement solutions.

Opportunities available for students during their year between school and university on the Horizons School Sponsorship Scheme.
The Scheme combines training with work experience where participants receive consultancy experience in and alongside major international organisations, as well as valuable technical and business skills. Students are given the chance to develop strengths and abilities and receive guidance and feedback from management consultants at the top of their profession. On assignment, participants are based at a client's site which could be anywhere in the UK. Those selected for the Scheme attend a training session which is a thought-provoking introduction to business and technology, delivered through business seminars, workshops and IT case studies. It gives a unique insight into Andersen Consulting's style of management consultancy.

Ages 18+. Open to students in their gap year between school and university only. Applicants must have 3 good A levels or equivalent and have secured a place at university. An interest in information technology is essential. All applications must be authorised by the student's headteacher. All nationalities welcome, although applications not accepted from students requiring work permits. **B D PH W**

8 months, September-May

35 hour week, Monday-Friday. Salary £10,000 pro-rata, plus £1,600 travel bursary awarded on completion of placement and possibility of full sponsorship throughout university. Travel and insurance provided and, if a placement is not found within commutable distance to the individual's home, accommodation is offered free of charge.

Apply by April

ARTHUR ANDERSEN

National Scholarship Programme Manager, Arthur Andersen, I Surrey Street, London WC2R 2PS

© 0171-438 3110

Ten offices throughout the UK

One of the largest professional services organisations, employing over 80,000 people throughout the world

Offers an opportunity for young people to gain insight into chartered accountancy, business and finance through a scholarship programme. The programme comprises paid training and work experience on an 8 months placement during the gap year, support during a university degree course, with further paid summer work experience and the potential offer of a full-time job on graduation.

Ages 17+. Applicants should anticipate gaining 3 A or B grades at A level (or equivalent), preferably including mathematics; a GCSE (or equivalent) grade A in mathematics is also essential. Applicants should have a keen interest in business and finance. Only EEA nationals, or other nationals not requiring a work permit. **B D PH**

Initial year out training and work experience programme lasts 35 weeks; entire scholarship programme lasts 4 years, including 6 weeks during each summer vacation. Participants are not obliged to continue with the scholarship once the course is over, nor are they made to take on a long-term commitment; it is simply hoped they will want to join the firm after graduation.

During the initial programme, work is for 37½ hours per week at a rate of £10,500 per annum (London office), plus additional pay for overtime. On completion of the programme in May there is a travel bonus of £1,000. At the beginning of each academic year participants receive £1,200, based on satisfactory performance over the previous period of work. Vacation work is paid at a rate commensurate with experience.

Throughout the programme, participants' performance is reviewed by the professionals for whom they are working, and during their time at university they are kept in touch with the firm's activities

Apply at the beginning of last year at school; interviews usually held from September onwards. There is no closing date.

AUSTRALIA WORK & TRAVEL PROGRAMME

Australia Work & Travel Programme, Council on International Educational Exchange, 52 Poland Street, London WIV 4JQ

© 0171-478 2000   ⊠ 0171-734 7322   ✉ infouk@ciee.org

Throughout Australia

The Council administers a variety of international programmes offering a unique way to develop personal and career goals in an international setting. Participation in one of the programmes enables students to work abroad without the stresses and uncertainties usually involved as a pre-departure advice and information service is provided and in-country support is available throughout the stay.

Australia Work and Travel is a new programme which offers the opportunity to undertake casual work anywhere in Australia. Two nights accommodation on arrival, orientation in Sydney, support during the stay and help with finding suitable jobs provided.

Ages 18-25. No qualifications or experience necessary. UK and Irish nationals only.

Up to 12 months

Terms and conditions of employment and accommodation provision varies according to placement. Programme fee payable.

Telephone or write for information about application procedures and deadlines

BINNIE BLACK & VEATCH
CONSULTING ENGINEERS

Mr ME Hannah, Human Resources Director, Binnie Black & Veatch Consulting Engineers, Grosvenor House, 69 London Road, Redhill, Surrey RH1 1LQ

℗ Redhill (01737) 774155

Redhill, England

A partnership of professional engineers, with a worldwide staff of over 800. Involved in water supply, irrigation, energy, waste water and infrastructure engineering, the firm employs engineers in many disciplines to provide a wide range of consultancy services.

Two school-leavers are recruited each year to work, applying their scientific knowledge in a computer-based environment

Ages 17-19. Applicants must have, or be expecting to gain, 3 good A levels (or equivalent) in mathematics, physics and one other maths or science based subject, and intend to read for a mathematics, physics or engineering degree. An interest in computing, an enthusiastic approach to problem-solving and an ability to think laterally essential.

6-12 months, usually September-August

Participants work a 37½ hour week and earn a salary of up to £9,000 per annum. Accommodation is provided for the first two weeks while participants look for somewhere to live.

Apply as soon as possible

BRITISH STEEL

British Steel, 9 Albert Embankment, London SE1 7SN

At various sites throughout the UK

An international steel producer which provides the manufacturing industry in the UK and overseas with a broad range of high-quality steel products. Its production facilities are split into businesses, according to their product type. Employs over 35,000 people in the UK.

Offers students a varied range of industrial experiences, from highly technical projects through international commercial work to demanding people-management roles. Most training places are for students studying scientific disciplines such as mechanical engineering, electronic engineering, materials science or chemistry, although some placements are offered to students from computing, business management and other commercial or numerical subjects. Students undertake a mixture of on-the-job experience, project work and formal training.
An individual training plan is drawn up for each student and reviewed frequently to ensure it remains relevant to the needs of the individual.

Applications accepted from students at almost all stages of their degree course, from the time they accept a place at university to their penultimate year. Applicants should be high academic achievers who can demonstrate enthusiasm, commitment to their discipline, drive, determination and the ability to function well as part of a team.

Placements available during the summer holidays or during a sandwich year. Students receive an attractive monthly salary. Possibility of substantial bursary through the sponsorship programme, paid holiday and, in some cases, subsidised accommodation.

Applications should be sent direct to individual sites. For further information and addresses of UK sites, contact the Personnel Department at the address above.

BRITISH UNIVERSITIES NORTH AMERICA CLUB (BUNAC)

BUNAC, 16 Bowling Green Lane, London EC1R 0BD

© 0171-251 3472 ⊡ 0171-251 0215 ⬚ bunac@easynet.co.uk

Australia, New Zealand and Canada

A non-profitmaking, non-political, educational student club venture which aims to foster international understanding, principally through student work exchange programmes

Offers various programmes - Work Australia, Work New Zealand, Work Canada - for students wishing to work and travel in their year out. Areas of work can include hotel, restaurant and shop work; selling ice cream, sandwiches, soft drinks and fast food; or working in a laundry or an amusement park.

Ages 18-30 (Canada and New Zealand); 18-25 (Australia). Applicants should have enthusiasm, motivation, confidence, initiative and be prepared to work hard. Work Canada: applicants will need to have proof that they have secured a place on a tertiary level course (degree, HND, two year BTEC), or else be a full-time tertiary level student. Participants must be British or Irish passport holders. Work Australia and Work New Zealand: applicants can be students or non-students, but must have proof of sufficient funds (minimum £2,000) for personal support whilst in the country. For Australia, applicants must have a UK, Irish, Dutch or Canadian passport; for New Zealand, UK passport-holders only.

Placements up to 12 months. Departures in February (Canada) and August-October (Australia and New Zealand). Workers are free to spend time after their placement travelling around the country.

Australia and New Zealand: £1,042-£1,500 covers flight and registration fee. Canada: £79 registration fee, approx £365 return flight and £4 membership fee. All work is paid, but participants will have to find their own accommodation.

Compulsory orientation programmes held throughout Britain and in host country on arrival, giving advice on finding and choosing a job, obtaining a visa, income tax, accommodation, travel, food and budgeting. Information also provided on onward travel.

Apply for information in November

CALEDONIA LANGUAGE COURSES

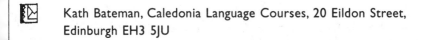

Kath Bateman, Caledonia Language Courses, 20 Eildon Street, Edinburgh EH3 5JU

©/☎ 0131-558 7118

Throughout Germany and Austria; southern Spain

Provides a free advisory and booking service for language courses abroad, mainly in Europe and South America. Detailed information on courses, accommodation, social and cultural activities based on personal visits to each school. Courses offered for all ages and levels throughout the year.

Work placements combined with an intensive language course available in Germany and Austria. Placements are in the tourism industry: in hotel receptions; as ski instructors; sales staff in retail outlets; waiting staff in restaurants or hotels.

Also au pair placements in southern Spain with the option of a Spanish language course before and during placement. Minimum 3 months. Pay approx £40 per month plus full board accommodation provided. Travel arranged by applicants. Administration and family placement fee £165.

Ages 18-30. All applicants should be EU citizens.

One month language course followed by a work placement lasting 2-10 months. Accommodation and full board usually provided by employers and a monthly salary of at least £200. These language and work placements are eligible for funding through the EU programme LEONARDO.

CANVAS HOLIDAYS

The Operations Department, Canvas Holidays, 12 Abbey Park Place, Dunfermline, Fife KY12 7PD

℗ Dunfermline (01383) 644018

Austria, France, Germany, Italy, Luxembourg, Spain, Switzerland

A tour operator providing ready-erected, fully equipped tents and mobile homes on campsites throughout Europe

Resident campsite couriers are required to help erect and clean out tents, check equipment, look after clients, organise activities, help with administration, and dismantle and store tents at the end of the season. Children's couriers are also needed on some sites. There are also some positions for montage assistants who must be aged 21+ and with a valid driving licence, to help set up and dismantle 200-250 tents on approx 12 campsites.

Ages 19+. Applicants should be sociable, enthusiastic, practical, reliable, self-motivated, able to turn their hand to new and varied tasks, and have a sense of humour. Montage assistants need to be fit and able to work long hours under pressure without supervision, and cope with living out of a rucksack. Children's couriers should have relevant experience/ qualifications. Knowledge of a mainland European language essential for resident couriers.

6 months, April-October

No fixed hours, as workload varies from day to day and is especially busy at beginning and end of season. Transport to site provided; return travel dependent on completion of contract. Salary £90 per week; insurance, accommodation in frame tents and bicycle for use on site provided.

Apply at any time; interviews commence early November for following season

CARISMA HOLIDAYS

The Operations Manager, Carisma Holidays, Bethel House, Heronsgate Road, Chorleywood, Hertfordshire WD3 5BB

℗ Chorleywood (01923) 284235

France

A family-run business organising holidays in tents and mobile homes on beach sites along the Atlantic coast of France, from Brittany to Biarritz

Recruits approx 25 resident couriers each year. Work involves welcoming families, providing information and advice, cleaning and maintaining tents and mobile homes, and babysitting for clients when necessary.

Ages 18+. Applicants should have a helpful and friendly disposition and experience of dealing with people. Good spoken French and English essential.

2-5 months, beginning early May or late June

Salary £65-£100 per week, depending on experience and level of responsibility. Self-catering accommodation provided on site in tents or mobile homes. Travel costs paid.

Full training given on site at start of season

Apply as early as possible

CLUB MED

Club Med, 106 Brompton Road, London SW3 1YY

✆ 0171-581 5454

Throughout Europe and Africa

Founded in 1950, Club Med runs 120 holiday villages throughout the world which offer restaurants, shops, theatres, night clubs, children's activities, sports facilities and a range of accommodation options including boats, huts, bungalows and hotels. The villages are either seasonal, opening for 4-6 months of the year, or permanent. Club Med also offers other holidays such as cruises and excursions.

Approximately 50 positions available including: hostesses; shop assistants; secretaries and administrators; tour guides; child workers; health workers; sound, lighting and wardrobe technicians; set decorators; bar stewards; domestic workers and catering staff; lifeguards and sports instructors.

Ages 20+. Applicants must speak fluent French and English. Some positions require older applicants with specific experience and qualifications, such as additional European languages, full driving licence or first aid skills. EU nationals only.

4-6 months, April/May to September/October

7 day week. Accommodation, insurance, food and travel provided. Salary £400 per month net.

Orientation course provided

DATA CONNECTION LTD

Justine McLennan, Recruitment Manager, Data Connection Ltd, 100 Church Street, Enfield, Middlesex EN2 6BQ

✆ 0181-366 1177   ✉ recruit@datcon.co.uk   🕸 http://www.datcon.co.uk

Enfield, England

A substantial UK software development company founded in 1981, focusing on leading-edge technology. For the past fifteen years has supplied key software technologies to companies such as Microsoft, Sun, Lotus and Hewlett Packard. Current projects range from Web audio access through cross-platform application sharing to high performance ATM switching support.

Employs a number of pre-university students each year to work on mainline projects with the support and guidance of world-class software developers. Students are assigned significant pieces of work to do as part of a small project team. Outstanding students may be offered sponsorship throughout their first and subsequent university years.

Ages 17+. Applicants should have a real interest in, and an aptitude for, software development. Successful candidates typically have, or are expecting, all A grades at A level or equivalent.

Minimum 8 weeks; many students stay for up to 12 months

Students work a 37½ hour week and receive approx £800 per month. Self-catering accommodation provided locally in a large house shared with other students.

Review at end of placement

Recruitment all year

DIRECT TRAINING SERVICES

Jackie Bufton, Proprietor, Direct Training Services, Crossmead Conference Centre, Barley Lane, Exeter, Devon EX4 1FT

℗ Exeter (01392) 495449   ✍ (01392) 495450
✉ jb@dtseuro.zynet.co.uk

England, Finland, France (including Corsica), Germany, Portugal, Spain and Switzerland

A privately-run training company established in 1992 to train people in information technology and business administration. Also organises work placements within Europe, particularly through the IT Europe programme which incorporates skills required for the use of information technology in business, with a European dimension being added through the development of occupational and business languages.

The information technology programme is designed to develop existing personal skills as well as providing invaluable new ones. The programme consists of a period of 7 weeks training in England, at one of the local training centres, where participants will receive training in information technology and language skills, followed by a period of 12 weeks on work experience with an organisation in a mainland European host country. NVQs in languages and information technology available.

Ages 16-27. Ages 27+ accepted, but not eligible for EU funding. Specific qualifications not required as training is provided. All nationalities welcome. **B D PH W** dependent on ability

Placements are a minimum of 4 weeks, maximum as required. 20-30 hour week with 2 free days. Accommodation provided with a host family or in student villages. Travel costs and accommodation charges levied according to whether candidates are eligible for funding.

EQUITY TOTAL TRAVEL

Equity Total Travel, Dukes Lane House, 47 Middle Street, Brighton, East Sussex BN1 1AL

© Brighton (01273) 886879   ☎ (01273) 203212
✉ travel@equity.co.uk   🔗 http://www.equity.co.uk

Austria, France and Italy

Tour operator, established in 1991, specialising in ski holidays for adult and school groups.

65 positions offered annually. Posts offered include resort representatives, who ensure the smooth running of clients' stay in the resort, liaise with suppliers and arrange evening entertainments; and hotel staff, including waiters, cleaners and bar staff.

Ages 18+ for hotel staff; 21+ for resort representatives. Previous experience an advantage for hotel staff. No previous experience required for resort representatives but they must speak fluent Italian, French or German, be hardworking, enthusiastic, dedicated to customer service and have strong organisational skills. Experience of skiing preferable. EU nationals only for positions in France; all nationalities welcome in resorts in Austria and Italy.

December-April

Hotel staff work 60 hours per week, over 6 days per week; no set hours for resort representatives. Salary £200+ per month for hotel staff and £300 per month plus commission for resort representatives. All staff are provided with full board accommodation, full medical and public liability insurance and a ski pass.

Resort representatives undertake a one week training course

EUROCAMP

Overseas Recruitment Department, Eurocamp, Canute Court, Toft Road, Knutsford, Cheshire WA16 0NL

✆ Knutsford (01565) 625522   📠 (01565) 654930

Austria, Belgium, France, Germany, Italy, Spain, Switzerland

Organises self-drive holidays providing fully equipped tents and caravans on campsites throughout Europe

Resident couriers are required to prepare and maintain tents and equipment, replenish gas supplies, keep the store tent in order, keep accounts and report back to England. They also meet holidaymakers on arrival, organise activities, provide information on local events and attractions and sort out any problems clients may have. At the beginning and end of the season they help erect and dismantle tents.

Ages 18+. Applicants should be familiar with working and travelling abroad, preferably with some camping experience. They should also be adaptable, reliable, independent, efficient, hardworking, sensible, sociable, tactful, patient and have a working knowledge of the relevant language.

Three or six months, beginning April or May

No set working hours or set free days, as these depend on unpredictable factors. Salary £95 per week. Accommodation provided in tents with cooking facilities, plus insurance, return travel and moped/bicycle for use on site.

Training provided

Apply as early as possible; interviews start September/October

FORD MOTOR COMPANY LTD

Recruitment Department, Ford Motor Company, Room 15/4B-A12, Research & Engineering Centre, Laindon, Basildon, Essex SS15 6EE

Global operations; sponsorship schemes and management accountancy scheme are UK-based

One of the largest automotive companies in the world. The Ford Motor Company designs, manufactures and sells car and trucks around the globe, and in addition Ford Credit are one of the largest automotive finance operations in the world.

Operates sponsorship schemes in engineering and systems, combining industrial training with support during a degree course.
The management accountancy scheme provides support for study towards membership of the Chartered Institute of Management Accountants.

Ages 17/18+. Applicants should have 5 GCSEs and relevant A levels or equivalent. Specific requirements for each scheme available on application. The company is committed to the principle of equal opportunity in employment, and will ensure that individuals are selected, promoted and treated on the basis of relevant skills and abilities.

Sponsored students work a minimum of 18 months during their sponsorship period. Those doing a pre-university year with Ford are therefore required to do two further 3 month placements during summer vacations. Accountancy trainees are full-time employees from hiring, subject to satisfactory progression through their studies.

Sponsored students and accountancy trainees work 37½ hours per week and are paid a salary related to the year of their course, starting from £1,012 per month. Tax free bursaries are paid during the first two academic years for sponsored students.

Applicants should first apply as early as possible in their last year at school

GAP CHALLENGE

Gap Challenge, World Challenge Expeditions, Black Arrow House, 2 Chandos Road, London NW10 6NF

✆ 0181-961 1122   📠 0181-961 1551
✉ welcome@world-challenge.co.uk

India, Nepal; Malawi, South Africa, Tanzania, Zanzibar; Belize, Ecuador; Australia, New Zealand, Canada

For ten years World Challenge has been providing overseas projects and adventure training opportunities for young people. The Gap Challenge programme provides year between students and graduates with professionally organised work placements in both the developing and the developed world.

Type of placement varies widely according to country - conservation projects, work in schools, homes for the handicapped, hotels, on farms and with trekking agencies

Ages 18-25. Placements are open to those taking a year out between school and university, and graduates. A high degree of motivation and commitment is required for all posts.

3-6 months; departures in September and January

Participants work in exchange for accommodation and pocket money. Costs from £1,474, Nepal, including return flight valid for 12 months.

All applicants are required to attend a selection course. Training given by qualified staff and former Gap Challenge students.

Applications are considered between 3-18 months in advance of intended departure date; early applications recommended

GEC - MARCONI
RESEARCH CENTRE

Personnel Department, GEC-Marconi Research Centre, West Hanningfield Road, Great Baddow, Chelmsford, Essex CM2 8HN

℗ Chelmsford (01245) 473331   Freephone 0800 581 738

Outskirts of Chelmsford, England

The GEC-Marconi Research Centre provides a research and development facility for both GEC-Marconi companies and external organisations. The Centre is organised in laboratories specialising in specific areas of technology. Topics of research cover optoelectronics, communication systems, signal processing, power electronics, information technology, microwave systems and computing. Established in 1939, the multidisciplined site now has some 800 employees.

Each year approx 5-10 university students are given the opportunity of an industrial placement or vacation work in one of the laboratories. Students are given clearly defined responsibilities and objectives to meet, and work alongside qualified engineers/scientists as part of a project team. They are expected to contribute fully to the work undertaken, helping to meet deadlines and fulfil contracts. The work is challenging and rewarding.

Students should have good grades at A level or equivalent in mathematics, physics and one other science and are usually studying for an electrical and electronic engineering, physics, mathematics, computer science or material science sandwich course, on either a 2-1-1 or thin sandwich basis. The company does have a list of preferred universities, but is prepared to consider applications from other places. Applicants should be interested in working in a research environment, with some business awareness. UK nationals only. **B D PH**

6 months-1 year, from July

37 hour week; salary £7,200-£8,000 per annum. Subsidised staff canteen available. At the end of their work experience period students may be considered for sponsorship for final year of degree course.

Each student is assigned an industrial tutor, a young professional scientist/engineer to act as an adviser. Assessment of work provided.

Applications for thin sandwich placements considered from October; for vacation work and 1 year placements from January

GEC - MARCONI SENSORS LTD

GEC-Marconi Sensors Ltd, Christopher Martin Road, Basildon, Essex SS14 3EL

© Basildon (01268) 522822

Basildon, England

GEC-Marconi Sensors is part of the multinational GEC Group, a world class technology and manufacturing group specialising in electro-optical aviation and thermal imaging equipment

A number of industrial year placements in engineering and computer science available each year, with a view to employing participants at the end of their degree course

Ages 19-23. No experience necessary. Applicants must have 3 good A levels, or equivalent, including mathematics and science. They should be looking for a career in the electronics industry and studying for an appropriate degree. UK nationals only. **B D PH** welcome, depending on severity of disability.

1 year

Salary paid. Approx 37 hour week. Limited number of self-contained flats available at £46.50 per week.

Apply before the end of December

GREEK   DANCES   THEATRE

A Raftis, President, Greek Dances Theatre, 8 Scholiou Street, Plaka, 105 58 Athens, Greece

℗ Athens (00 30 1) 324 4395

Athens, Greece

Founded as a living museum for Greek dance, with a troupe of 60 dancers and a collection of some 2,500 traditional costumes from all regions of Greece. Evening performances held during the summer at an open-air theatre on Philopappou Hill, Athens.

Placements available for those wishing to gain experience in arts/theatre management or in traditional culture, as volunteer assistants helping with costume maintenance, theatre administration and stage management

Ages 18+. Knowledge of Greek not necessary, but good English or French essential.

Placements arranged May-October. 20-30 hours per week. Pocket money provided.

Apply one month in advance. Opportunity to attend dance courses, lectures and workshops.

HOOGEWERF & CO

Hoogewerf & Co, PO Box 878, 19 rue Aldringen, 2018 Luxembourg

℗ Luxembourg (00 352) 460025   (00 352) 460027

Luxembourg

A small, professional firm of accountants and lawyers established in 1971

Two gap year students are recruited per year to work in the office

Ages 18-23. Applicants must have 2 A levels or equivalent and be able to speak French and English. All nationalities welcome.

1-12 months

40 hour week. Accommodation and return travel to Luxembourg provided. Applicants must arrange their own insurance cover.

HORIZON HPL

Horizon HPL, I East Passage, Off 87 Long Acre, London ECIA 9ET

℅ 0171-600 7595/7686   ✉ 0171-600 7599

France

A French and British linguistic training organisation that can place candidates in hotels and companies throughout France in order to gain professional experience

Opportunities for training placements in hotels and companies selected according to the quality and content of the training they offer. During the training placement Horizon organises French courses in Paris (3 hours per week) for those who wish to improve their spoken and written French. In addition there are opportunities for candidates who would like to increase their knowledge of business French and develop their computer skills. Responsibilities include computing, finance, secretarial and marketing placements, general assistant and receptionist work. All trainees will be advised and guided according not only to their linguistic and professional skills, but also to their personality and their ability to adapt to a new environment.

Ages 18-35. No experience necessary. Candidates should have basic French and be motivated to work and learn in a new environment. EU nationals only.

One, three or six months depending on placement

Cost £240 hotel placement; £300 company placement; £400-£600 French tuition and placement; £500 computer training and French tuition. Accommodation provided with a family or at hotel. Insurance an additional FF200. £50 per week pocket money provided.

Orientation course held prior to placement. A follow-up is organised during the stay in order to ensure progress, both professional and linguistic, and to help with any problems.

Recruitment all year

HOVERSPEED LTD

Linda Oliver, Personnel Executive, Hoverspeed Ltd, International Hoverport, Western Docks, Dover, Kent CT17 9TG

℗ Dover (01304) 240101   ▭ (01304) 209393

Cross-Channel operator established in 1982, operating an airline-style service with a hovercraft service from Dover to Calais and a catamaran service from Folkestone to Boulogne. Also offers holidays in the south of France and on the Costa Brava, luxury coach services to Belgium, France, Germany and the Netherlands, and special train fares.

Work placements available as cabin crew; retail assistants; customer service assistants; and telesales agents

Ages 18-45. Applicants must be outgoing, confident and of smart appearance; travel and tourism qualifications useful. Preference given to those who can speak an additional European language. Applicants for telesales positions must be proficient in computers and keyboarding. In-house training provided for all positions. All nationalities welcome; where required applicants must have a valid work permit.

Placements scheduled March-September. 45 hours per week. Salary from £4.02 per hour plus shift allowance. Limited accommodation in own room with shared facilities charged at £35 per week.

Apply from January

INTERNSHIP CANADA PROGRAMME

Internship Canada Programme, Council on International Educational Exchange, 52 Poland Street, London W1V 4JQ

✆ 0171-478 2007   📠 0171-734 7322   ✉infouk@ciee.org

Canada

The Council on International Educational Exchange is a non-profit, non-governmental organisation dedicated to helping people gain understanding, acquire knowledge and develop skills for living in a globally independent and culturally diverse world. Founded in 1947, it has a variety of programmes and services for students and teachers at secondary through to university levels. Administers a variety of international work programmes offering a unique way to develop personal and career goals in an international setting. Joining one of the programmes enables students to work abroad without the stresses and uncertainties usually involved as a pre-departure advice, an information service and in-country support throughout the stay are provided.

Opportunities for students to experience the Canadian work environment and, if required, improve French skills at the same time by doing an internship in one of the country's French-speaking regions. The placements are arranged independently. CIEE helps to obtain the Work Authorisation Number needed.

Ages 18-35. Applicants must be year between students with a secured place at an institution of higher education or enrolled in full-time higher education, where the placement forms an integral part of the course. Participants have to prove means to finance the visit. UK and Irish nationals only.

Placements last 6-12 months

Working hours and conditions vary according to host employer. Administration fee £135.

Applications must be received at least two months before applicants wish to travel

INTERNSHIP USA
PROGRAMME

Internship USA Programme, Council on International Educational Exchange, 52 Poland Street, London W1V 4JQ

℗ 0171-478 2007   ☎ 0171-734 7322   ✉ infouk@ciee.org

Throughout the United States

Administers a variety of international work programmes offering a unique way to develop personal and career goals in an international setting. Participation in one of the programmes enables students to work abroad without the stresses and uncertainties usually involved as a pre-departure advice and information service is provided. In 1996 over 800 students took advantage of the opportunities offered by the Programme.

The Programme is aimed at students needing course-related work experience and for recent graduates who wish to gain experience in their chosen field. Placements can be in a large variety of fields such as architecture; tourism management; law; engineering; and business studies. Examples include continuing legal training in a Chicago law firm; developing understanding of hospitality management US-style at a New England hotel; and learning and working alongside New York architects in the city. In-country support provided by the New York office throughout the stay.

Ages 18+. All applicants must be enrolled in, or a recent graduate of, full-time higher education in the UK at HND level or above, and must prove that the placement forms an integral part of their studies and future career developments. All participants must secure a full-time work placement in the United States and must be able, through payment from the employer or other means, to finance the entire visit.

Placements of up to 18 months, all year round. The terms and conditions of employment vary according to the host employer. Most positions are paid. Accommodation not included.

All applications must be submitted at least two months before applicants wish to travel. Administration fee £185 for up to 6 months, £215 for 6-12 months and £250, 12-18 months.

INTERSPEAK LTD

David & Irene Ratcliffe, Managing Directors, Interspeak Ltd, The Coach House, Blackwood Estate, Blackwood, Lanarkshire ML11 0JG

✆ Lanark (01555) 894219   ☐ (01555) 894954

Mainly the UK, France, Spain and Germany

Specialises in finding quality *stages* in the UK for students from mainland Europe who have a reasonable level of spoken and written English. Also finds placements abroad for UK students.

Placements are available in the fields of marketing, international trade, secretarial, computing, engineering and hotel and catering. Places up to 1,000 students each year in the UK and abroad.

Ages 18+. Applicants should have an enquiring and open mind, and an interest in the world of business and commerce. Initiative and commonsense are key attributes, as is the ability to work as part of a team. Applicants should have at least A level qualifications or equivalent; school leavers should be planning to go on to further or higher education. Previous work experience is highly desirable, and a reasonable written and spoken level of the relevant language is essential. **B D PH**

2-6 months

Participants work 30-40 hours a week; remuneration varies depending on employer. In order to maximise the linguistic, social and cultural benefit to participants accommodation is in host families; cost approx £100 per week. Participants pay their own travel and insurance costs. Booking fee from £250.

Individual monitoring takes place throughout the placement, and participants are encouraged to prepare a short report

Apply at least 2 months in advance

JOBS IN THE ALPS AGENCY

The Proprietor, Jobs in the Alps Agency, 17 High Street, Gretton, Northamptonshire NN17 3DE

France, Germany, Switzerland

Established in 1972, Jobs in the Alps can place young people in Swiss alpine resort hotels, and carries out aptitude tests on behalf of hotels in France and Germany.

The work is mainly as hall or night porters, waiting staff, receptionists, barmaids, chambermaids or kitchen helpers, in hotels with an international clientele. Some 400+ placements available.

Ages 18+. Good knowledge of French or German required for the more interesting jobs. Applicants must be prepared to work hard and to a high professional standard, alongside an international workforce. Preference given to those with previous work experience.

3-4 months, December-April or June-September

Employees work 8-9 hours each day, with 1-2 days free per week. Pay approx £100-£130 per week; board, lodging and insurance provided. £30 service charge and £20 per month fee depending on length of contract for placements in Switzerland; subscription fee to JITA Club required for placements in France or Germany. Interview fee £1 for postage.

Apply by 15 September for winter placements; by 15 April for summer placements. Interviews held in London and other major cities.

JOHN LAING PLC

Trainee Resourcing Department, John Laing plc, Page Street, Mill Hill, London NW7 2ER

© 0181-906 5314

Throughout the UK

One of Britain's largest construction and civil engineering groups

Offers work at construction sites and offices to students wishing to embark on a career in the construction industry. Limited number of opportunities available for students to work for a year prior to sponsorship on a degree course; generally only a few of the students sponsored opt for a year out before their degree. The benefits are that it can help candidates decide whether they have made the right career choice; the major drawback is that of returning to academic life after a year as a wage-earner.

Ages 16-19. UK nationals only. Applicants should have an interest in the construction industry and evidence that they have what it takes to work in this challenging environment. Previous experience not essential.

Usually 3 months, or 12-15 months for year out placements

Participants work a 40 hour week, with salary and employers' public liability insurance provided

Apply as soon as possible

K P M G

KPMG, 8 Salisbury Square, Blackfriars, London EC4Y 8BB

℃ 0171-311 1000   ▭ 0171-311 5883

London and local offices, England

One of the world's leading firms of accountants and business advisers, who are proud of the fact that they can take a broader view whilst focusing on their clients' individual needs. Over the next few years they expect to increase their global penetration and promote further the KPMG hallmark of quality service within the profession.

Opportunities to gain experience in the areas of audit and accountancy; tax; public sector; corporate recovery; and information risk management. Also run an Accountancy For Fun scheme, a 2 day skills course covering interview skills, presentation skills and insight into accountancy.

Open to 6th form students only. Must have or be predicted to obtain 22 UCAS points and have grade A GCSE mathematics or equivalent

3-6 months, starting with an induction in October. 35 hours per week. Insurance provided. No accommodation arranged. Travel costs paid for those on the Accountancy For Fun scheme. Unable to accept applications from those requiring a work permit. **B D PH W**

No application deadline

LISHMAN SIDWELL CAMPBELL & PRICE

Personnel and Training Manager, Lishman Sidwell Campbell & Price, 68 North Street, Ripon HG4 1EN

℗ Ripon (01765) 690890   📖 (01765) 690296

22 offices in Yorkshire and north east England

An accountancy practice established in 1938 offering a full range of financial services to its clients. Offers financial work experience to chartered, certified accountant, ATT and other students from colleges and universities on secondments, attachment or through summer work.

On-the-job training is given and each student is supervised by a senior student, a manager or a member of senior staff. Each student then undergoes a 6 monthly review with their mentor. After 3 months the student in turn becomes responsible to assist a new student. This is a very structured placement with opportunities to study for professional examinations. Number of positions offered annually varies, but approx 30 students may be on placement at any one time.

Ages 15-22. Qualifications required vary according to work experience placement, but student accountants should have either 22 UCCA points or a 2:1 appropriate degree. All nationalities welcome. **B D PH W**

Placements available all year, length varies. 37½ hour week with weekends free. No accommodation, travel or insurance provided.

LOCAL GOVERNMENT
STUDENT SPONSORSHIP

Local Government Student Sponsorship, PO Box 1540, Homer Road, Solihull, West Midlands B91 3QB

© 0121-704 6040   ☎ 0121-711 1294

Throughout England and Wales

Local Government manages a diverse range of functions; everything from architecture to accountancy, green belt management to law, and are constantly striving to provide a more caring, cost-effective and quality service to the local communities. The student sponsorship was founded in 1989.

A structured, paid work experience placement with a local authority for students during their final summer vacation. Approx 30 placements available. The project is designed to give an insight into how a local authority is managed and enhance students' job prospects. At the end of the placement students produce a management report which is then entered into a competition for further cash prizes up to the value of £500.

Applicants must be in penultimate year of degree, HND or postgraduate study. No experience necessary, but fluent English essential. UK nationals only. **B D PH** welcome

Approx 37 hour week, minimum 5 weeks, June-October

Minimum salary £120 per week. Possible assistance in finding accommodation.

Orientation course available prior to placement

End April closing date for receipt of completed applications

MENTOR LANGUAGE TRAINING

Marion Garbotz, Mentor Language Training, ICG-Bürohaus, Siegfriedstraße 183, 10365 Berlin, Germany

✆ (00 49 30) 5586 245   📖 (00 49 30) 5586 246

In and around Berlin, Germany

A language training company whose motto is learning by doing. Offers an interesting way of learning German as a foreign language by total immersion into the culture, achieved by spending time living and working in Germany.

Work placements arranged according to individual requirements, in small and medium-sized companies in and around Berlin. The stay can be combined with a language course suited to personal needs; various combinations possible. This enables trainees to enhance their grasp of German as well as to gain contact with German enterprises. Short educational trips also organised. The scheme is open to people who have received funding through an EU educational programme, eg LEONARDO, or anyone who wishes to privately fund the work placements.

Those who receive funding through an EU programme are restricted by those guidelines on age and qualifications. Participants who privately fund their stay are not subject to any restrictions. All applicants must speak basic German and be ready to immerse themselves in the culture.

Those receiving funding through the LEONARDO programme must stay for a minimum of 3 months; includes 80 language lessons of 45 minutes each. Other participants must stay a minimum of one month. Accommodation found with host families or in budget hotels.

Applications accepted all year

PFIZER LTD
(CENTRAL RESEARCH)

Personnel Adviser, Pfizer Central Research, Ramsgate Road, Sandwich, Kent CT13 9NJ

📞 Sandwich (01304) 618722

Sandwich, England

An international research-based company established in New York in 1849 and concerned with the development and manufacture of pharmaceuticals, Pfizer's business is in health care. Over 4,500 people around the world are employed in Pfizer's research centres, and the Sandwich centre is the second largest in the group, employing some 1,420 scientists and support staff.

3-6 work placements are available in data management, helping to set up and maintain databases, reviewing and inputting data from clinical trials. Occasionally, work is also available in chemistry or biology research laboratories.

Ages 17/18+. Applicants must have relevant A levels or equivalent, such as mathematics, statistics or computer studies, or appropriate science subject for work in laboratories. They should be well-motivated, with an interest in pharmaceutical research and development. **PH**

12 months

Trainees work a 37 hour week in return for a salary of approx £8,500. 2½ days holiday per month. Local accommodation can be arranged.

Training programme arranged covering the usage of the computer systems and introduction to the company

Recruitment all year

PGL TRAVEL LTD

Recruitment Officer, PGL Travel Ltd, Alton Court, Penyard Lane, Ross-on-Wye, Herefordshire HR9 5NR

℗ Ross-on-Wye (01989) 767833

Throughout Britain and France

Organises activity holidays for young people

Positions are available for activity instructors and support staff, including kitchen/domestic assistants, cooks, site assistants, stores organisers, drivers and administration assistants. Also more senior posts such as couriers, group leaders, TEFL teachers and supervisors. Approx 2,000 young people work for PGL each year.

Ages 18+ (20+ for work abroad and for more senior positions). Applicants must have plenty of energy, enthusiasm and a good sense of humour. They must enjoy working in a team and be able to work and play hard. Qualifications in outdoor activities an advantage, and experience of working with children essential.

2-6 months preferred. Work available February-November.

Salary approx £45 per week, depending on position. Full board and accommodation provided on site. Medical insurance cover provided, and travel from port of exit for staff working abroad.

Full training provided for all staff, including the opportunity to take examinations for BCU, RYA and Open College Network qualifications

Apply December-April. Applicants available before May have a greater chance of selection.

PROEUROPA

Support Services Manager, ProEuropa, 59 High Street, Totnes, Devon TQ9 5PB

© Totnes (01803) 864526   ☐ (01803) 865793

Throughout EU member states

Has been involved in organising work experience placements, language tuition and vocational training since 1989. Aims to provide the opportunity for young Europeans to become sufficiently acquainted with different European countries to enable them to live and work freely in another EU country, thus opening up to them a far greater geographic and economic area in which to seek employment.

Placements are organised in a number of sectors: hotel & catering; accountancy; marketing; engineering; photography; international business; secretarial; retail; construction; art restoration; horticulture; and translation. Language courses and cultural and social activities also organised for large groups to supplement their learning experience.

Placements for young Britons in EU countries normally funded from EU and private sources; some programmes arranged for young Jobseekers. Programmes normally consist of 4 weeks intensive language training in Totnes followed by a 9 week work placement in another EU country.

Placements in the UK for participants from both western and eastern Europe; programmes contain combinations of English language tuition, vocational training, work experience, and social and cultural activities

Ages 19-30. Qualifications required depend on the placement. Nationals of a member state of the EU do not require either a visa or a trainee work experience permit for placements in other member states.

Placements throughout the year, from 2-52 weeks. Approx 35 hour week. Accommodation normally in private homes, halls of residence or hostels. Work experience providers carry employers liability insurance.

One month minimum notice required for applications

SHELL RESEARCH LTD

Personnel Division, Shell Research Ltd, Thornton Research Centre, PO Box 1, Chester CH1 3SH

© 0151-373 5000/5464

Thornton Research Centre, near Chester, England

One of the major Shell Research and Development Centres, employing over 600 people with a wide range of scientific skills. Much of the work is concerned with the development of products such as fuels, lubricants and bitumen and the additives that go into them. The Centre also studies methods of storing and distributing petroleum products, provides advice on design and durability of equipment in hostile environments, and has a large fund of expertise in combustion science. The Centre sees the year out as beneficial both to the company and to the student. The company achieves completed projects and the student learns skills, improves competencies, matures, communicates and acquires some savings before starting university.

Placements are available for approx 12 school-leavers each year who intend to read science or engineering at university

Ages 17-20. Applicants need to be keen and self-motivated and must have above average A level (or equivalent) passes in mathematics, physics and chemistry.

Ten months, beginning September

Students work an arranged 37½ hour week and receive a salary of £8,901. They are responsible for finding their own accommodation and paying their own travel costs.

Compulsory safety, security and fire induction courses organised, and a placement exit interview

Apply by December for following July; places are limited

THE SMALLPEICE TRUST

The Smallpeice Trust, Smallpeice House, 27 Newbold Terrace East, Leamington Spa, Warwickshire CV32 4ES

℗ Leamington Spa (01926) 336423   ☏ (01926) 450679
✉ gen@smallpeice.co.uk   🌐 http://www.smallpeice.co.uk

Study in England and work placement in mainland Europe

An independent, registered charitable trust founded in 1966 by Dr Cosby Smallpeice, the inventor of the Smallpeice Lathe. The Trust aims to enhance perceptions of engineering as a career, to help students gain practical experience, increase awareness of engineering and industry and create worthwhile links between education and industry. It specialises in the provision of free and sponsored courses for students aged 13-25.

The Engineering Careers Foundation Year is a vocational training scheme and exchange/placement programme for gap year students intending to do an engineering degree at university. The scheme is made up of a 12 week academic study course in England, which covers basic engineering, management skills, computer-aided design, a one week outward bound course, 4 weeks language tuition and a 13 week placement in European industry. The course is not intended to replace all or any part of university education, which addresses the more advanced levels of the science of engineering.

Ages 18+ at the commencement of the academic programme. Applications are invited from A level, Higher, CSYS or equivalent students who are taking a year out before entering university to take up an engineering-related degree course.

Scheme runs September-mid May

Costs of travel to and from the European work placement, accommodation and training covered. Students are required to partially finance their subsistence and to take out their own insurance whilst working overseas.

Applications must be submitted by end October

SOLAIRE HOLIDAYS

Personnel Manager, Solaire Holidays, 1158 Stratford Road, Hall Green, Birmingham B28 8AF

✆ 0121-778 5061

France and Spain

A family-run company organising camping and mobile home holidays at sites in the Normandy, Paris, Brittany, Loire, Vendée, Dordogne, Southwest and Mediterranean regions of France, and on the Costa Dorada in Spain

Couriers are required to prepare tents and mobile homes at the beginning of each season, ensure the smooth running of the camps, undertake maintenance work and look after campers, and close down at the end of the season. Children's couriers are also required.

Ages 18+. No previous experience necessary. Knowledge of French or Spanish preferable but not essential. Experience of working with children essential for children's couriers.

Six months, May-September/October

Due to the nature of the job there are no fixed hours of work. Salary £55-£80 per week; accommodation provided in tents or mobile homes on site. Insurance and travel expenses provided.

Apply between January and March

SUPERCHOICE

Superchoice, Personnel Department, 191 Freshfield Road, Brighton, East Sussex BN2 2YE

© Brighton (01273) 676467   (01273) 676290

Throughout the UK and Ireland

Operates adventure-based educational activity holidays for school groups and unaccompanied young people aged 8-18 at various centres

Offers placements as multi-activity, information technology and field study instructors

Ages 18-30. Experience in outdoor pursuits useful but not essential as full training given. Staff are given the opportunity to gain nationally recognised qualifications. Applicants must be dedicated, enthusiastic and keen to work with children in a residential outdoor environment. They should be energetic and outgoing with a good sense of humour. UK nationals only.

Placements last a minimum of 6 weeks, February-October. 6 day week. Salary £45+ per week. Public liability insurance, full board and accommodation provided, plus use of all sports and leisure facilities.

Apply December-April

UK/US CAREER DEVELOPMENT PROGRAMME

UK/US Career Development Programme, Council on International Educational Exchange, 52 Poland Street, London W1V 4JQ

© 0171-478 2006   ✆ 0171-734 7322   ✉ infouk@ciee.org

Throughout the United States, and in the UK for US citizens

In cooperation with Association for International Practical Training (AIPT) in the United States, administers the Career Development Programme to promote international training for qualified individuals

The programme aims to enable young professionals to gain practical work experience by facilitating the issue of the necessary work permits/visas. Applicants are responsible for finding their own paid work placements which must be full-time and at a level suited to the applicant's qualifications and training, but CIEE can provide advice and information on how to start the job search. Placements can be in a variety of fields such as business, hospitality, architecture or information technology.

Ages 18+. Applicants must have relevant academic, professional or vocational qualifications and/or previous work experience in the relevant field.

Placements from 3-18 months, all year round

Terms and conditions of employment vary according to the host employer. Host employers generally assist trainees in finding accommodation or provide housing directly. Trainees must carry insurance which can be their own policy, arranged through the host employer or by AIPT. No travel provided. Salaries are comparable to that paid to US employees with similar background and work experience. Registration fee £75, which includes US Embassy visa fee.

Allow 10-12 weeks between applying and intended date of travel. Applicants in the United States should apply to AIPT, 10400 Little Patuxent Parkway, Suite 250, Columbia, MD 21044-3510
© Baltimore (410) 997 2200   ✆ (410) 992 3924   ✉ aipt@aipt.org
🌐 http://www.aipt.org

UK/US HOSPITALITY & TOURISM EXCHANGE PROGRAMME

UK/US Hospitality & Tourism Exchange Programme, Council on International Educational Exchange, 52 Poland Street, London WIV 4JQ

✆ 0171-478 2000   ▭ 0171-734 7322   ✉ infouk@ciee.org

Throughout the United States, and in the UK for US citizens

In cooperation with the Association for International Practical Training (AIPT) in the United States, administers this programme to promote transitional training for qualified individuals

The programme aims to enable participants to gain practical work experience by facilitating the issue of the necessary work permits/visas. The programme is divided into two parts: the Reserved Programme for individuals who have located their own training programme with an employer in the hotel, catering or tourism industry; and the Open Programme for those who require assistance in finding a work placement. Details of applicants are advertised in AIPT's monthly newsletter, distributed to host employers.

Ages 18+. Applicants must be currently enrolled in or have academic, professional or vocational qualifications in hotel management or tourism/leisure studies or have at least one year of relevant work experience. They should have good written and oral communication skills in English, and be in good health.

Placements from 1-72 weeks, all year round

The work is full-time, with a minimum of 30-35 hours per week. The conditions of an offer of training vary considerably depending on the employer. The prospective training organisation is asked to pay a salary sufficient to cover the trainee's living expenses, plus a reasonable amount for recreation. Applicants must be covered by medical insurance.

Reserved Programme applications take 8 weeks to process. The Open Programme takes an average 6-8 months to locate a suitable placement. Applicants in the United States should contact the AIPT, 10400 Little Patuxent, Suite 250, Columbia, MD 21044-3510   ✆ Baltimore (410) 997 2200   ▭ (410) 992 3924   ✉ aipt@aipt.org   🖳 http://www.aipt.org.

THE YEAR IN INDUSTRY

The Year In Industry, c/o University of Manchester, Simon Building, Oxford Road, Manchester M13 9PL

☎/✉ 0161-275 4396   🌐 http://www.yini.org.uk/yini/

Throughout England and Wales

Set up in 1986, a registered charity organising industrial placements and training for students

The scheme offers approx 500 positions annually in over 250 different companies. Most of the placements are suited to those interested in engineering, science, computing and business studies, but students of all disciplines are welcome as some non-technical places are available. Most companies prefer local students; however, if applicants prefer to work away from home or if there is no local placement to suit, they can be considered for opportunities in other regions.

Ages 18-19. The scheme is open to students taking deferred entry to university. Companies require good examination grades, but will also be influenced by non-academic achievements. UK nationals only. **D**

Programme runs from mid August-mid July; exact start and finish times vary between companies and regions

Students are employed on the normal terms and conditions applied by the individual companies. Formal training given to help students adapt to the industrial environment and scheme tutors are on hand to help with training assignments and performance appraisals. Salary rates vary from company to company; students will normally be paid the typical rate for 18 year old employees, subject to The Year In Industry's recommended minimum of £130 per week.

Apply in the summer term of lower 6th or autumn term of upper 6th to the relevant regional office:
Devon & Cornwall ☎ (01752) 232557; East Midlands ☎ 0115-948 6498; Eastern ☎ (01480) 476665; Northern ☎ 0191-374 3912; North West ☎ 0161-275 4395; South ☎ (01703) 592430; Thames Valley ☎ (01865) 483558; Wales ☎ (01792) 295494; West of England ☎ 0117-928 8119; West Midlands ☎ 0121-414 4136; Yorkshire ☎ 0114-222 0936.

YOUTH HOSTELS ASSOCIATION

National Recruitment Department (YBI), YHA (England and Wales) Limited, PO Box 11, Matlock, Derbyshire DE4 2XA

© Matlock (01629) 822074   (01629) 824571

Throughout England and Wales

The YHA aims to help all, especially young people of limited means, to achieve a greater knowledge, love and care of the countryside, in particular by providing hostels or other simple accommodation

Recruits seasonal assistant wardens to assist in the running of its many youth hostels throughout England and Wales. Work involves domestic and catering duties, reception work and other general duties.

Ages 18+. Applicants should have a cheerful, outgoing personality; an interest in the countryside and in the work of the YHA is also desirable. A proven ability to cater for large numbers or perform clerical work would be an advantage.

2-6 months, all year; peak periods March-September. Preference given to applicants prepared to work for most of a season.

Assistant wardens work a 5 day week, with 2 days off or payment/time in lieu. Salary approx £360 per month, depending on location; full board accommodation and insurance provided. Applicants pay their own travel expenses. Opportunity to attain recognised NVQs.

Recruitment all year; send SAE for further information and application form

DISCOVERY/
LEADERSHIP

This section covers organisations who can offer you the chance to learn new skills and develop ones you already have in the context of an expedition, usually to some remote corner of the world, designed to test and stretch the abilities of participants. Also covered are short-service schemes run by the Armed Forces, which provide the opportunity to train and join a unit, develop leadership skills, and possibly travel overseas.

Expedition programmes generally involve an aspect of community service or environmental research, giving participants an awareness of the problems faced by local communities and the natural world, and the opportunity to work in some small way towards resolving them. In this way topics covered in school geography and biology lessons can become realities. And as a result of the challenges they present to participants' endurance and problem-solving abilities, many of the expeditions covered here qualify participants for Duke of Edinburgh awards.

Groups are supervised by fully trained and experienced leaders, and will tend to be made up of young people from different backgrounds. Once they are thrown together far from home, perhaps in a hostile environment, a spirit of companionship, loyalty and teamwork develops, as each participant depends on the others for the success of the project. Learning to survive in an Arctic climate or jungle terrain, taking responsibility for actions which will affect other members of the group, overcoming physical hardships and tackling practical problems, all these aspects of expeditions go to develop participants' self-confidence, maturity and leadership ability.

Although leadership experience, scientific knowledge and outdoor skills are obviously very valuable qualities for potential expedition members, they are not necessarily the first things that the organisers are looking for. They will usually want a broad range of people to make up a group, and qualities such as a sense of humour, enthusiasm, determination and commonsense are the most likely to help a group gel. Physical fitness is important, but you don't have to be an Olympic athlete. Many organisations encourage applications from people with disabilities. Above all, it is having the right motivation that counts.

For most expeditionary projects, you will be required to raise the finances to fund your participation. In some cases this is considered to be part of the challenge of joining an expedition, and participants are usually discouraged from depending on their parents' generosity, or may be asked to help out participants who have not benefited from the same advantages as them. Help and advice on fundraising may be given, but participants are expected to rely mainly on their own resourcefulness and imagination.

The International Scientific Support Trust's expeditionary arm, Trekforce Expeditions, provides a unique opportunity to work with scientists and/or conservation bodies in remote Indonesian rainforest reserves, experience a different culture as well as an education and training in outdoor living and self awareness. Trekforce believes that taking a year out is very beneficial, as long as the year is used sensibly, and that expeditions mature, broaden and prepare school-leavers for further education. Clare Browne-Clayton took a year out, travelling to Australia first, and then joining Trekforce in Jakarta to work on a turtle project:

My expedition in the jungles of Java was a great success and definitely the most brilliant and valuable experience of my life so far, one I shall never forget. I have learnt a great deal about the Indonesian way of life, the jungle, how to cope with people 24 hours a day, how to help each other through thick and thin and how to cope with hardship. I have made friends for life.

The expedition programmes demand a lot from the participants, but give a lot in return. If you are concerned that your scientific, sport or physical skills may not come up to the standards required, take heart from Teresa Fenoughty, who interviews applicants for the BSES expeditions. She stresses that at the outset of the expedition they are not necessarily looking for the winners in life:

They don't have to be the toughest rock rats. We pick students who have a real interest and potential, who might give a lot or even gain a lot from such an experience, either because they are under confident, arrogant or immature.

BSES expeditions create the challenge of adventure in remote environments, fostering dedication, companionship and personal initiative. The majority of destinations are Arctic/sub-Arctic environments such as Greenland, Iceland and Alaska. Lucy Wright appreciated the challenges the environment imposed on her expedition:

I've become more tolerant since the trip. Under survival conditions you have to look after those around you and take responsibility for the

community. Your mistake could mean a fatal accident.

Mark Mullen joined the 2nd King Edward VII's Own Gurkha Rifles in Brunei under the Army Short Service Limited Commission (SSLC) scheme before taking up his place at London University:

Having completed a basic Nepali language course, I returned to the battalion to become platoon commander, under the watchful eye of the platoon sergeant who was always on hand to offer that vital piece of advice. Though often tired and hot in the jungle, I found it one of the most exciting and interesting environments I have ever been in. The experience of serving an SSLC has taught me a lot about myself and others. I feel my confidence has grown and my horizons have been broadened from that of a schoolboy.

Jennifer Clee also undertook an Army Short Service Commission in her year between before going on to Nottingham University:

Having passed the selection I arrived at Sandhurst for the three week course very apprehensive, and with no idea of what to expect ... my time spent there was probably the hardest, most challenging and the most rewarding of my life. When I arrived at 28 (British) Signal regiment, part of the northern Army Group in Germany, I was whisked straight off on a NATO exercise for ten days. Upon arriving back at camp I became 2IC of a troop, enabling me to see the role of a troop commander, and later with a little help to fulfil that role. However the Army does not believe in all work and no play, so whilst with the unit I took the rounders team to the championships in Berlin. I was also a member of the winning women's shooting team as well as representing the regiment at swimming. I managed to fit in some adventure training in the Mosel: canoeing, swimming, cycling and walking, plus some compulsory wine tasting!

Before taking up his place at Brunel University, Paul Hayhurst served his Commission in Hong Kong and Hawaii with the 1st Battalion The Royal Regiment of Wales:

In Exercise Union Pacific, B Company, of which I was a member, went over to Hawaii for seven weeks to exercise with the United States Marine Corps and the US Army. This was by far the most beneficial part of my SSLC ... we were taught the principles and tactics behind a beach assault and then did a night time main assault with the Americans acting as enemy, an experience that not many British officers can boast. The Exercise also gave me an opportunity to see another country and we had sufficient time off to get out and about. I managed to go big game fishing, diving and to visit a lava flow.

Most of my time, however, was spent in Hong Kong. It was here that I learnt how the battalion ran and had the opportunity to carry out Orderly Officer duties. It was a very valuable experience and I had a wide variety of challenges to sort out, from compassionate cases to domestic and disciplinary problems. In Hong Kong there was also an excellent opportunity for adventure training, from water-skiing to abseiling. There were also a lot of sports played in the battalion which I was strongly encouraged to take part in, such as rugby, water polo, boxing, football and many more.

Army Short Service Limited Commission

Brathay Exploration Group

BSES Expeditions

Dorset Expeditionary Society

Four Corners School of Outdoor Education

Outward Bound Trust

Raleigh International

Sail Training Association

Trekforce Expeditions

THE ARMY SHORT SERVICE LIMITED COMMISSION

The Army Short Service Limited Commission, ATRA, Ministry of Defence, Building 38B, Trenchard Lines, Upavon, Pewsey, Wiltshire SN9 6BE

UK and overseas

Aims to give young men and women a unique opportunity to develop their self-confidence and maturity in the testing environment of a frontline unit. In return, the Army gains the services of a number of young officers who make an important contribution to the life of their units, and who, it is hoped, will carry a favourable impression of their Army service into their later careers.

Open to young men and women with time between leaving school and going to university. SSLC Officers serve as second lieutenants in Regular Army units, where possible overseas, but not on active-service operations. Recruits 40-60 SSLC officers annually.

Ages 18-20. The most successful candidates are of high academic ability who have usually been prefects or leading members of school societies or sports teams. They should have wide interests with a taste for outdoor pursuits and a sense of adventure. Applicants must have a confirmed place at a UK university to read for a recognised degree, with all academic work and examinations completed before commencing the placement. UK nationals only.

4-18 months, beginning October and March

Hours vary depending on the work of the unit where officers are placed. SSLC officers receive a salary of £10,544 per annum, from which they pay for board and lodging. They live in their own study bedroom in the officers' mess, with all meals provided. Travel costs provided.

All applicants must attend a 3 day selection at the Regular Commissions Board in Westbury, Wiltshire. Successful candidates then attend a 3 week course at the Royal Military Academy, Sandhurst. SSLC Officers receive a report from their commanding officer at the end of their tour.

Applications should be made through careers teachers to local Army Schools Liaison Officers. Recruitment all year.

BRATHAY EXPLORATION GROUP

The Administrator, Brathay Exploration Group, Brathay Hall, Ambleside, Cumbria LA22 0HP

℗ Ambleside (0153 94) 33942

UK and worldwide

Established in 1947, a non-profitmaking, voluntary organisation running expeditions aimed at increasing members' understanding of the natural environment, people and cultures of the places visited

Applicants are invited to become members of expeditions, usually exploring wild, rugged, remote or mountainous areas. Members have the opportunity to develop outdoor skills, carry out scientific work or take part in conservation tasks. Expeditions planned for the future include ornithology and archaeology on the Shetland island of Foula, environmental investigations on Mull, carrying out rural surveys in southern China, scientific work and adventure in Iceland or Norway, a visit to the Atai Mountains in Siberia, living with the Sherpa people in Nepal, or trekking in the French Alps.

Ages 16-25. Most expeditions require applicants with a good level of fitness. **PH**

1-4 weeks, April-September

Members pay an expedition fee which covers all travel from a specified meeting point, food and accommodation (usually in tents), scientific and camping equipment, and insurance. Bursary funds are available, as is advice on raising funds for those who may have difficulty raising the expedition fee.

Training weekends held. Expedition members are generally given training on the spot with any special skills such as snow and ice work or climbing techniques.

Early application advised; expeditions are popular

BSES EXPEDITIONS

The Executive Director, BSES Expeditions, Royal Geographical Society, 1 Kensington Gore, London SW7 2AR

℡ 0171-591 3141 📠 0171-591 3140

Generally Arctic/sub-Arctic environments such as Greenland, Iceland, Spitzbergen, Norway, Canada and Alaska; destinations have also included Botswana, Kenya, Namibia, Zimbabwe, India and Papua New Guinea

Founded in 1932, BSES provides opportunities to take part in exploratory projects led by experts from universities, teaching and medical professions, industry and the Services. Expeditions create the challenge of adventure in remote and hostile environments, fostering dedication, companionship and personal initiative.

Expeditions planned in the next 2 years include mountain climbing and trekking in the Indian Himalayas; glacier travel, climbing and scientific research (geology, glaciology and survey) in south Greenland; camel trekking, geology, archaeology and scuba diving in Sinai; climbing, trekking and the study of local cultures in Morocco; scientific research, wildlife study, climbing and canoeing in Lesotho; conservation, botany, glaciology, mountaineering and glacier travel in east Greenland.

Ages 16½-20. Applicants should be keen on taking up the challenges offered, interested in the natural world and related science projects, and willing to work as part of a team. Knowledge of camping and hill walking necessary; specialised mountaineering skills not essential. Ability in natural/life sciences desirable. **D PH** full walking ability essential.

3-4 months, usually beginning in spring; or 6 weeks, mid July-late August. 72 members on the 6 week summer expedition, formed into five groups with 2 leaders, each group working independently on specific tasks.

Participants are expected to contribute equally to the costs of the expedition, from £2,000-£2,800 depending on destination and length. Advice and assistance given with fundraising, which is considered to be part of the challenge, involving participants' drive and initiative.

Participants issued with expedition handbooks and attend informal get-togethers, plus at least one training weekend. Each expedition makes an audiovisual presentation, and reports are published.

Apply as soon as possible for 3/4 month expeditions; selection weekends in late autumn. Apply by 31 October for 6 week programme.

DORSET EXPEDITIONARY SOCIETY

Dorset Expeditionary Society, c/o The Budmouth College, Weymouth, Dorset DT4 9SY

✆ Weymouth (01305) 775599   📠 (01305) 766389
🌐 http://www.wdi.co.uk/des

Africa, Asia, America and Europe

Established in 1986, a registered charity founded to encourage safe adventurous opportunities for young people. By training and challenging young people it seeks to cultivate and promote the personal qualities of service, self-sufficiency and leadership. The Society's leaders are volunteers and its programmes are specifically targeted at increasing the scope and depth of challenge to all participants. Schemes include residential courses for groups from schools, colleges and clubs where participants undertake activities such as rock climbing, mountain biking, parachuting and canoeing in the wild country areas of Dartmoor, Wales and Scotland, and overseas expeditions.

Organises overseas expeditions throughout the world. Previous ventures have involved participants undertaking environmental work in the Arctic Circle, completing the Inca Trail to Machu Picchu, surviving on a desert island in the South China Sea and trekking across the Moonlands of Ladakh. Participants are actively involved in the planning and preparation stages of each expedition. 100 places offered annually.

Also holds courses for aspiring young leaders throughout the world which can lead to the Basic Expedition Training Award, the Mountain First Aid Certificate, and the Cave Leadership and Mountain Leadership Awards. Many young leaders go on to organise their own expeditions.

Ages 15-20 when applying. Experience not necessary as training is given, but high motivation is essential. Participants for the overseas expeditions are selected on a 48 hour course. All nationalities welcome. The Society actively encourages participation of disadvantaged young people. **B D PH W**

Expeditions last 2-6 weeks, most take place June-September

Cost £250-£1,500 which covers selection, training, equipment, visas, climbing permits, guides, flights, insurance, hotels, food, laundry, hire of rafts/canoes and society membership

FOUR CORNERS SCHOOL
OF OUTDOOR EDUCATION

Four Corners School of Outdoor Education, PO Box 1029, Monticello, Utah 84535, United States

© Monticello (00 1 801) 587 2156

The Colorado Plateau, United States

The Colorado Plateau extends for 160,000 square miles through Utah, Colorado, New Mexico and Arizona, in the south-western corner of the United States. Using this magnificent wilderness as an outdoor classroom, Four Corners School is dedicated to educating people of all ages and backgrounds about the need to preserve the world's natural and cultural treasures.

A wide range of programmes is offered, including archaeology and geology adventures; environmental and cultural studies; photography and writing courses; natural history and wilderness advocacy; river rafting and hiking; houseboat exploring; van touring; backpacking and cultural sharing. Programmes are led by expert instructors who are happy to share their enthusiasm, knowledge, leadership skills and concern for the environment.

Ages 16+ for unaccompanied participants. No special qualifications are necessary, apart from an interest in the outdoors and in environmental education. Programmes range in level of difficulty; for the more strenuous programmes some camping, hiking and/or whitewater experience may be required.

Programmes run January-October and last 5-14 days

Costs range from $695-$1,800 depending on subject and length. Fees cover supplies, group equipment, instruction, food, accommodation and transportation within the programme area. Accommodation is in basecamps which can be fairly primitive. Participants arrange and pay own insurance and travel to and from programme location.

Apply all year round

OUTWARD BOUND TRUST

Outward Bound Trust, Watermillock, near Penrith, Cumbria CA11 0JL

☎ (0990) 134227

Three national centres in Wales, Scotland and the Lake District, England

A charitable trust which has offered a variety of multi-activity, personal and team development programmes for over 50 years. Approx 12,000 participants attend programmes each year. The Trust believes that everyone is capable of achieving more than they realise, and that too few people have real appreciation of what can be achieved by teamwork and mutual support. Outward Bound courses are designed to address both issues.

Participants are given the opportunity to safely explore independence, perfect the art of relating to other people and cultivate the skills of leadership, problem-solving, goal-setting and group cooperation.
Each course provides a carefully integrated complementary range of activities involving all aspects of personal development including physical, emotional, mental and social aspects, using the sea, lakes, rivers and mountains as a classroom for exciting activities such as mountain trekking, sailing, fell walking, raft building, orienteering, caving and expeditions.

Ages 11+. No qualifications or experience necessary. All nationalities welcome; participants should speak English. **B D PH** welcome.

I, 2 or 3 week courses; programmes all year round

Cost from £100-£662, inclusive of VAT, depending on course. Limited funds available to help people who otherwise could not afford fees. Accommodation in single sex dormitories and self-service dining area available. Tuition, specialist clothing and equipment provided.

Advisers help participants prepare for courses and are available to them for advice and support after the course

Recruitment all year

RALEIGH INTERNATIONAL

Raleigh International, 27 Parsons Green Lane, London SW6 4HZ

✆ 0171-371 8585   ✉ 0171-371 5116   ✉ info@raleigh.org.uk
🌐 http://www.raleigh.org.uk

Worldwide

Raleigh International is a charity running a series of expeditions across the world for people from many nations. It aims to provide a unique opportunity for young people to develop their self-confidence and leadership skills by stretching themselves mentally and physically whilst at the same time helping others.

Venturers join expeditions based on community work, scientific research and conservation, with a strong ingredient of adventure. Expeditions consist of some 100 Venturers split into groups of 5-15 to tackle individual projects, which may include improving primary health care; constructing schools, bridges, and water supplies; studying the effects of pollution on ecology; or gathering information for scientific surveys. Adventure projects are an essential feature of expeditions: Venturers go trekking across deserts, climbing glaciers and exploring little-known corners of the earth.

Ages 17-25. No formal qualifications necessary. Applicants must understand basic English and be able to swim 200 metres. An intensive selection and assessment process is held to discover those with the motivation, determination, compatibility and humour to cope with the demands of expedition life. Evidence of leadership ability and a genuine commitment to help others also required. **B D PH**

Ten weeks

Initial assessment weekend fee £25. Once selected, each Venturer is asked to raise £2,995 to help fund the work; advice and support given on fundraising. 150 places available each year through a programme for young people from disadvantaged backgrounds.

Problem solving and teamwork exercises take place over a weekend and are tough, challenging and rewarding. Those on the Youth Development Programme receive a week's special pre-expedition training.

Applications accepted all year round

SAIL TRAINING ASSOCIATION

Sail Training Association, 2A The Hard, Portsmouth, Hampshire PO1 3PT

☎ Portsmouth (01705) 832055/6   ✉ (01705) 815769
✉ tallships@sta.org.uk   🌐 http://www.sta.org.uk/sta/

UK and Continental ports, and the Canary Islands

A registered charity which organises adventure voyages on Tall Ships for young people. Aims to give young people the opportunity to learn about themselves and their own capabilities, and develop an awareness of others by working together in a team. The Association is also responsible for organising the Cutty Sark Tall Ships Race each year.

Up to 39 participants join the crew to sail a 150 ft, 3-masted schooner on voyages to northern continental waters, visiting 2-3 Continental ports during each voyage. As well as helping with the care and maintenance of the ship, duties include look-out, steering, sail-trimming, galley work and ship cleaning. Voyages qualify for the Duke of Edinburgh's Gold Award.

Ages 16-24. No experience necessary; participants should have a reasonable understanding of English and be eager to meet a unique challenge. All nationalities welcome. **B D PH** depending on extent of ability; ships do not have special adaptations

Voyages sail between March-November in Europe, and between November-April in the Canary Islands, for 10-20 nights. A watch system is operated whereby participants work 4 hours on, 4 hours standby and 4 hours off.

Fees vary from £49-£70 per day, and cover full board dormitory accommodation in bunks on board ship, and the provision of safety equipment. Insurance cover is provided for a premium of £12 per voyage. Participants should supply own pocket money. Help given in cases of financial hardship, and advice given on fundraising/sponsorship.

Briefing available through volunteer support groups in the UK. Debriefing at the end of each voyage.

Apply throughout the year

TREKFORCE EXPEDITIONS

Trekforce Expeditions, 134 Buckingham Palace Road, London
SW1W 9SA

① 0171-824 8890   ▱ 0171-824 8892   ▢ trekforce@dial.pipex.com
🕏 http://www.ds.dial.pipex.com/town/parade/hu15

Belize, Indonesia, Kenya

Run by the International Scientific Support Trust, a registered charity.
Work involves projects in remote areas in support of science and
conservation. Offers the chance to experience other cultures as well as
gain education and training in outdoor living and self-awareness.

Recent expeditions include building a turtle hatching pen in southern
Sumatra; building huts for the forestry department, in national parks in
Indonesia; mapping ancient Mayan temples with GPS systems, and
building signposts in national parks, in Belize; and protecting a scarce
water supply, essential to the lives of the nomadic tribes in Kenya

Ages 17+. No special skills required; trekkers should be enthusiastic,
able to work as part of a team and enjoy a challenge. Expedition and/or
scientific experience not essential.

Expeditions run throughout the year. Each expedition lasts 6 weeks and
trekkers have the opportunity of independent travel after the
expedition. Also 2, 3 or 4 week expeditions to Belize only.

As the first part of the challenge trekkers are asked to contribute
£2,700; this covers all expedition costs and goes towards the cost of
providing the project. Most trekkers fund participation through raffles,
sponsorship and organising sponsored events.

Interested potential trekkers are asked to attend an introduction
weekend to enable them and Trekforce to find out if an expedition is for
them. Previous trekkers are on hand to talk about their
experiences, and help and advice on fundraising is given. Each
expedition starts with a few days pre-expedition training. This enables
the trekker to learn about all facets of jungle/desert living as well as
enhancing and strengthening the group as a whole.

Recruitment all year. Interviews for those unable to attend the
introduction weekends.

All the essential advice and information you need to arrange a successful and enjoyable seasonal job is in the Central Bureau's information guide **WORKING HOLIDAYS**, acknowledged as *the* authoritative guide.

WORKING HOLIDAYS lists hundreds of employers offering over 99,000 temporary or seasonal jobs in Britain and 70 other countries. Whatever the job, in whatever country, **WORKING HOLIDAYS** gives very full details. Any age or nationality restrictions are noted, the period of work on offer, salary and terms, including whether travel, accommodation or insurance is included is listed, and application deadlines are given. But it doesn't stop there.

WORKING HOLIDAYS carries information on a wide range of other useful details: where and how to advertise for a job in a foreign newspaper, services of local youth information centres, useful publications to help you plan your visit, what work or residence permit you'll need and how to go about getting it, what medical precautions you should take, what insurance cover you should have, and what passports or visas will get you across borders. It lists addresses and telephone numbers of embassies,

From picking pears in Australia to being an au pair in Greece; from excavating Inca remains in South America to restoring medieval castles in France; from teaching sports in the US to cooking in Switzerland, **WORKING HOLIDAYS** has the opportunities and the information to help you see the world.

high commissions, youth and student travel offices, youth hostels, passport and tourist offices & other organisations to help you, tells you all about accommodation, insurance, health requirements, money and travel, and provides just about everything else you'll need not only to get a holiday job but to make the whole experience as fulfilling and trouble-free as possible.

Unlike some other guides, every piece of information in **WORKING HOLIDAYS** is checked each and every year, and updated against reports and other received information. Combine this with the databases and computerised information we use to edit and produce the guide and you can be sure that the information you will be using to choose your holiday is right up to date.

WORKING HOLIDAYS has opportunities for those aged 12-70+; from 3 days up to a year; from Au pairs to Zoo staff; from Austria to Zimbabwe. It is available from all good bookshops or direct from the Central Bureau. For further information on the Bureau's publications & programmes contact the Information Desk on © 0171-389 4004.

WORKING HOLIDAYS is published each November for the following year.

This section covers a range of opportunities offering you the chance to contribute in a practical way to the health of this planet as well as to community development.

Conservation The Earth is 4,600 million years old; over the last 150 years we have come ever closer to upsetting the ecological balance that has developed since the planet's creation. Earth's human inhabitants have raided the planet for fuels, used the land, sea and air as rubbish tips, and caused the extinction of over 500 species of animals. The world is changing so rapidly that many fear the environment left to us now may no longer be available to our children. If these threats to our natural and cultural heritage give you cause for alarm, why not use your year between to take positive action through volunteering?

The destruction of habitats threatens whole populations, and the extinction of a single species may put countless others at risk. So in order to develop a strategy for planetary survival, we first need to discover as much as possible about different species, how they survive and how their behaviour affects others. For this reason, much of the work done by conservation volunteers involves detailed studying, surveying or monitoring to determine the current population levels, habits or optimum environment of a particular plant or animal species. Such work does not necessarily require you to have any knowledge of the species in question or experience in surveying techniques, as these can be learned on-the-job. Conservation volunteers also work to solve or prevent problems caused by human or natural activity. For example, you may get involved in combating erosion, cleaning up pollution or protecting against encroachment by an introduced species which poses a threat to native flora and fauna. There is also a need to promote growth in dwindling native populations through a programme of wildlife management - this may involve work such as digging ponds to create a new habitat, collecting seeds for revegetation, or breeding animals for later release into the wild.

As well as hands-on work with nature, there are also plenty of opportunities to preserve the built or managed environment, including the restoration of railways, canals and other aspects of our industrial heritage; renovating churches, castles, stately homes and gardens; rebuilding abandoned hamlets; carrying out coppicing and hedge-laying; and building drystone walls. This presents a real opportunity to learn about a region's history, culture and heritage and perhaps find out what ordinary life was really like in days gone by. The human heritage is not necessarily destructive to nature - there are countless examples of areas such as railway cuttings, canals, managed woodlands, hedges, walls and meadows where plants and animals can flourish. Such environments need to be preserved and developed to encourage a diversity of wildlife, even in the most urban surroundings.

One of the most important aspects of conservation work is to encourage other people to take an interest in the world around them and to realise that parts of it are under threat. The range of tasks that this encompasses is quite considerable - for example, building a waymarked trail through a national park will encourage people to visit, and by keeping to the path they will reduce their impact on other areas. Working as a warden or environmental interpreter at a nature reserve will bring you into contact with those who are eager to find out more about the local environment. You could also get involved in projects devoted to campaigning and raising awareness about conservation, pollution, waste recycling, energy use, nature protection and alternative lifestyles in general. Environmental groups such as Friends of the Earth, Greenpeace and the Worldwide Fund for Nature are always looking for members who can devote spare time and energy to fundraising and campaigns. Your library should be able to give you the address of your local group. In addition to the recruiters detailed in the following pages, the organisations below undertake conservation work in Britain and recruit volunteers accordingly. Most of these organisations have a local group network and the regional headquarters should be able to provide you with details of the group nearest to you. Projects tend to be limited to 10 days at the most, and will therefore only be of interest as short-term options during a year out. However, if you have previous experience of this type of work there may be longer term opportunities as a task leader or field officer.

British Trust for Conservation Volunteers
36 St Mary's Street, Wallingford, Oxfordshire OX10 OEU
© Wallingford (01491) 839766

National Trust Acorn Projects
PO Box 84, Cirencester, Gloucestershire GL17 1ZP
© Cirencester (01285) 644727

The Scottish Conservation Projects Trust
Balallan House, 24 Allan Park, Stirling

FK8 2QG
© Stirling (01786) 479697

National Trust for Scotland Thistle Camps
5 Charlotte Square, Edinburgh EH2 4DU
© 0131-243 9470

Conservation Volunteers (Northern Ireland)
159 Ravenhill Road, Belfast BT6 0BP © Belfast (01232) 645161

National Trust, Northern Ireland Region
Rowallane House, Saintfield Ballynahinch, Co Down BT24 7LH
© Saintfield (01238) 510721

Due to the nature of the work and the fact that much of it carries on outdoors, there is a wider variety of projects in Britain during the summer months, although opportunities do exist all through the year. Further details of organisations arranging short-term conservation projects and workcamps throughout Britain, Europe and even further afield are given in the Central Bureau's annual guidebook **WORKING HOLIDAYS**. The more longer-term options for conservation tend to be based overseas, and volunteers can thereby combine the work project with a period of travel or exploration. Frontier is the expeditionary arm of the Society for Environmental Exploration, established in the belief that volunteers can assist with practical solutions to some of the world's environmental problems. On its projects in Africa and South East Asia many of the volunteers are students taking a year out. Frontier believes that its volunteers benefit significantly from the experience of living and working in such a vastly different environment, rather than just passing through as tourists. Working in a team with people from diverse backgrounds and cultures is an education in itself, which matures the volunteers' outlook and helps prepare them for university life. Gillian Bell was one such volunteer, on an expedition to Uganda:

Raising the funds to take part was quite a challenge, but I definitely feel I got my money's worth. I made a lot of friends, both among the other volunteers and the Ugandans we were working with. I came away with the satisfying feeling that I had really done something positive to help the environment. I think that taking part broadened my horizons and gave me the confidence and the craving to set out on other adventures.

Whatever type of project you choose it is still important to remember that we all have a part to play in caring for the environment. If you can accept some personal responsibility and resolve to reduce your own impact on the world around you, this is taking a step in the right direction. A good code to follow, wherever you travel, is to *take nothing but photos* and *leave nothing but footprints*.

Kibbutzim/moshavim There are hundreds of kibbutzim and moshavim all over Israel, offering the opportunity to experience the challenge of living and working in a small, independent community. This in itself is potentially rewarding, as is living in a country whose society and culture are so different from one's own. The first **kibbutz** was established in 1909 by a group of pioneers who wanted to form a community where there was no exploitation and no drive to accumulate individual wealth. The desire to establish a just society is the basic principle guiding kibbutz life, together with a commitment to undertake tasks important to the development of Israel and the Jewish people. There are now some 270 kibbutzim throughout Israel providing a way of life for nearly 100,000 people, in which all means of production are owned by the community as a whole. The workforce consists of all members and any volunteers, who receive no wages but give their labour according to ability and in return receive in accordance with their needs.

Kibbutzim are democratic societies and all members have a voice in determining how the kibbutz is run. A general assembly meets weekly and committees discuss and resolve specialist problems. Kibbutzim welcome volunteers who are prepared to live and work within the community and abide by the kibbutz way of life. Volunteers share all communal facilities with kibbutz members, and should be capable of adapting to a totally new society. The work may be based indoors or outdoors and may include farming, citrus, melon, soft fruit and vegetable harvesting, market gardening, haymaking, working in fishponds, cowsheds or chicken houses, and even light industry. In addition, everyone is expected to take their turn in doing household chores such as helping with cooking, cleaning and washing for the whole community. Volunteers work approximately an 8 hour day, 6 day week with Saturdays free and 2 additional days off at the end of each month. Additional hours' work may be necessary at busy periods, such as the harvest. During the summer, work outdoors often starts early in the morning with the afternoons free to avoid the hottest part of the day. Volunteers live together in wood cabins or stone houses, with food provided in the communal dining area. Male and female volunteers generally sleep in separate 2-4 bedded rooms. Laundry, toilet requisites, medical care and other basic needs, such as stamps and cigarettes, are usually available as required, and some kibbutzim have bars and discos.

Sally was a kibbutz volunteer for six months. She worked in the kitchen of Kibbutz Sha'ar Ha'amakim, on a placement organised through Project 67:

I found this experience to be absolutely incredible. I made wonderful friends from all over the world and had an excellent time travelling throughout the country. I would recommend Israel to many people.

Moshavim are collective settlements made up of between 10-100 individual smallholders. As opposed to the collectivity of a kibbutz, a moshav is far more centred on private enterprise and the family unit. Each family works and develops its own area of land or farm while sharing the capital costs of equipment, marketing and necessary services. There are almost 1,000 moshavim where volunteers can live and work as a member of an Israeli family, mainly in the Jordan valley, the Arava and the western Negev. Most of the work is on the land, particularly in flower growing, market gardening, specialist fruit farming, chicken rearing or dairy farming. Moshav placements differ from kibbutz placements in that there is greater emphasis placed on the individual volunteer, who is placed within a family and paid a small allowance; moshav volunteers may have travel to Israel alone, rather than as part of a group.

Kibbutzim or moshavim volunteers should be aged 18-32, in good physical and mental health, and will need references, a medical certificate and a special entry visa. Prospective volunteers should bear in mind that the work is often physically arduous, that conditions can be uncomfortable, and the hours long. The effect of living in relatively close confinement with a group of fellow volunteers is also something that should not be underestimated. There are fewer placements now than previously and applicants should understand that a serious attitude to work is required, as well as a genuine desire to become involved in the life of the community. Placements can last from 8 weeks upwards.

Agriculture/horticulture Trainee placements abroad are available for young people considering an agricultural/horticultural career, and applications can be made through the international farm exchange organisations listed in this section. Such placements are likely to involve fairly strenuous work, so applicants should be physically fit, with a strong practical streak. A valid driving licence is essential, and general maintenance skills come in very useful. The following is just one of the enthusiastic comments that trainees placed on farms abroad have made about their experiences:

I enjoyed becoming part of another family, learning and experiencing their way of life in the home and on the farm. I was able to meet local Americans of my own age and be part of their social life. It was a good way to get hands-on experience in American agriculture, and it was great to meet so many people from different countries and all having one common interest - farming. There have been no arguments as such between groups and everybody got along well. I must say the social life of a trainee is the best I and many others have ever had. It is a terrific programme - I have benefited enormously.

There are also opportunities available in Britain for people, preferably with basic skills or qualifications in horticulture, to work on community garden projects involving horticultural therapy. Projects are based at hospitals, day centres, residential homes or urban farms and can range from small gardens to large commercial nurseries, reclaiming derelict land or creating new amenities. Volunteers may work alongside elderly or disadvantaged people, or people with physical handicaps, visual or hearing impairments, mental or psychiatric problems. They help to prepare and cultivate sites and train people in basic horticultural tasks, playing a key role in encouraging a team spirit amongst the project's gardeners. The rewards, in both shared experience and therapeutic benefit, can be many.

AFS/Intercultural Education Programmes

Artemis Cloudforest Preserve

Australian Trust for Conservation Volunteers

Casa Rio Blanco Rainforest Reserve

Coral Cay Conservation Ltd

Frontier (The Society for Environmental Exploration)

GAP Activity Projects (GAP) Ltd

Genesis II Talamanca Cloudforest

International Agricultural Exchange Association

International Farm Experience Programme

Involvement Volunteers

IPP Environmental Projects

Kibbutz Representatives

L'Ouvre Tête

Project 67

Student Conservation Association Inc

Willing Workers On Organic Farms (WWOOF)

AFS / INTERCULTURAL
EDUCATION PROGRAMMES

The National Director, AFS/IEP, Arden House, Wellington Street, Bingley, West Yorkshire BD16 2NB

✆ Bingley (01274) 560677   📠 (01274) 567675

A wide range of countries in Latin America, Africa and Asia

AFS is an international, voluntary non-profitmaking organisation represented in 55 countries. It has operated in the UK since 1947 and is a registered charity. Provides intercultural learning opportunities to help people develop the knowledge, skills and understanding needed to create a more just and peaceful world. The only organisation of its kind to receive a citation from the United Nations in recognition of its work for world youth.

Opportunities to spend 6 months abroad living with a volunteer host family whilst working alongside local people on community social projects dealing with environmental issues and conservation, gaining another language and an insider's appreciation of the culture

Ages 18-29. Applicants should be flexible, adaptable and interested in other cultures and ways of life. It is not a requirement to speak the language of the intended country before departure.

6 months departing in January/February or July

Cost £2,750. All participants are given advice and support on doing their own fundraising. The fee covers travel to and from the host country, expenses involving the project, medical insurance, orientation courses and ongoing support from volunteers and staff in the host country and in the UK.

Orientation courses held before departure to help participants prepare for the experience, and at regular intervals during the 6 months. Intensive language training provided during the first month.

Applications accepted up to 18 months in advance of departure. Prefer to receive applications at least 6 months before departure, but can occasionally accept late applicants.

ARTEMIS CLOUDFOREST PRESERVE

Rafael & Hilda Pina, Co-owners, Artemis Cloudforest Preserve, Apdo 937, 2050 San Pedro, Montes de Oca, Costa Rica

© (00 506) 253 72 43

Costa Rica

A recently-established, private cloudforest preserve in the Talamanca mountains of Costa Rica. Situated at an elevation of approx 2,700 metres, the preserve comprises 25 hectares of primary forest and is home to a great diversity of trees, flowers, birds and insects. The owners wish to protect the forest and open it up to visitors.

Volunteers are required to build a trail system, help with the reforestation of cleared areas and share in maintenance, fencing and gardening tasks

Ages 18+. No experience necessary, but relevant skills welcome. Knowledge of English or Spanish essential.

1+ months, all year

6 hour day, 5 day week, or 10 days followed by 4 days off. Each volunteer contributes at least US$150 per week to cover food, accommodation and laundry. Volunteers must take their own sleeping bag, wellingtons or hiking boots, warm clothing and waterproofs, and must organise and pay for their own travel and insurance.

Write for further information. Completed application forms together with US$150 returnable deposit should reach Artemis at least 1 month in advance (post is very slow).

AUSTRALIAN TRUST FOR CONSERVATION VOLUNTEERS

Australian Trust For Conservation Volunteers (ATCV), Box 423, Ballarat, Victoria 3353, Australia

℗ (00 61 053) 331 483   ☐ (00 61 053) 332 290
☐ atcv@netconnect.com.au   ☀ http://www.peg.apc.org/~atcv/atcv.html

Throughout Australia

Set up in 1982, the Trust is a non-profit, non-political, community-based organisation which undertakes practical conservation projects involving volunteers in the management and care of the environment

Echidna package scheme enables overseas volunteers to work on ATCV projects. ATCV undertake approx 1,200 projects each year, including tree planting, constructing walking tracks and vermin-proof fences, seed collection and flora and fauna surveys. Volunteers work in teams under the guidance of an ATCV team leader, and must be prepared to undertake domestic duties such as cooking, washing and cleaning.

Ages 17+. Applicants should be fit and willing to work in a team to the best of their ability. Sound knowledge of English necessary. Anti-tetanus immunisation essential. Applicants must hold a valid visitor's visa.

6+ weeks. 08.00-16.00, Monday-Friday. Part of each weekend may be spent travelling to the next project. Package cost from AU$840 includes food, accommodation, travel to and from projects and ATCV membership. Accommodation varies according to the nature of the project and the location. Advice on medical and travel insurance provided.

Contact the Trust for detailed information on costs, terms and conditions

Apply at least 3 months in advance

CASA RIO BLANCO RAINFOREST RESERVE

Thea Gaudette, President, Casa Rio Blanco Rainforest Reserve, Apdo 241-7210, Guapiles, Pococi, Costa Rica

Guapiles, Costa Rica

Run by a husband and wife team, the reserve has been open to the public for four years, and offers lodging, education and guided hikes

Opportunities available for volunteers to work on a variety of projects: recycling, teaching in local schools, developing educational materials, trail work and organic gardening. Approx 4 positions offered annually.

Ages 19+. Applicants should be flexible, enthusiastic and able to follow instructions independently. As the reserve is very isolated, there are very few means of entertainment available. No skills or experience necessary except for teaching posts, which require a knowledge of Spanish. All nationalities welcome.

4 week placements available throughout the year. 30 hour, 5 day week. Accommodation provided with host family, cost £150 per month. No travel or insurance costs provided.

Apply 4 months in advance; send 5 International Reply Coupons with application

CORAL CAY CONSERVATION

Volunteer Recruitment, Coral Cay Conservation (CCC) Ltd,
154 Clapham Park Road, London SW4 7DE

℅ 0171-498 6248   📠 0171-498 8447
📧 ccc@coralcay.demon.co.uk   🌐 http://www.coralcay.com.org

Belize, Indonesia, Philippines, Maldives, Papua New Guinea, Red Sea

A non-profit organisation established in 1986, providing resources to
assist with the conservation and sustainable use of coastal forests and
coral reefs through research, education and training. Coral reefs and
coastal forests are under serious threat; within 40 years over half of the
world's reefs will have vanished if action is not taken now to help
protect them. CCC volunteers have helped create eight new marine
reserves and wildlife sanctuaries, including four World Heritage Sites.

Volunteers are invited to join one of a series of expeditions to help
survey tropical forests and coral reefs. Based on remote islands, up to
30 international volunteers work together with local counterparts as an
integrated team to meet the challenges of living and working amongst
some of the most unexplored environments on Earth.

Ages 16+. No previous scientific or expedition experience required but
applicants should be open minded and willing to take an active role in all
aspects of expedition life. All training, including scuba diving where
necessary, provided at the expedition base and includes tropical marine/
terrestrial ecology and coastal zone management, survey methods,
equipment operation and maintenance, and a variety of other skills.

2-12 weeks

Approx 60 hour week. Monday-Friday the team concentrate on survey
work. Weekends are reserved for recreational diving/exploration,
advanced training courses and equipment maintenance. One weekend
in every four volunteers are offered opportunities to visit local villages
and explore mainland attractions such as rainforests, mountains and the
relics of ancient civilisations. Costs from £750, 2 weeks, to £3,000, 12
weeks, and include full board, lodging, training and equipment. Flights
cost approx £550, insurance approx £40.

Volunteers are trained to work effectively and safely as a self-sufficient
team in remote tropical environments

Expeditions depart monthly throughout the year

FRONTIER (THE SOCIETY FOR ENVIRONMENTAL EXPLORATION)

Frontier (The Society for Environmental Exploration), 77 Leonard Street, London EC2A 4QS

© 0171-613 2422   ▭ 0171-613 2992
✉enquiries@frontier.mailbox.co.uk
🕭 http://www.mailbox.co.uk/frontier

Mozambique, Tanzania, Uganda and Vietnam

Expeditionary arm of the Society for Environmental Exploration, established in 1989 in the belief that volunteers can assist with practical solutions to some of the world's environmental problems. Expeditions carry out priority research and conservation projects identified by governments, scientists and research institutions of collaborating countries, and provide support for international research workers.

Volunteers work with fellow recruits under the direction of research scientists in the setting up of specific projects. In general the work is basic scientific research. Examples of projects include monitoring tidal currents in a mangrove delta; setting up underwater tourist diving trails on a coral reef; or studying chimpanzees in a forest reserve. Recruits approx 200 volunteers each year.

Ages 17+. Expeditions are often in remote, inaccessible and inhospitable environments, so volunteers must be capable of operating efficiently under difficult circumstances. A high value is placed on enthusiasm, tolerance, willingness to learn and an interest in environmental and development issues. Scientific qualifications and experience not essential.

3 months, beginning January, April, July and October. Each expedition lasts 10 weeks, but air tickets are valid for longer, allowing volunteers to travel independently after work has finished.

Relies largely on contributions from volunteers to run the expedition; these amount to approx £2,850 for 3 months including return flight, medical insurance, vehicles, equipment, food and fuel. Advice given on raising funds. Living conditions are basic, with accommodation under canvas and simple food.

Recruitment all year

GAP ACTIVITY PROJECTS (GAP) LIMITED

The Registrar, GAP Activity Projects Ltd, GAP House, 44 Queen's Road, Reading, Berkshire RG1 4BB

℡ (0118) 959 4914   📠 (0118) 957 6634

Australia, Ecuador, Falkland Islands, Israel, Jordan, Mexico, Paraguay, Zambia

A charity founded in 1972 to give those with a year between leaving school and going on to further/higher education or vocational training the opportunity to undertake voluntary work in another country

Arranges placements for practical conservation/land management work in Australia, Ecuador, Jordan and Paraguay. Farm placements available in Australia, Falkland Islands, Mexico and Zambia, and on kibbutzim in Israel.

Ages 18-19. UK nationals only. Males only for farm placements in Australia and Paraguay. Applicants should be reliable, possess initiative and intelligence, and be prepared to work hard. For projects in Latin America applicants must speak Spanish.

6-9 months

Board and accommodation provided, and usually a small amount of pocket money. Volunteers must find their own travel and insurance costs, plus the placement fee of £440.

Candidates attend a briefing session before departure

Apply from September of last year at school or college; early application advisable. Interviews held from October.

GENESIS II TALAMANCA CLOUDFOREST

Steve & Paula Friedman, Co-owners, Genesis II Talamanca Cloudforest, Apdo 655, 7050 Cartago, Costa Rica

Costa Rica

A privately-owned cloudforest situated at a height of 2,300 metres in the Talamanca mountains of central Costa Rica, Genesis II was established in 1983 as a preserve for academic research and recreational activities such as birdwatching. Within its 15.5 hectares can be found many species of birds, ferns, orchids and fungi, as well as the towering white oak.

Volunteers are required to help build and maintain trails through and around the forest, and with other projects as the need arises

Ages 21+. Relevant experience preferred, but some training can be given. Some knowledge of Spanish helpful. Applicants must be very fit and strongly motivated.

4+ weeks, all year

Volunteers work for two 10 day periods, 6 hours a day, with 4 days off at the end of each period. Contribution of at least US$150 per week covers dormitory-style accommodation, all meals and laundry facilities. Volunteers must arrange and pay for their own travel and insurance. Non-refundable loss/breakage fee of US$25 payable on arrival.

Recruitment all year. Competition for places is strong and it is advisable to apply well in advance.

INTERNATIONAL AGRICULTURAL EXCHANGE ASSOCIATION

The Coordinator, International Agricultural Exchange Association, YFC Centre, National Agricultural Centre, Stoneleigh Park, Kenilworth, Warwickshire CV8 2LG

℗ Coventry (01203) 696578

Australia, Canada, Japan, New Zealand, United States. Two-country placements available; stopovers in Singapore, Thailand and Pacific can be arranged en route.

Operates opportunities for young people involved with agriculture, horticulture or home management to acquire practical work experience in the rural sector and to strengthen and improve their knowledge and understanding of the way of life in other countries

Participants are given the opportunity to study practical methods on approved training farms, and work as trainees, gaining further experience in their chosen field

Ages 18-30. UK or Irish passport-holders only. Applicants should have a real desire for a farming and cultural experience abroad. They must be single, have good practical experience in the category of work they have chosen and hold a valid driver's licence.

6-14 months, depending on placement

Cost from £1,695, depending on country chosen. £200 deposit payable. Costs cover airfare, work permit, administration fee, insurance, supervision, placement, information and orientation. Trainees live as members of host family and receive £60-£70 per week. Supervisors visit trainees and host families at least once during programme. All programmes include at least 3 weeks unpaid holiday.

All trainees attend an information meeting prior to departure, where they meet past trainees and support staff. Compulsory orientation seminars are conducted in the host country.

Apply at least 4 months in advance

INTERNATIONAL FARM EXPERIENCE PROGRAMME

The Organiser, International Farm Experience Programme, YFC Centre, National Agricultural Centre, Stoneleigh Park, Kenilworth, Warwickshire CV8 2LG

℡ Coventry (01203) 696544   (01203) 696559 ifep@nfyfc.org.uk

Austria, Belgium, Bulgaria, Denmark, Finland, France, Germany, Greece, Hungary, Italy, Latvia, Netherlands, Poland, Portugal, Spain, Sweden; Canada, United States; Australia, New Zealand; Brazil; South Africa; China

Provides assistance to young farmers and horticulturalists by finding them places on farms/nurseries abroad. This enables them to broaden their knowledge of the industry and agricultural methods, learn new skills and techniques, make new friends and expand their personal horizons.

Opportunities for practical agricultural, horticultural or equestrian work on a variety of farms and nurseries. Participants usually live and work with a farmer's family, and work is matched as far as possible with participants' requirements. Au pair positions also available for young women in some countries.

Ages 17-30. Applicants must have some relevant experience and intend to make a career in agriculture/horticulture. Valid driving licence essential.

Usually 3-6 months for Europe; 6-12 months preferred for Australia and the United States

Participants generally work a 40-50 hour week, with one free day. They receive a basic wage plus board, lodging and holiday, and pay their own fares and insurance. Registration fee £125/£175. Placement, travel and visas arranged.

Some of the programmes in the United States include a university course, where participants can study an aspect of the industry in detail

Apply at least 2 months in advance

INVOLVEMENT VOLUNTEERS

The Director, Involvement Volunteers, PO Box 218, Port Melbourne, Victoria 3207, Australia

℗ Melbourne (00 61 3) 9646 9392   ▭ (00 61 3) 9646 5504
▢ ivimel@iaccess.com.au

Australia, Fiji, Germany, Ghana, Greece, Kenya, Lebanon, Malaysia (Sabah), New Zealand, South Africa, Thailand, United States (California)

Through networked international volunteering, aims to assist people travelling overseas to participate as volunteers to gain experience while assisting community-based, not-for-profit organisations around the world

Individual or team placements include conservation projects in urban or rural areas: on farms planting trees; marine archaeology; zoology research; bird observatory operations; zoo species breeding operations; researching, restoring or maintaining historic sites or gardens; developing National Parks, steam railways or passive recreation areas; assisting native villages or agricultural education programmes related to sustainable agricultural development.

Ages 17+. Relevant experience welcome but only necessary for certain projects. Understanding of spoken English essential.

2+ weeks, but no limit to the number of placements

Cost AU$460. Provides advice on placements, itinerary planning and arrangements. Board and accommodation varies according to placement, and may be provided free of charge. Volunteers arrange their own visitor visa, international travel and insurance. In Australia, meeting on arrival, initial accommodation, introductions to banking and a communications base provided. Discounted internal travel, eco introductory trip and scuba diving instruction also available.

Apply at least 3 months in advance, but more planning time is recommended if possible

IPP ENVIRONMENTAL PROJECTS

Ed Bentham, Projects Coordinator, Proyecto Ambiental Tenerife, IPP Environmental Projects, 54 Monmouth Street, Covent Garden, London WC2H 9DG

℡ 0171-240 6604   ℻ 0171-240 5795

The Canary Islands, Cuba, Turkey and Brazil

A rural development charity established in 1992, organising conservation and environmental projects. Volunteers work on rural development projects alongside local people, helping to develop small businesses. Also conducts projects in the conservation of whales and dolphins.

Work placements can be made for volunteers to work on the rural development and whale and dolphin conservation projects. Approx 30 positions offered annually.

Ages 18+. No skills or experience required. All nationalities welcome.

Placements arranged May-October for individuals; groups can go anytime. 1-5 weeks. 40 hour week, 2-3 days per week. Accommodation provided in a kibbutz. No travel or insurance provided. Cost £65 per week covers half board accommodation, language training and generally funds the project.

KIBBUTZ REPRESENTATIVES

Kibbutz Representatives, 1a Accommodation Road, London NW11 8ED

© 0181-458 9235   ▭ 0181-455 7930   ▯ enquiries@kibbutz.org.uk

Israel

The official representatives in Britain of all kibbutzim, established in 1967, with the aim of raising awareness and introducing youth to kibbutz life. The kibbutz is a communal society in which all the means of production are owned by the community as a whole. Private property is limited to personal possessions. It is a classless, egalitarian society whose members do not receive wages or salaries, but all their needs are supplied regardless of the kind of work they do.

Operates a working visitor scheme throughout the year whereby volunteers spend 8-12 weeks on a kibbutz, working alongside members of the kibbutz, either in agriculture, services (ie dining room, laundry, clothes store, kitchen) or industry. There will be many opportunities to take part in the everyday life of the community.

Ages 18-32. Applicants must supply a medical certificate and two character references. No formal skills, qualifications or experience necessary.

8-12 weeks

Volunteers work a 6-8 hour day, 6 day week and receive full board, lodging and an allowance. Volunteers pay their own travel costs.

All applicants are expected to attend an orientation interview

Apply at least 2-4 months in advance. Limited places during July and August; apply before Easter.

L'OUVRE TÊTE

L'Ouvre Tête, Les Maurels, 04300 Pierrerue, France

✆/☎ (00 33 4) 92751065

Provence, France

Established in 1990, L'Ouvre Tête is involved in the restoration of a 16th century farmhouse in the heart of Provence. The home is used by a small group of disadvantaged children and disabled people, as well as housing the homeless and former drug addicts.

Volunteers required for classical restoration work or to help with the maintenance of the farmhouse and to entertain the group. Four positions offered annually.

Ages 24+. Basic French essential. No qualifications required, but applicants must be team workers, with good communication skills and be able to adapt to uneasy circumstances. Previous experience of working on kibbutzim/moshavim an advantage. EU, Australian and New Zealand nationals only.

Minimum 2 months; mid September-mid May. Only those who work during the winter can continue through the summer.

32 hours per week. The first two weeks are probationary, then volunteers receive 75FF per week. Accommodation provided in comfortable dormitories or rooms, with hot showers available. Travel costs and insurance not provided.

Apply one month in advance

PROJECT 67

Project 67, 10 Hatton Garden, London EC1N 8AH

℗ 0171-831 7626

Israel

Has organised working holidays on kibbutzim and moshavim in Israel for the past 29 years

A kibbutz is a communal society in which the means of production are owned by the community as a whole. Volunteers work alongside permanent residents and other volunteers; work can include farmwork, market gardening and light industry. A moshav is a collective of individual smallholders where each family develops its own land whilst sharing capital costs. Volunteers live and work as part of a family; work can include flower, vegetable or fruit growing, or chicken and dairy farming.

Ages 18-32 (kibbutzim); 21-35 (moshavim). Applicants must be physically and mentally fit. No formal skills, qualifications or experience necessary.

8 weeks-12 months

Cost from £269 (kibbutzim) or from £239 (moshavim) covers return flight, registration and support from Tel Aviv office. Normal working hours are 8 hours a day, 6 days a week. Additional hours may be worked at harvest time. Early morning start to avoid the heat of the day. Full board, lodging and an allowance provided.

Briefing held in London to advise on conditions and provide the opportunity to meet fellow volunteers. No briefing necessary for moshavim.

Apply as early as possible, as places are limited. Last-minute applications sometimes accepted.

STUDENT CONSERVATION ASSOCIATION INC

Resource Assistant Program, Student Conservation Association Inc, PO Box 550, River Road, Charlestown, New Hampshire 03603-0550, United States

✆ (00 1 603) 543 1700   🖷 (00 1 603) 543 1828

Throughout the United States, including Hawaii and Alaska

Founded in 1957, the Student Conservation Association is a national non-profitmaking educational organisation committed to conservation, resource management and volunteer service

The SCA works with state, federal and private organisations to place volunteers in over 250 national parks, forests, wildlife refuges and similar areas each year. Duties vary with location, but may include trail patrol, wildlife management, visitor contact, natural science interpretation, forestry, archaeological surveys or recreation management.

Ages 18+. Applicants should have an interest in conservation or resource management. Some positions may require experience in public speaking, hiking or other outdoor activities, or in a particular academic field.

12+ weeks

Volunteers receive $50-$100 per week to cover food expenses, and a uniform allowance if required. Accommodation is provided in an apartment, trailer or ranger station. SCA offer information and assistance with visas, and partial travel reimbursement within the US. Application fee $20 must accompany completed application form.

Training, guidance and supervision provided by professional staff

SCA supply application forms and a current listing of positions available. Write 2-3 months in advance for application materials.

WILLING WORKERS ON ORGANIC FARMS (WWOOF)

Willing Workers On Organic Farms (WWOOF), 19 Bradford Road, Lewes, Sussex BN7 1RB

Working weekends organised on organic farms, smallholdings and gardens throughout Britain

A non-profitmaking membership organisation which aims to help organic farmers and smallholders whose work is often labour-intensive as it does not rely on the use of artificial fertilisers or pesticides

Unskilled voluntary workers can gain first-hand experience of organic farming and gardening, and get a chance to spend an energetic weekend in the country. The work can include hedging, haymaking, fruit, vegetable and dairy work, beekeeping, sheep shearing, rearing kids and ducklings, building renovation, peat cutting, hooking and scything, seaweed spraying and compost making.

Ages 16+. No experience necessary. **D**

Placements available all year round

8 hour day. Positions are unpaid, but full board and accommodation provided in farmhouse or outbuildings. Volunteers should take a sleeping bag. Insurance and anti-tetanus vaccination recommended.

Membership fee £10. Members receive a bi-monthly newsletter which details places needing help on specific weekends and job opportunities in the organic movement. After completing 2 scheduled weekends members may apply for the complete list of places, including some overseas, so independent arrangements for longer periods can be made.

Partner organisations operating in Australia (WWOOF W Tree, Buchan, Victoria 3885); Canada (WWOOF RR2, Carlson Road, S18 C9, Nelson, British Columbia VIL 5P5); Germany (WWOOF Stettiner Straße 3, 35415 Pohlheim); Ghana (WWOOF/FIOH, PO Box 154, Trade Fair Site, La - Accra); Ireland (WWOOF, Harpoonstown, Drinagh, Co Wexford); New Zealand (WWOOF, c/o Andrew and Jane Strange, PO Box 1172, Nelson); and Switzerland (WWOOF Thomas Schwager, Postfach 615, 9001 St Gallen).

A period of voluntary service can be enriching and rewarding, involving volunteers in improving the quality of life and community environment. Opportunities to take on a demanding challenge exist in developed and developing countries, and all the essential advice and information needed to arrange a successful, constructive placement is in the Central Bureau's guide **VOLUNTEER WORK**, the authoritative guide that has found worthwhile placements for thousands of volunteers.

VOLUNTEER WORK has comprehensive details on volunteer-sending agencies recruiting and placing volunteers for medium and long-term service, from a few months up to several years, in Britain and 120 countries worldwide. Advice is given on selecting an agency and a personal checklist is provided to evaluate potential. Each agency is profiled, giving information on its origins, orientation and philosophy, countries of operation, projects arranged, personal qualities and skills required, length and terms of service, briefing and relevant literature. Practical information and advice includes everything from invaluable insights from development workers and

A quarter of the world's population still lives in poverty; almost a fifth is non-literate; the opening up of Eastern Europe and the need to rebuild economies has revealed another skills shortage which volunteers can help fill. Even in so-called developed countries working to overcome the problems caused by poverty, bad housing and illiteracy, presents a worthwhile challenge. **VOLUNTEER WORK** offers invaluable information and advice to those considering volunteering.

returned volunteers, through preparation and training, advisory bodies, to health, travel and insurance.

Typical projects include assisting in the provision of vocational training in the South Pacific islands; helping run women's literacy classes in rural India; organising nutrition programmes with the Guruani Indians of Bolivia; working with the homeless poor at a creative non-violence community in the US; helping with the resettlement and education of refugees in Britain; and protecting the rights of the disadvantaged to education and representation in France.

VOLUNTEER WORK has opportunities for those aged 16+; from 3 weeks to 3 years; from agricultural projects to town planning schemes; from placements for business advisers to midwives; from Antigua to Western Samoa. For short-term opportunities, the Central Bureau guide **WORKING HOLIDAYS** provides information on thousands of placements lasting from a long weekend to 3 months. For further information on the Bureau's publications and programmes contact the Information Desk on © 0171-389 4004.

VOLUNTEER WORK is published biannually.   Sixth edition 1995   ISBN 1 898601 04 6   £8.99

TEACHING/
INSTRUCTING

English today is spoken by some 320 million native speakers, and by an estimated 450 million as a second language. This makes it the most widely spoken language in the world after Mandarin Chinese. English is now the language of international business and commerce, air traffic, popular music, science and technology. As a consequence there are millions of non-native speakers around the world eager to learn, practise and perfect it, and Teaching English as a Foreign Language (TEFL) provides an interesting opportunity to undertake a challenging period of work in either Britain or abroad.

However, teaching a language is not just a question of being able to speak it properly. This is particularly the case when the language in question is your mother tongue; the way you speak it may be based more upon instinct and intuition than upon any knowledge of the rules of grammar. A good TEFL course will give you a basic grounding in grammar, teaching materials and classroom techniques, with the chance of some teaching practice, and for many placements some kind of qualification in TEFL is a requirement.

Many language schools in Britain offer introductory TEFL training and their own qualifications. However, the initial qualifications that are the most widely recognised on an international level are the Cambridge/RSA Certificate in English Language Teaching to Adults (CELTA) and the Trinity College of London Certificate in the Teaching of English to Speakers of Other Languages (TESOL).

Candidates should generally be aged 20+ and have a standard of education which would allow entry to higher education in their country. Courses leading to these certificates last from 4 weeks and are very intensive; participants should ensure they have no other commitments for the duration of the course. Part-time courses are also available. Cambridge have also introduced a pilot Certificate in English Language Teaching to Young Learners in Language Schools (CELTYL) which is available at selected centres worldwide. Course fees vary from centre to centre and individual centres will give you full details.

Further details about these certificates, and also the diploma courses for experienced teachers, can be obtained by writing to the CILTS Unit, University of Cambridge Local Examinations Syndicate, Syndicate Buildings, 1 Hills Road, Cambridge CB1 2EU ✆ (01223) 553789 ⌨ (01223) 553086 or Trinity College London, 16 Park Crescent, London WIN 4AH ✆ 0171-323 2328.

As well as the opportunities covered in this section, many TEFL posts are advertised in the national press, such as the Educational Appointments section of the *Guardian* (every Tuesday) or the specialist education press such as the *Times Educational Supplement* (every Friday) or the *EFL Gazette* (monthly). Applicants should find out as much as possible about the school and make sure they have a proper contract and work permit (where necessary) before accepting a position. Schools that are approved or recognised by a national inspecting body are likely to operate to good standards. As a rule, you should not be expected to teach much more than 25 hours per week, with a maximum of 20 students per class, but on top of this you will need to prepare classes and may also be required for supervisory duties.

The Central Bureau's annual guide **WORKING HOLIDAYS** has details of short-term TEFL opportunities including opportunities to teach overseas teenagers in summer schools in Britain. For those with some teaching or instructing skills, qualifications or relevant experience, **WORKING HOLIDAYS** also offers a variety of other opportunities, including instructing on activity holidays or sports coaching during the summer holidays. If you are more seriously interested in a career in TEFL or long-term placements abroad, the Central Bureau's guide **TEACH ABROAD** offers vital information and advice.
Further details of all Central Bureau publications available on © 0171-389 4880 or 🖱 http://www.britcoun.org/cbeve/.

Opportunities for school leavers to undertake TEFL teaching are limited, and usually consist of acting as helpers to English language teachers or teaching on a voluntary basis in the Third World. Work is also available in Britain, and occasionally abroad, for post-A level students to act as student teachers or assistant matrons in independent schools. As well as teaching, work usually involves domestic and supervisory duties. Those interested may either approach schools direct or apply through the relevant organisations listed in this section.

Graduates have a wider range of opportunities open to them, especially if they have previously gained some informal experience of teaching or of working with children. Opportunities are not simply limited to English teaching, but also cover subjects such as mathematics, sciences, languages or computer studies for those with a degree in a relevant subject.

Keran, Tania, Fiona and David worked as junior language assistants during their year between. Under this scheme, run by the Central Bureau for Educational Visits & Exchanges, participants work under the supervision of the English teaching staff, improving the pupils' command of spoken English and introducing them to British life, customs and institutions. Keran relished the challenge of teaching in a French state secondary school:

I have undoubtedly experienced the best six months of my life, learning how to live independently. My French is now fluent and I have integrated very well into the French way of life. Teaching a class of thirty rowdy children who are almost the same age as you is the greatest challenge, but a very enjoyable and satisfying one. I learnt exactly what it was like to be standing in front of the blackboard. This six months helped me decide that I want to be a teacher. This is a very productive and pleasurable way of spending six months before going into higher education.

Tania also worked in France, and felt that the time as an assistant gave her increased confidence and forced her to use her creative imagination:

I have learned a lot about how to deal with children and about how to teach. I have learned a lot about life in France, my French has improved no end and I have gained a lot of confidence by coming to a foreign country and discovering such a lot, meeting so many people and having such a good time. I have exercised my imagination as I haven't done since I was a child, thinking up entertaining and useful lessons. I also have enjoyed having time to relax - time I never gave myself at home.

Fiona worked in a boarding school near Düsseldorf in Germany. She outlines the benefits:

The work's really rewarding and enjoyable but also quite hard. I've made a lot of new friends and greatly improved my German. I got a great sense of achievement when my pupils improved and, I hope, I've gained the ability to teach kids and make them understand.

David also worked in Germany, helping pupils with their homework and taking part in English lessons:

My command of German has improved so that I am now capable in any situation. I have become more mature and independent, making my own decisions and setting my own goals. I have also had time to reflect on my priorities and attitudes, leaving me better prepared for the future.

If you are going to teach as part of your year out you should be aware that your students are likely to be young teenagers, and you will need patience and energy if you are to make a success of the task in hand. Your creative resources may be tested to the limit in order to put over imaginatively the language concepts you are attempting to teach. Having just completed years of continuous education yourself you will need to have the ability and understanding to motivate others who may be only reluctantly committed to additional learning. That apart, the rewards to be gained from a period of teaching are not to be underestimated. The work may be challenging and exhausting but it can also be deeply satisfying, using your creative skills to pass on knowledge and to awaken interest in even the most seemingly uninterested and unmotivated student.

Africa Venture

AFS/Intercultural Education Programmes

The Daneford Trust

Escuelas de Idiomas Berlitz de España

French Encounters

Gabbitas Educational Consultants Ltd

GAP Activity Projects (GAP) Ltd

Gap Challenge

i to i International Projects Ltd

Insight Nepal

Involvement Volunteers

Japan Exchange & Teaching (JET) Programme

Junior Assistant Programme with France

Junior Assistant Programme with Germany

Language Assistants

Marlborough Brandt Group

Outdoor Adventure

The Project Trust

Q E D

SOCRATES - Lingua Action C

Assistantships

S P W

Syndicat Mixte Montaigu Rocheservière

Teach in China

UNIPAL (Universities' Educational Trust

for Palestinians)

WorldTeach

AFRICA VENTURE

The Director, Africa Venture Limited, 10 Market Place, Devizes, Wiltshire SN10 1HT

✆ Devizes (01380) 729009   ☐ (01380) 720060
✉ aventure@aol.com   🌐 http://members.aol.com/aventure

Kenya, Malawi, Uganda, Zimbabwe

Aimed at hardworking school leavers wishing to spend time in Africa, combining constructive and rewarding work experience with companionship and adventure

Participants are placed in pairs as assistant teachers in selected African secondary schools for one term. Depending on their skills and attributes, and the requirements of the schools, they assist in a variety of subjects ranging from English, the sciences, music and vocational activities to clubs and sports. Schools are chosen with location, work opportunities, accommodation and security in mind, and placements do not deprive local teachers from working. There are also a few opportunities for attachments to community-related projects. Following the placement, participants have 2 weeks for independent travel and the complete programme is rounded off with a group safari to places of interest such as Lake Turkana or the Zambesi.

Ages 17½+ (on leaving school). At the time of applying applicants should be studying A levels (or equivalent) and intending to go on to further education. They must be highly motivated, in good health, and interested in working with young people of other cultures.

Four months, departing late August, early January or late April

Cost approx £1,950 covers comprehensive health and personal effects insurance, orientation and in-country back up, living allowance commensurate with local wages, self-catering accommodation in school grounds, all-inclusive safari, and a contribution towards educating an African child. It does not cover airfare to Nairobi or Harare, or spending money, which are the responsibility of the participant. Advice given on raising sponsorship.

Applicants attend an interview where their suitability is assessed. Those selected attend an orientation course on arrival and have the support of an in-country director throughout their stay.

Apply as early as possible

AFS / INTERCULTURAL EDUCATION PROGRAMMES

The National Director, AFS/IEP, Arden House, Wellington Street, Bingley, West Yorkshire BD16 2NB

℗ Bingley (01274) 560677   ▭ (01274) 567675

A wide range of countries in Latin America, Africa and Asia

AFS is an international, voluntary non-profitmaking organisation represented in 55 countries. It has operated in the UK since 1947 and is a registered charity. Provides intercultural learning opportunities to help people develop the knowledge, skills and understanding needed to create a more just and peaceful world. The only organisation of its kind to receive a citation from the United Nations in recognition of its work for world youth.

Opportunities to spend 6 months abroad living with a volunteer host family whilst working alongside local people on community social projects dealing with education issues, gaining another language and an insider's appreciation of the culture

Ages 18-29. Applicants should be flexible, adaptable and interested in other cultures and ways of life. It is not a requirement to speak the language of the intended country before departure.

6 months departing in January/February or July

Cost £2,750. All participants are given advice and support on doing their own fundraising. The fee covers travel to and from the host country, expenses involving the project, medical insurance, orientation courses and ongoing support from volunteers and staff in the host country and in the UK.

Orientation courses held before departure to help participants prepare for the experience, and at regular intervals during the 6 months. Intensive language training provided during the first month.

Applications accepted up to 18 months in advance of departure. Prefer to receive applications at least 6 months before departure, but can occasionally accept late applicants.

THE DANEFORD TRUST

The Daneford Trust, PO Box 11190, London E2 6LB

©/☐ 0171-729 1928

Bangladesh, Botswana, Jamaica, Namibia, St Lucia, St Vincent and Zimbabwe

The Trust exists to help promote educational and working exchanges between young people from inner city areas and their contemporaries in Africa, Asia and the Caribbean

Approx 25 placements a year for teaching, working with people with disabilities and general administration work. Participants are able to work within and adapt to differing cultures and values, and engage in a mutual learning experience with young people from other countries.

Ages 18-26. Volunteers must demonstrate a sense of individual commitment. No formal qualifications required; A levels or equivalent useful on some placements. In some cases, knowledge of Bengali required. UK nationals from London boroughs only. **B D PH** welcome.

Three, six or twelve month placements

Cost £1,500-£4,000 depending on length of placement. Basic accommodation and some expenses provided. Advice and help given on raising funds and sponsorship.

Seminars for participants at the beginning and end of placements

Recruitment all year

ESCUELAS DE IDIOMAS
BERLITZ DE ESPAÑA

Susan Taylor, Method Director, Escuelas de Idiomas Berlitz de España, Gran Via 80, 4°, 28013 Madrid, Spain

© Madrid (00 34 1) 542 3586   (00 34 1) 541 2765

Madrid, Barcelona, Bilbao, Sevilla, Valencia and Palma de Mallorca, Spain

One of a network of language centres providing tuition in English as a foreign language to various levels and in different disciplines

Opportunities for graduates of any discipline to teach English as a foreign/second language to adult professionals at beginner through to advanced levels at various language centres. Also possibility of teaching English for Special Purposes in commerce, finance, science and engineering. Work may involve frequent travel within and around the city of allocation.

Ages 21+. Applicants should be mature, responsible and flexible regarding timetable, and have an outgoing personality. TEFL training/ experience not necessary; full in-house training provided.

Placements last 9 months. Irregular timetable hours, 08.00-21.30, including Saturday mornings. Details of salary on application.

Applicants should send cv and recent photograph. Interviews held in Spain in early September.

FRENCH ENCOUNTERS

Soula Callow & Patsy Musto, Directors, French Encounters,
63 Fordhouse Road, Bromsgrove, Worcestershire B60 2LU

℗ Bromsgrove (01527) 873645   ☎ (01527) 832794

Normandy, France

A small, independent enterprise running language field trips for
10-13 year old children, based in two *châteaux* in Normandy

Animateurs/trices are required to help run the courses. Work involves
preparing equipment and activities; assisting in general organisation;
accompanying coaches and giving commentaries on places to be visited;
supervising children on excursions and picnics; organising indoor and
outdoor activities and evening entertainment; encouraging children to
speak French and eat French food; and generally making their stay a
pleasant and rewarding one. Opportunities to develop organisational
and administrative skills and perfect spoken French. Participants also
have the chance to familiarise themselves with the cultural, historical,
economic and social aspects of an important area of France. Recruits
4-8 *animateurs/trices* annually.

Ages 18-22. UK nationals only. Applicants should have enthusiasm,
good organisational and social skills, the ability to work as part of a
team, self-discipline and a sense of humour. Experience of working with
10-13 year old children, plus A level or equivalent French with very
good oral skills essential.

3/4 months, beginning mid February

Animateurs/trices work approx 45 hours per week, with some periods of
intense activity and others of rest and relaxation, but as they are
resident in the *châteaux* they are on call 24 hours a day. Full board and
lodging provided, plus approx FF400 per week pocket money.
All transport costs and insurance provided.

Compulsory 2 week training course and debriefing provided before and
after period of work

Apply before 15 September. Interviews are usually held end September/
beginning October.

GABBITAS EDUCATIONAL CONSULTANTS

Gabbitas Educational Consultants Ltd, Carrington House, 126-130 Regent Street, London WIR 6EE

℗ 0171-734 0161 or 0171-439 2071
✉ 0171-437 1764   ✉ admin@gabbitas.co.uk

Throughout the UK

Offers expert advice and guidance to parents and students, covering the choice of independent schools, colleges and courses; planning and preparing for higher education; career guidance and options for a year out

Recruits teaching and non-teaching staff for independent schools and colleges

Ages 17/18+. No experience or qualifications necessary, but school leavers should have A levels or equivalent and be going on to university. A good school record and plenty of outside interests are desirable. Overseas applicants must have appropriate visa/work permit and be available for interview.

3-9 months

Terms and conditions of work vary according to placement. Full board accommodation usually provided within the school, in addition to salary.

Apply by June/July to begin the following academic year

GAP ACTIVITY PROJECTS (GAP) LIMITED

The Registrar, GAP Activity Projects Ltd, GAP House, 44 Queen's Road, Reading, Berkshire RG1 4BB

© (0118) 959 4914   ▭ (0118) 957 6634

Morocco, Namibia, South Africa; India, Nepal, Pakistan; Czech and Slovak Republics, Hungary, Poland, Russia, Romania; China (Hong Kong), Japan, Malaysia, Vietnam; Argentina, Chile, Ecuador, Mexico, Paraguay; Israel, Jordan; Canada, United States; Australia, New Zealand, Fiji and the South Pacific

A charity founded in 1972 to give those with a year between leaving school and going on to further/higher education or vocational training the opportunity to undertake voluntary work in another country

Attachments are available in schools and colleges, which may involve assisting in the teaching of English, or in English-speaking countries, acting as teachers' assistants and coaching in games, music or drama

Ages 18-19. UK nationals only. Applicants should be reliable, possess initiative and intelligence, and be prepared to work hard. Placements in Latin America require an ability to speak the relevant language.

Most placements are for 6-9 months

Board and accommodation provided, and usually a small amount of pocket money. Volunteers must find their own travel and insurance costs, plus the placement fee of £440. For many of the teaching placements applicants must attend a 1 or 2 week TEFL course, cost from £110 per week.

Candidates attend a briefing session before departure

Apply from September of last year at school or college; early application advisable. Interviews held from October.

GAP CHALLENGE

Gap Challenge, World Challenge Expeditions, Black Arrow House, Chandos Road, London NW10 6NF

℗ 0181-961 1122   ☎ 0181-961 1551
✉ welcome@world-challenge.co.uk

Belize, India, Malawi, Nepal, South Africa, Tanzania, Zanzibar

For ten years World Challenge has been providing overseas projects and adventure training opportunities for young people. The Gap Challenge programme provides year between students and graduates with professionally organised placements in the developing world.

In India there are opportunities to undertake voluntary work as an English teacher in institutions ranging from orphanages to public schools, in locations varying from the northern Indian Himalayas to Goa. Some of the work may be with disadvantaged children. In Nepal, placements range from teaching in a Tibetan refugee school to teaching in a village school. In Tanzania, placements are all based near Moshi, a small town on the flanks of Kilimanjaro, where there are opportunities to work as a teacher in a state secondary school.

Placements are open to those taking a year between school and university. A high degree of motivation and commitment is required for all posts.

3-6 months, paid and voluntary placements

Costs from £1,474, Nepal, includes return flight valid for 12 months

All applicants are required to attend a selection interview. There is also an obligatory 2 day training course before departure where participants receive briefings from qualified staff and former Gap Challenge students.

Departures in September and January. Applications are considered between 3-18 months in advance of intended departure date; early application recommended.

i TO i INTERNATIONAL PROJECTS LTD

i to i International Projects Ltd, Notre Dame Sixth Form College, St Marks Avenue, Leeds LS2 9BN

☎ 0113-245 3515   ▭ 0113-245 3350   ✉ 106144.174@compuserve.com
🔖 http://ourworld.compuserve.com/homepages/i-to-i

Courses take place throughout the UK; placements in Greece, Turkey, Sri Lanka, Russia and occasionally Poland

Offers a range of services to help young people work and travel abroad, including workshops, introductory TEFL courses and placements for EFL teachers and teaching assistants

Introductory TEFL weekend courses are suitable for year between students who wish to teach English abroad, enabling them to plan and prepare lessons. Successful participants receive a TEFL Certificate which is acceptable to a large number of private language schools throughout the world and in the UK.

Also offers placements for teaching assistants and TEFL teachers to help students practise and improve their conversational and written English.

Ages 17+. Teaching assistants and TEFL teachers should have the i to i Introductory TEFL certificate; TEFL teachers should be graduates. Applicants must be prepared to live and work abroad and be lively and enthusiastic. UK nationals only.

Teaching placements available throughout the year; 1-6 months for teaching assistants and 10 months, usually September-June, for TEFL teachers

25 hours per week. TEFL teachers receive a full salary. Teaching assistants are provided with full board and lodging with a host family, plus 50% teacher's salary for those working in Greece. Applicants must provide their own insurance. Help in arranging work permits and visas provided.

TEFL Introductory course costs £175, or £135 at concessionary rate

INSIGHT NEPAL

Insight Nepal, PO Box 6760, Kathmandu, Nepal

℡ Kathmandu (00 977 1) 418964   🖷 (00 977 1) 416144

Nepal

A recently-established organisation offering language training, cultural tours and homestays in Nepal

Very limited number of volunteer placements available in both urban and remote areas of the country. Work involves teaching English, science, mathematics and computer studies in schools ranging from primary through to technical school.

Ages 21+. Applicants must be educated to at least A level or equivalent, preferably with some teaching experience. Skills in games, sports or art an advantage. **B D**

3-4 months, beginning February, April or August

20-25 hour, 5-5½ day week. Half board accommodation provided. Cost US$600 plus visa fee depending on length of work period. Application fee US$20. No fares, wages or insurance paid.

One week orientation includes language instruction, cross-cultural training and homestay. Tours and excursions arranged (for a week).

Completed application forms must be submitted at least 3 months in advance

INVOLVEMENT VOLUNTEERS

The Director, Involvement Volunteers, PO Box 218, Port Melbourne, Victoria 3207, Australia

℡ Melbourne (00 61 3) 9646 9392   (00 61 3) 9646 5504
✉ ivimel@iaccess.com.au

Australia, Fiji, Germany, Ghana, Greece, Kenya, Lebanon, Malaysia (Sabah), New Zealand, South Africa, Thailand, United States (California)

Through networked international volunteering, aims to assist people travelling overseas to participate as volunteers to gain experience while assisting community-based, not-for-profit organisations around the world

Placements are available to suit local needs which vary from teaching children with learning difficulties to assisting local teachers of English as a spoken second language; occupational therapy for the rehabilitation of retarded children; recreation for older adults; social welfare related training for volunteer organisations; and health care instruction to villages.

Ages to suit the placements. Relevant experience welcome, but not always necessary for certain placements. Usually best for a pair of girls to provide mutual support in a foreign country. Understanding of spoken English essential.

6-12 weeks or more

Cost AU$460. Provides advice on placements, itinerary planning and arrangements. Board and accommodation varies according to placement, and may be provided free of charge. Volunteers arrange their own visitor visa, international travel and insurance. In Australia, meeting on arrival, initial accommodation, introductions to banking and a communications base provided. Discounted internal travel, eco introductory trip and scuba diving instruction also available.

Apply at least 3 months in advance, but more planning time is recommended if possible

JAPAN EXCHANGE & TEACHING (JET) PROGRAMME

JET Programme Desk, Council on International Educational Exchange, 52 Poland Street, London WIV 4JQ

℘ 0171-478 2010 ⊡ 0171-734 7344 ⊡ infouk@ciee.org

Japan

Seeks to promote mutual understanding between Japan and other countries, and fosters international perspectives by promoting international exchange and intensifying foreign language education in Japan. Conducted under the co-sponsorship of the Japanese Ministries of Foreign Affairs, Education and Home Affairs and local governments.

Approx 500 vacancies each year for English teaching assistants, coaching in English language and pronunciation, preparing teaching materials and participating in extra-curricular activities, under the guidance of Japanese academic staff. Placements are in lower and upper secondary schools. Approx 30 vacancies for coordinators of international relations, Japanese-speakers who work in local government offices.

Ages 21-35. Applicants must be mentally and physically fit, with an interest in Japan and the ability to adapt themselves to significantly different living and working conditions. They should be interested in education and teaching in general, and in the teaching of English in particular. Applicants must be British nationals holding a Bachelor's degree, have excellent English pronunciation, rhythm, intonation and voice projection, and good English writing skills and grammar usage. Teaching experience or training an advantage. Knowledge of Japanese not essential, but candidates are expected to devote some effort to learning the language before leaving for Japan and while they are there.

Twelve months, beginning late July

Participants work on average 35 hours per week. Salary Y3,600,000 per annum; paid holiday on similar terms to Japanese colleagues. Return air ticket provided, and assistance given with finding accommodation.

Participants receive written information on the programme and on basic Japanese before departure, as well as a two day pre-departure orientation in London. Further orientation provided on arrival in Tokyo.

Apply by early December; interviews take place January/February. Application forms available from October.

JUNIOR ASSISTANT PROGRAMME WITH FRANCE

Junior Assistant Programme with France, Central Bureau for Educational Visits and Exchanges, 10 Spring Gardens, London SW1A 2BN

© 0171-389 4228   ☎ 0171-389 4594
🐾 http://www.britcoun.org/cbeve/

Throughout France

Administered by the Central Bureau for Educational Visits & Exchanges, the UK national office for the provision of advice and information on all forms of educational visits and exchanges. Incorporating the UK Centre for European Education and Education Partners Overseas, the Bureau forms part of the British Council, the UK's international network for education, culture and development services. It is funded by the Education Departments of the UK, and is the UK national agency for many of the European Union education and training programmes.

Placements as teaching assistants, to teach English in state secondary schools (mainly ages 11-15) in small towns all over France. Assistants work either in teams or independently with groups/half classes. The aim is to improve pupils oral/aural skills and give them an insight into British life, customs and institutions. 50 positions offered annually.

Ages 18-20. Applicants must have a secured place at university/ institution of higher education or show proof that they intend to apply. A or AS level or equivalent in French also required. Participants must either be UK nationals or have been educated in the UK from age 11.

Assistantships last from the first week in January to 30 June. 11 hour, 5 day week. Assistants should seek to participate fully in the life of the school outside classroom hours. Accommodation and pay of FF2,782 provided, but not board. Social Security provides 70% cover of medical expenses. No travel costs or insurance for possessions included.

Apply by end May. Application forms available from end March. Interviews are compulsory and are held during the first 10 days in July. Applicants in Scotland should apply to the Central Bureau office in Edinburgh © 0131-447 8024   ☎ 0131-452 8569; applicants in Northern Ireland to the office in Belfast © (01232) 664418   ☎ (01232) 661275.

JUNIOR ASSISTANT PROGRAMME
WITH GERMANY

Junior Assistant Programme with Germany, Central Bureau for Educational Visits & Exchanges, 10 Spring Gardens, London SW1A 2BN

© 0171-389 4228   ▭ 0171-389 4594
▶ http://www.britcoun.org/cbeve/

Germany: Bayern, Baden-Wüttemberg, Hessen, Niedersachsen, Nordrhein-Westfalen, Rheinland-Pfalz, Schleswig-Holstein and Thüringen; some of the posts are in eastern Germany

Administered by the Central Bureau, the national office for the provision of advice and information on all forms of educational visits and exchanges. The Bureau forms part of the British Council; it is funded by the UK education departments and is the UK national agency for many of the European Union education and training programmes.

Placements in boarding schools for helpers, working under the guidance of the teaching staff. Duties vary, and include supervising pupils with homework, giving extra tuition where necessary; taking small groups for English conversation; and giving an insight into British life, customs and institutions. Helpers must be prepared to join in the communal life of the school and look after the general welfare of the students; opportunities to attend classes where the subject is of particular interest. The isolation of some schools means that helpers have to entertain themselves during free periods. 15 positions offered annually.

Ages 18-20. Participants must have A level or equivalent German and have been accepted on a course of undergraduate study (not necessarily German) at an institute of higher education.

Placements from August/September and April/July

12-16 hours per week. Board and accommodation provided within the school or nearby, and an allowance of not less than DM200 per month. Participants responsible for their own travel arrangements and expenses to and from their destination. Schools tend to be located in small towns or isolated country districts, often with limited public transport.

Once appointments have been confirmed, candidates are put in direct contact with the school and the previous year's helper, so as much information can be obtained before the appointment commences

Applications should be submitted in March

LANGUAGE ASSISTANTS

Cherry Winchester, Language Assistants, Central Bureau for Educational Visits & Exchanges, 10 Spring Gardens, London SW1A 2BN

℗ 0171-389 4594   ▭ 0171-389 4594
🌐 http://www.britcoun.org/cbeve/

Hungary, Romania, Russia, Slovenia and Ukraine

The Language Assistant scheme is administered by the Central Bureau for Educational Visits & Exchanges, the UK national office for the provision of advice and information on all forms of educational visits and exchanges. Incorporating the UK Centre for European Education and Education Partners Overseas, the Bureau forms part of the British Council, the UK's international network for education, culture and development services. It is funded by the Education Departments of the UK, and is the UK national agency for many European Union education and training programmes.

Opportunities to teach in schools, colleges and universities overseas. Around 100 positions offered annually.

Ages 22-35. Applicants must be graduates; for posts in Russia applicants must also speak the language. TEFL experience will be an advantage. UK nationals only. **B D PH** but there is little provision for disabled people in Eastern Europe.

Placements start in the autumn and last one academic year. Exact conditions vary according to country. 15-18 hours per week. Salary is sufficient to provide reasonable standard of living for one person in the country concerned. Accommodation arranged by host institution. Insurance cover available. Travel not provided.

Apply by spring prior to the autumn in which post commences. Applicants in Scotland should apply to the Central Bureau office in Edinburgh ℗ 0131-447 8024   ▭ 0131-452 8569; applicants in Northern Ireland to the Central Bureau office in Belfast ℗ (01232) 664418   ▭ (01232) 661275.

MARLBOROUGH BRANDT GROUP

Marlborough Brandt Group, c/o Mr Ken Wright, IA London Road, Marlborough, Wiltshire SN8 IPH

©/☎ Marlborough (01672) 514078

The Gambia

Founded in 1981, the Marlborough Brandt Group successfully formed a link with Gunjur in The Gambia, West Africa, and since 1984 there has been a regular interchange of visits between the two towns

Four or five teaching placements are available each year at the middle school in Gunjur; volunteers stay with an African family and participate in village life

Ages 18+. Applicants should be educated to A level standard or equivalent, have a commitment to teaching and a willingness to adapt to a very different environment.

10-12 months; September-July

Participants work 30+ hours per week, plus preparation and marking time. Cost £3,000 for the year. This includes board and lodging with a family in a compound where there is no running water or electricity. Advice given on fundraising; significant support from charities usually available. Permits/visas arranged. Arrangements are made for travel and insurance.

Orientation course provided prior to placement. One day debriefing on return from placement. Volunteers are encouraged to continue their involvement with the group and provide input into the preparation of future volunteers.

Formal application should be made by October/November

OUTDOOR ADVENTURE

Outdoor Adventure, Atlantic Court, Widemouth Bay, near Bude, Cornwall EX23 0DF

✆ Widemouth Bay (01288) 361312   ▭ (01288) 361153

Cornwall, England

Runs leisure/activity holidays and courses in all kinds of outdoor pursuits. Set in 10 acres of heritage coastland along the rugged north Cornwall coast, Widemouth Bay is one of the few beaches with a maximum 4 Dolphin award for water quality. The centre caters for 26 people and the programmes are run by experienced trainers and instructors who provide tuition on a 1:1 basis.

The Personal Development Programme is an instructor course which aims to provide tuition in people, coaching and sports skills. Sports include canoeing, surfing and surf life-saving, windsurfing, powerboat skills, dinghy sailing and climbing. The programme also provides coaching in centre management, safety, selling techniques and knowledge about the industry, useful for those who are looking to develop a career in outdoor pursuits. Participants work towards achieving four National Governing Coaching Awards.

Ideally suited to those taking a gap year, but open to all ages. Applicants must have a love of outdoor sports, a desire to work with people and a motivation to enhance their life and career. Pre-entry requirements: windsurfing at RYA Level 2; dinghy sailing at RYA Level 3; canoeing (kayak) at BCU Two Star; plus 20 hours experience for climbing, if chosen, and two years experience and strong swimming abilities for surfing, if chosen. All nationalities welcome.

13 week programme run twice a year, spring and autumn

No specific hours; work involves evenings and many weekends. Programme fee £3,750, includes accommodation, linen, room towels, meals, equipment, transport, all training and assessment, RYA log books and selected handbooks, and programme file. Participants may be eligible for vocational tax relief, career development loans or local authority grants.

THE PROJECT TRUST

The Director, The Project Trust, The Hebridean Centre, Isle of Coll, Argyll PA78 6TE

© Coll (01879) 230444   ▭ (01879) 230357
▯ 101553.2560@compuserve.com

Botswana, Egypt, Namibia, South Africa, Uganda, Zimbabwe; China, Hong Kong, Indonesia, Japan, Malaysia, Sri Lanka, Thailand, Vietnam; Brazil, Chile, Cuba, Guyana, Honduras, Peru; Jordan

Founded in 1968, a non-sectarian educational trust. Aims to enable a new generation to experience life and work overseas, gaining some understanding of life outside Europe, particularly in the Third World, placing volunteers in a way which is of real benefit to the community.

Projects chosen to ensure volunteers are not taking work from local people. Opportunities include teaching English in schools, colleges and universities; teaching in primary and secondary schools, assisting with extra-curricular activities such as arts and sports; and on outdoor activity projects in Outward Bound schools. Recruits approx 220 volunteers annually.

Applicants must be at least 17.3 years, maximum 19 at time of going. They should have initiative, commonsense, flexibility, sensitivity and be fit and healthy to cope with the climate and conditions. Open to UK passport-holders in full-time education, taking 3 A levels or equivalent. **B D PH** where projects suitable

One year, starting August/September

Volunteers live in the same type of accommodation as a local worker, with food usually provided. Insurance, travel and pocket money paid. Leave is at the discretion of the host country. Cost £3,175 of which volunteers must earn at least £150 and raise the rest through sponsorship.

Initial interviews June-January at a location close to the applicant's home; between September-January successful candidates attend 4 day selection course on Coll; cost deductible from sponsorship money. The island's few inhabitants play a major role in the selection and training of volunteers and this, plus the history of Coll, gives volunteers an invaluable insight into the conditions to be met overseas. Training course in July; candidates learn the rudiments of teaching and are briefed. Two day debriefing on return.

Applications open 14 months before proposed date of departure

Q E D

Angela Forsyth, Managing Director, QED Educational Consultants, 90 Gloucester Place, London W1H 4BL

℗ 0171-935 4909   ▭ 0171-486 9922   ▯ qedl@aol.com

Throughout the UK

An educational consultancy offering a specialised recruitment service for teachers and students, and training in interview techniques, cv preparation and career guidance

Places a number of school leavers and new graduates each year, usually in independent preparatory schools for 8-13 year olds, where they work as games assistants or general teaching assistants

Ages 18-21. Applicants should have good A levels or equivalent and be willing to contribute to a range of extra-curricular activities.

1-3 terms

Pay and conditions of work vary according to the placement, but in general year between students are provided with full board accommodation in addition to a modest salary

Recruitment all year

SOCRATES - LINGUA ACTION C ASSISTANTSHIPS

Julia Stone, Lingua Action C Assistantships, Central Bureau for Educational Visits & Exchanges, 10 Spring Gardens, London SW1A 2BN

✆ 0171-389 4596/4955   ⊡ 0171-389 4594
🌐 http://www.britcoun.org/cbeve/

All countries in the EU and EEA

The Lingua Action C programme is part of SOCRATES, the European Union education programme, funded by the European Commission and running since 1995/96

A Lingua Action C assistantship involves assisting teachers in primary, secondary, vocational or special schools in other member states of the EU/EEA. Lingua assistants are required not only to teach English, but also to contribute to the whole school curriculum. Approx 150 positions offered annually.

Ages 20+. Applicants must either be holders of the necessary qualifications for teaching foreign languages or must have completed a minimum of two years of study at higher education level providing access to a career as a teacher. Applicants must also be native speakers of English and EEA nationals. **B D PH W** depending on availability of suitable school.

3-8 month placement, scheduled during the academic year. 12-16 hours per week. Free days dependent on timetable. Assistants receive a monthly grant of approx £500, according to the cost of living in the country of appointment, from the European Commission. Return travel to destination provided (one return journey only). Accommodation not provided, but help is given in finding it. No insurance provided.

Apply by 1 February. Applicants in Scotland should apply to the Central Bureau office in Edinburgh ✆ 0131-447 8024   ⊡ 0131-452 8569; applicants in Northern Ireland to the Central Bureau office in Belfast ✆ (01232) 664418   ⊡ (01232) 661275. Applicants in other EU/EEA member states should apply through the SOCRATES National Agency in their own country.

S P W

Jim Cogan, Director, SPW, 17 Dean's Yard, London SW1P 3PB

℃ 0171-222 0138/976 8070   ⌷ 0171-233 0008/963 1006

Namibia, Tanzania, Uganda, Zimbabwe; India, Nepal

An educational charity set up in 1985 to organise placements for young people wanting to work in developing countries. Its main purpose is to provide those on a year between with challenging experiences outside formal education and focus their efforts on developing countries where educational and social services are poor.

Overseas teaching placements where participants work as a teaching assistant, providing English language support and organising extra-curricular activities. During the programmes volunteers are also involved in spending funds raised in the West, on mini-projects to benefit the local schools and communities. Examples of these projects include levelling and equipping playing fields, setting up poultry, piggery and beekeeping projects, and setting up libraries. These projects are intended to benefit and involve as many young people as possible.

Ages 18-25. Applicants are usually taking a year out before, during or after going into further education and are expected to have/to be about to gain high A level (or equivalent) grades and have a real commitment to teaching; relevant experience an advantage. Flexibility and an openness to other cultures essential, as is the resourcefulness to cope with living in spartan conditions. **D PH** where practicable

7-11 months, beginning September/November or January

Cost approx £1,750, of which £1,000 covers expenses such as travel, insurance, inoculations and £750 sponsorship which provides basic living allowance, training and administration overseas. All volunteers are asked to raise extra money to contribute towards the mini-projects which they carry out whilst overseas. Optional school sponsorship scheme through which schools agree to provide financial support for their participating students.

Obligatory pre-departure and in-country training sessions, including basic local language and TEFL training

Early application advised

SYNDICAT MIXTE MONTAIGU ROCHESERVIÈRE

Mrs J Legreé, Responsable du Service Anglais, Syndicat Mixte Montaigu Rocheservière, 35 avenue Villebois Mareuil, BP 44, 85607 Montaigu, Cedex, France

℗ (00 33 2) 51 46 45 45   (00 33 2) 51 46 45 40

The Montaigu area of Vendée, France

An organisation financed by local government and in operation since 1990, which aims to introduce the English language to children in primary schools

Two posts available to teach English in French primary schools and one in a *lycée* or *collège* as an assistant

Ages 18-25. UK nationals only. Applicants must have A level French or equivalent with good oral skills. A love of children and a desire to teach are also essential, as are good organisational skills, independence, initiative and an interest in the French way of life.

8 months, beginning October

Participants work 20 hours per week and receive a salary of FF1,800 per month. Board and lodging provided with local families. Participants pay their own travel and personal insurance costs.

Training is given during the first week, and participants are expected to write a report during their placement

Apply in January for the following October, enclosing full *cv* and photograph plus two references

TEACH IN CHINA

Teach in China, Council on International Educational Exchange,
52 Poland Street, London W1V 4JQ

℅ 0171-478 2000   ☐ 0171-734 7322   ☐ infouk ciee.org

People's Republic of China

The Council on International Educational Exchange is an international,
non-profit, non-governmental organisation dedicated to helping people
gain understanding, acquire knowledge and develop skills for living in a
globally interdependent and culturally diverse world. Founded in 1947,
it offers a range of work, study and travel opportunities around the
world.

On behalf of the State Bureau of Foreign Experts, the Council recruits
educators for English teaching positions with universities across China.
As well as teaching English, duties may include introducing cross-cultural
issues, directing communicative activities, developing original teaching
materials, coordinating English clubs and leading discussion groups.

Applicants must be graduates, with excellent English communication
skills, both written and spoken. Personal qualities include maturity,
flexibility and adaptability. Previous experience in teaching and in living
and working overseas desirable but not essential.

10 months, starting late August/September

10-20 hours per week, Monday-Friday. Participants receive a monthly
stipend RMB1500-RMB2500 (approx 12 RMB = £1) and have to pay a
fee, from £600-£1,300 depending on qualifications. This covers the cost
of all administration, return travel to China, insurance, and the support
services of the office in Beijing.

Participants with no prior qualifications/experience may be required to
take a week-long course, covering issues related to TEFL and living in
China. All participants receive a 2 day orientation on arrival in Beijing,
which includes a general introduction to life in China and visits to the
Great Wall and the Forbidden City.

Apply by June 15

UNIPAL
(UNIVERSITIES' EDUCATIONAL
TRUST FOR PALESTINIANS)

Peter Williams or Neil Quilliam, UNIPAL, CMEIS, University of Durham, South Road, Durham DH1 3TG

℗/☎ 0191-386 7124

Palestinian communities in Lebanon, the West Bank and Gaza Strip

Founded in 1972, UNIPAL is a small educational charity which aims to provide forms of help which will benefit not only individuals but also Palestinian communities and especially over 700,000 refugees still in camps. Palestinian teachers of English are brought to the UK for extra training; where possible financial aid is given to Palestinian educational institutions that are helping deprived children and young people; and volunteers are sent to the Middle East to share their skills and learn at firsthand about the Palestinian situation.

A limited number of volunteers are needed. Work generally involves teaching English as a foreign language (TEFL). There are occasional openings for other placements such as manual work or work with children.

Ages 20+. Applicants should have sensitivity, tolerance, readiness to learn, political awareness, adaptability and a sense of responsibility. Previous relevant experience necessary. Background reading on the Middle East situation essential.

Volunteers usually placed on 2-3 month projects in the summer (July/August), or 1 year projects for those with a TEFL qualification

Food and simple shared accommodation provided. Summer volunteers pay own fares and insurance and take own pocket money. Volunteers serving 6+ months have all expenses paid.

Interviews held in March and successful applicants are then briefed on their placement

Recruitment principally in January/February

WORLDTEACH

Director of Recruiting, WorldTeach, Harvard Institute for International Development, One Eliot Street, Cambridge, Massachusetts 02138-5705, United States

✆ (00 1 617) 495 5527   ▭ (00 1 617) 495 1599
🖳 http://www.igc.org/worldteach

Namibia, South Africa; Lithuania, Poland, Russia; China, Thailand, Vietnam; Costa Rica, Ecuador, Mexico

Founded in 1986 with the goal of contributing to education overseas and creating opportunities for individuals to gain experience in international development. The administration of the programme is financed primarily by participants' fees, with additional contributions from the Harvard Institute for International Development, Harvard University, foundations and individual donors.

Most volunteers teach English as a Second Language (TESL); also opportunities to teach science, mathematics and sports. Establishments include primary and secondary schools, colleges, universities, non-profitmaking and public enterprises, in urban and rural areas.

Ages 18+. Applicants must have a Bachelors degree from an accredited college or university by their date of departure. Before leaving they must also have taken a course in TESL or have spent at least 25 hours teaching or tutoring English. Knowledge of the host country's language helpful but not essential. Applicants should be independent and adaptable, with a commitment to teaching, and have strong communication and interpersonal skills. All nationalities may apply, but fluency in English is required. **B D PH W**

One year minimum; also 6 month programmes in China and Mexico

Programme fee from $3,600 covers the cost of airfare from the US, health insurance, orientation and training and support during the year. Accommodation provided with a host family or in a dormitory, and volunteers receive a small stipend equivalent to the pay of a local teacher. WorldTeach maintain a field representative in each country to assist in emergencies and help with any problems.

3-4 week orientation held on arrival in host country

Departures and application deadlines vary depending on programme

A work placement not only helps you gain valuable experience, enabling you to increase your practical understanding of an area of work and use job-related equipment, but gives you the chance to develop personal skills such as responsibility, teamwork and time management.

Increasing numbers of students recognise the value of work experience and work placements in helping them pursue their chosen careers. The Central Bureau guide **WORKPLACE** provides up-to-date information to help you find that important placement, and includes over 260,000 opportunities for work experience in the UK and abroad. It profiles 120 companies and organisations offering work placements, locally, nationally and internationally, and each listing is presented in a clear, user-friendly format. Full details of the opportunities available, the terms and conditions of the placement, eligibility requirements and the application procedures are all included.

WORKPLACE covers a wide range of sectors including accountancy; arts, broadcasting and the media;

From working in TV production in Britain to learning about farming in Canada; from assisting at a child development centre in the US to a placement with a consultancy firm; from helping on photo shoots for a fashion magazine to working in a marine research centre in Iceland; from programming with a major software company to helping children learn English in Italy **WORKPLACE** has thousands of opportunities and a wealth of information to help you gain work experience.

care work; computing; conservation; engineering; hotel & catering; IT; law; management; marketing, retail; teaching; travel & tourism; youth work.

WORKPLACE also includes an A-Z of practical advice on issues such as assessment, briefing, funding, health & safety, insurance and resources, and alternatives to work placements, from one day work visits to 18 month management traineeships.

WORKPLACE also includes selected case studies giving the views of those who offer work placements and of teachers and other work experience programme organisers. It also includes contributions from those who have undertaken work experience and work placements either at school, during a gap year, as part of a university course or when they were in employment.

WORKPLACE has details of placements from 1-500 days. For further information on **WORKPLACE** and the Central Bureau's other publications and programmes contact the Information Desk on ℂ 0171-389 4004.

WORKPLACE will be published biannually   First edition, 1997   ISBN 1 898601 08 9   £9.99

COMMUNITY
& SOCIAL
SERVICE

There are many opportunities for those taking a year between to embark upon a period of community service. This can be a particularly valuable experience for everyone, especially those contemplating a career in health care or social work. The work is classed as voluntary, but this does not necessarily mean that you work for nothing. Most placements provide board and lodging, and possibly a certain amount of pocket money, or if the placement is in the Third World, a wage according to local rates of pay. Applicants should, however, be aware that any type of community work involves commitment. The ideas and attitudes of voluntary service which used to be expressed as *helping those less fortunate than ourselves* or as *giving benefit to people in need* are inappropriate and patronising in society today. You should also bear in mind that opportunities for unskilled volunteers in the Third World are now extremely limited. However, there are a number of volunteer-sending agencies who specialise in placing school-leavers during their year out. You could also try to find a placement through contacts with friends abroad, or by using links set up by your school or church.

Many agencies organising placements in the Third World will require you to raise money towards the cost of participation, or at least pay your own travel and living costs. There are a number of reasons for this, the overriding one being to reduce to a minimum any costs involved on the part of the agency, who have to finance the project in terms of equipment, materials and administration. The host community itself is likely to be too poor to be expected to contribute; Britain in comparison is rich and a little effort

on your part is all that is required to finance your trip. There is also the philosophy that those fortunate enough to have the opportunities of higher education or travel abroad have benefited from the resources available in their society, resources which are extremely limited in the Third World. From this angle a voluntary project can be seen as an educational and cultural experience, as well as a period of service to the community. However, you don't have to travel abroad to find out about other cultures. Britain's population, for example, is made up of many cultures and many faiths, and there are plenty of opportunities to work with them. You could also do a period of community service in another European country or in North America. Working to overcome problems caused by disability, poverty, bad housing, illiteracy, unemployment and discrimination against an immigrant population is a very worthwhile challenge in itself, and you won't need to raise a large sum of money to participate.

Community Service Volunteers is one of the largest organisations placing volunteers in Britain. Everyone aged 16 to 35 who can spend 4-12 months working full-time, away from home with people who need their help can be a Community Service Volunteer. Nearly 62% of the 3,000 CSVs placed each year are aged 18-25. They come from all walks of life: no one is ever turned away. For many the experience of community work marks a milestone in their life. Zoe Crosskey lost her place at university because of disappointing A levels:

I panicked. I nearly rushed into the first place I was offered, but my parents persuaded me to take a year off. They wanted me to see another

aspect of life and think about what
I really wanted to do.

After an interview at one of CSV's
local offices, Zoe was given a six
month position at a day centre in
London helping adults with disabilities
to develop new skills. She helped
teach assertiveness training,
supervised pottery workshops or
spent time taking someone out to the
shops. Zoe admitted it could be
tough, but she'd recommend it to
anyone, and thinks that doing badly in
her A levels might have been the best
thing that could have happened.
Partly because of her volunteer work,
Zoe was offered a place at a college in
Southampton to study social
administration. Richard Washington,
from Brenchley in Kent, worked on
two CSV placements during a year
between public school and reading
history at Oxford. Richard's first
project was in Birmingham, helping a
man with muscular dystrophy live in
his own home, rather than in a
residential institution. His second
CSV placement took him to London,
where he worked at a day centre for
people with learning difficulties. The
placements were an eye-opener for
him, as was his close contact with
people with disabilities:

The concept that people who have
disabilities are perfectly useless in
society is so wrong; there is so much
they have to give. CSV changed my
whole outlook. I feel I've matured
mentally. Although it's difficult to pin
down how, I feel different from the
way I did 6 or 7 months ago. I would
recommend it very strongly.

Being a CSV is tough, hard work, but
it is also fun. CSVs take on serious
responsibility, face new challenges and

develop confidence and independence.
Young people taking a year between
benefit from their time as a CSV - and
the community does too. Angie
Dobson has cerebral palsy. She is
able to live in her own home through
the support of CSV volunteers:

If it wasn't for the CSVs, I wouldn't be
able to live in this flat and live my own
life. I need a lot of help every day to do
the things I want to do. Having CSVs
means I can be my own person and be
independent - which means a lot to me.

Many aspects of community and social
service can be physically and
emotionally draining, and you should
read carefully all the literature
provided on the project and consider
your own strengths and weaknesses
before formally applying. If you have
any doubts or questions, discuss them
thoroughly with the people running
the project. The ability to take
initiatives within the framework of the
project team, to cope with crises, to
exert discipline without being
authoritarian, and to maintain a sense
of humour and perspective, is usually
essential. You may not be aware of
possessing all these capabilities, but
the training and experience provided
by a period of community service may
well bring them to the fore. This can
only stand you in good stead and
prepare you for the challenges you
may face in your future career.

Clare Hall-Matthews worked as a
volunteer in Kent's L'Arche
Community after graduating:

I was looking for something different -
I wanted to work on relationships, on
the heart, after years of educating the
head. I certainly found it. Living
closely with others, in a caring and

open atmosphere, I learned a lot about myself. I didn't like all of it -
I discovered my anger, tension and frustration; I realised there were people I didn't get on with. Sometimes I felt I was pushed to my limits. But still I was accepted and supported. L'Arche has been a place of enormous growth for me.

Marek worked as a full-time volunteer for Independent Living Schemes in Lewisham. The job consisted of working alongside a team of two volunteers, helping a severely disabled man to live an independent life in his own home in the local community:

I found the experience both challenging and rewarding. It proved interesting getting to know the user and other volunteers, plus the other people that were involved more indirectly on the project, all of whom were from a varied background.

Of course working there was not all a bed of roses. One had to learn to live on a small amount of money, budget oneself, and live alongside and get on with the other volunteers who stayed in the workers' flat. But I felt that all this was a very good learning experience.

Working on an Independent Living Scheme can teach independence and gives an opportunity to get to know a different area away from one's home background. Whatever one's reasons are for becoming a volunteer I am sure everyone gains something from the experience, like I did, through learning a bit about oneself and others.

Sarah was a volunteer working in the Israeli-occupied Gaza Strip for the Universities Educational Trust for Palestinians (UNIPAL):

For me it was the first time I had got outside the European/American eyeview to see a different kind of society, a different way of thought and action ... this was made possible by the incredible welcome I was given by the Palestinians themselves.
Throughout my stay I felt greatly my privilege at being welcomed by them as a sister.

Whilst voluntary work abroad is an ideal opportunity to really experience a different way of life on a daily basis, it can be extremely challenging. In addition to developing your skills and undertaking tasks that are new to you, you will have to get to grips with living in a foreign country which may have a very different climate, unusual foods and a lack of basic amenities. In addition to these environmental factors, there will be cultural differences which may seriously challenge your own values and beliefs, forcing you to re-examine what you have always taken to be normal or right. Luc Bertrand, UNAIS (United Nations Association International Service) Field Coordinator in Burkina Faso who has lived in a small African village, advises prospective volunteers to prepare psychologically:

There will be no cinema, nowhere to go out and you may find it difficult to make local friends. Moreover, there will be little or no cultural activity and any intellectual exchanges will be at the most basic level. You must therefore be able to adapt yourself to your surroundings, and cultural adaptability is a most important characteristic for a successful project worker.

When you first arrive you will attract a great deal of attention. The people living around you will be very curious and may appear somewhat intrusive. The way of life of a westerner is very different from what they are used to; his or her possessions and how they are used will also be novelties. You need to accept and even expect visitors who will come to your home merely to 'be there' and not necessarily to talk or chat to you. From their point of view, the fact that they are there is enough.

At the same time, the person at the receiving end of this strange experience has a need for a degree of solitude or privacy. He or she has to integrate into the village and therefore requires time to take in all these new and disconcerting experiences.

Despite increasing demand from overseas for their volunteers, Project Trust keep their numbers low so that every volunteer is known personally to the Trust and is looked upon as an individual. Project Trust wants each volunteer to obtain maximum benefit from his/her time overseas, and they believe this is best achieved by getting the volunteers to identify with and learn as much as they can, from the host community. The community involvement can take many forms: Mary and Kate worked as teachers at a vocational training centre in a rural community in Botswana. They taught a range of science subjects and English to pupils aged 16-24. Ian and Charles worked at Ikhwezi Lokusa, a community home for physically handicapped children in the Transkei. Generally the children were crippled from diseases connected with malnutrition and poor living conditions, but the atmosphere of the home was one of hope. In Jordan, Simon and Tom lived and worked at a home for the mentally handicapped on the outskirts of Amman, stimulating the children's interests by teaching them all forms of art. For many the year between is their first long-term job experience, and can reinforce or radically alter preconceived views on a future area of study, a career or life generally. One returning Project Trust volunteer had this to say:

Looking back I see my year as an important factor in my successful university career. It taught me self-motivation and a knowledge of the wide world outside the classroom window. I entered university confident that this was what I wanted to do.

Active Assistance

AFS/Intercultural Education Programmes

Arbeitskreis Freiwillige Soziale Dienste

L'Arche

ATD Fourth World

BREAK

Camphill Village Kimberton Hills

Camphill Village Trust

Camphill Village USA Inc

Casa de Los Amigos

Centro Studi Terzo Mondo

The Children's Trust

Churchtown Farm

Community Service Volunteers

The Corrymeela Community

Crisis

Dorfgemeinschaft Tennental

Edinburgh Cyrenians

FARM Africa

Fellowship of Reconciliation Taskforce on Latin America & Caribbean

Föreningen Staffansgården

Frontiers Foundation/Operation Beaver

GAP Activity Projects (GAP) Ltd

Great Georges Project

The Guide Association

Health Projects Abroad

Independent Living Alternatives

Independent Living Schemes

Indian Volunteers for Community Service

Innisfree Village

Inter-Cultural Youth Exchange (ICYE-UK)

International Partnership for Service-Learning

Internationaler Bund

Involvement Volunteers

Joint Assistance Centre

Kith and Kids

Lanka Jathika Sarvodaya Shramadana Sangamaya

The Leonard Cheshire Foundation

Lifestyles Independent Living Partnership

Loch Arthur Village Community

Lothlorien (Ropka Trust)

The Ockenden Venture

Oxfam

The Prince's Trust Volunteers

The Project Trust

Quest Overseas

St David's (Africa) Trust Ghana Project

St David's (Africa) Trust Morocco Project

Service Protestant de la Jeunesse - Année Diaconale

SHAD - Support & Housing Assistance for people with Disabilities

SHAD Wandsworth

Simon Community (Ireland)

Simon Community (London)

Society of Voluntary Associates

Sue Ryder Foundation

Survival

Tourism Concern

Winant Clayton Volunteers Association

Youth Action for Peace

ACTIVE ASSISTANCE

Karen Powell, Active Assistance, 3 Staveley Mill Yard, Staveley, Kendal, Cumbria LA8 9LR

℗ Kendal (01539) 822212   ☎ (01539) 822201

Throughout the UK and Ireland

Established in 1992, an employment agency with high professional standards and direct personal experience of the needs of disabled people, working with both private clients and social services. Member of the UK Home Care Association. Places personal care assistants with young physically disabled clients, most of whom have a spinal injury, others being stroke victims and MS sufferers.

Trainee or experienced personal care assistants required to live and work with disabled clients, mostly aged 20-45, helping in various areas, with the objective of allowing the clients to live independently and improve their quality of life. Duties may include making and changing beds, laundry, cooking, cleaning, preparing meals, assisting/escorting in social activities and personal care such as washing, toiletting, changing, dressing and movement in and out of beds/cars. Placements provide those looking to work or study further in the social, welfare and health fields with valuable practical experience.

Ages 21-35. No experience or qualifications necessary, but applicants must be able to demonstrate initiative and maturity, as care assistants often work on their own, with sole responsibility for a client. Ability and willingness to drive cars/small vans essential. Applicants must provide two good references. EU nationals only; good English essential.

3+ months or 6-12+ months

Care assistants receive £200-£250 per week gross wages plus board and lodging. Respite workers who travel to various clients also receive travel expenses. Employees liability insurance cover provided.

Full specialist training given, with certificate for successful candidates

Apply 2-3 months in advance of placement if possible

AFS / INTERCULTURAL EDUCATION PROGRAMMES

The National Director, AFS/IEP, Arden House, Wellington Street, Bingley, West Yorkshire BD16 2NB

℗ Bingley (01274) 560677   ▭ (01274) 567675

A wide range of countries in Latin America, Africa and Asia

AFS is an international, voluntary non-profitmaking organisation represented in 55 countries. Has operated in the UK since 1947 and is a registered charity. Provides intercultural learning opportunities to help people develop the knowledge, skills and understanding needed to create a more just and peaceful world. The only organisation of its kind to receive a citation from the United Nations in recognition of its work for world youth.

Opportunities to spend 6 months abroad living with a volunteer host family whilst working alongside local people on community social projects for underprivileged children and young people, gaining another language and an insider's appreciation of the culture. Projects deal with issues such as working with underprivileged children, the elderly and people with disabilities, drug rehabilitation, community development, health and women's issues.

Ages 18-29. Applicants should be flexible, adaptable and interested in other cultures and ways of life. It is not a requirement to speak the language of the intended country before departure.

6 months, departing in January/February or July

Cost £2,750. All participants are given advice and support on doing their own fundraising. The fee covers travel to and from the host country, expenses involving the project, medical insurance, orientation courses and ongoing support from volunteers and staff in the host country and in the UK.

Orientation courses held before departure to help participants prepare for the experience, and at regular intervals during the 6 months. Intensive language training provided during the first month.

Applications accepted up to 18 months in advance of departure. Prefer to receive applications at least 6 months before departure, but can occasionally accept late applicants.

ARBEITSKREIS FREIWILLIGE SOZIALE DIENSTE

Arbeitskreis Freiwillige Soziale Dienste, Postfach 101142, 70010 Stuttgart, Germany

© Stuttgart (00 49 711) 2159 0   (00 49 711) 2159 288

Throughout Germany

A Christian organisation coordinating the Voluntary Social Year throughout Germany, aiming to help society, develop Christianity and widen the experiences of the volunteer through practical work and discussions

Volunteers are invited to work in a social institution such as a hospital, a home for elderly people, a home for the handicapped or on other social projects

Ages 18-26. Applicants should be prepared to participate fully in their placement by working and learning with others, and be sound in body and mind. Experience and qualifications not always necessary, but at least basic spoken German essential.

1 year, beginning August, September or October

Board, lodging, approx DM300 per month pocket money, health and accident insurance provided. Five weeks holiday per year.

Counselling courses held throughout the year with groups of volunteers, covering responsible citizenship, education and personal development

Apply preferably 12 months in advance

L'ARCHE

The General Secretary, L'Arche, 10 Briggate, Silsden, Keighley, West Yorkshire BD20 9JT

© Keighley (01535) 656186   ☐ (01535) 656426

Bognor Regis, Brecon, Kent, Lambeth, Liverpool, Preston; Edinburgh, Inverness; some opportunities also exist to serve with L'Arche overseas

An international federation of communities in which men and women with learning disabilities and those who help them live, work and share their lives together. Founded in 1964 in northern France, there are now over 100 communities worldwide. L'Arche believes that each person, whether disabled or not, has a unique and mysterious value; people with a learning disability are complete human beings and as such have the right to life, care, education and work. They also believe that those with less capacity for autonomy are capable of great love, and have a particular contribution to make to the community and society. L'Arche was founded on a deep belief in the teachings of the Gospels and the simple, spiritual life is considered very important to the daily life of L'Arche communities.

Assistants are required to share their lives with people with learning disabilities, living and working as members of L'Arche communities. Some 60-70 assistants are recruited each year.

Ages 18-50. No previous experience necessary, but applicants must have a commitment to living in a community and be interested in caring for and have an openness to learn from disabled people. Communities are Christian based, but welcome people of all faiths, or none.

Twelve months minimum

Full board and lodging provided, plus £25+ per week pocket money and insurance (employers' liability and personal). Applicants pay their own travel and personal expenses.

All placements involve a trial period of a week or weekend to see whether volunteers are suited, a 1 or 2 month probationary period, ongoing training and monitoring, and an exit interview

Apply as far in advance as possible; no deadline

ATD FOURTH WORLD

The Director, ATD Fourth World, 48 Addington Square, London SE5 7LB

℗ 0171-703 3231   ☎ 0171-252 4276

Belgium, Britain, France, Germany, Luxembourg, Netherlands, Spain, Switzerland. Placements in other countries, including a number of developing countries, for those able to offer a commitment of at least two years.

An international human rights organisation founded in 1957. Aims to explore all possibilities of partnership with the most disadvantaged families. Encourages private citizens and public officials to support their effort in overcoming poverty and taking an active role in the community.

Full-time volunteers run programmes in very poor communities, building on the strengths and hopes of these families. They provide a forum for the disadvantaged and ensure that the voice of the Fourth World is heard at local, national and international levels. International workcamps and street workshops also take place during the summer.

Ages 18+. No professional or academic requirements; all welcome. Applicants need a genuine interest in learning from the experiences and hopes of very disadvantaged communities as a vital first step to building a future with them, and a willingness to work hard in a team.

3 months minimum period to volunteer full-time in the UK, 6 months minimum for placement in another European country

Those interested in becoming long-term volunteers can find out more through working weekends held at the beginning of each month.
The first 3 months of voluntary service are seen as a training period. Volunteers are required to pay their food expenses for the first month; for the following 2 months food and accommodation are provided. Those who stay on are paid in increments up to the minimum salary which all permanent volunteers receive after 1 year. Accident insurance, accommodation and travel expenses paid.

Volunteers receive a full introduction into the work of ATD Fourth World and during the first 2 years on-the-job training as well as supervision

Recruitment all year

BREAK

Glenys Gray, BREAK, 7A Church Street, Sheringham, Norfolk NR26 8QR

℗ Sheringham (01263) 822161 ⊠ (01263) 822181

Norfolk, England

A charity founded in 1968, providing holidays, short-stay and respite care for children and adults with learning disabilities/mental handicap and families with special needs

Volunteers are needed for residential work at three holiday homes in Sheringham and Hunstanton on the Norfolk coast. Work as care assistants involves helping with the personal welfare of the guests, their recreational programmes and with essential domestic duties. Recruits 80-100 volunteers annually.

Ages 18+. Applicants should be mature, stable, patient, understanding, conscientious, and able to accept physical and emotional pressures. No previous experience or qualifications necessary. All nationalities considered. Good command of English essential.

2-12 months

Board, lodging, insurance and £23 per week pocket money provided, plus travel expenses within the UK. 40 hour week.

Recruitment all year

CAMPHILL VILLAGE
KIMBERTON HILLS

The Admissions Group, Camphill Village Kimberton Hills, PO Box 155, Kimberton, Pennsylvania 19442, United States

℗ (00 1 610) 935 0300

Pennsylvania, United States

An agricultural and craft community based on a 430 acre estate in the rolling hills of southeast Pennsylvania. There is a total population of 120, including nearly 50 adults with mental handicaps. The community raises vegetables, fruits and meat, and produces milk and cheese from a small dairy herd. The community has a bakery, which sells to the local health foodstore, and a coffee shop open to the public. The community is a registered, non-profit charity.

Volunteers are required to live as co-workers within the community, working shoulder-to-shoulder with mentally handicapped adults. Work takes place on the farm and in the orchards, in the bakery, store, craft workshop, coffee shop and the administrative office and in expanded-family homes. Some 10-15 volunteers are recruited each year.

Ages 19+. Volunteers should have idealism, enthusiasm and an interest in personal growth. **B D PH**

Six months minimum, except for summer placements

Board and lodging and other incidental needs provided in a Village home. In the first 3 months volunteers receive $75 per month pocket money, after which they may choose to join the community's system of spending flexibly according to the perceived need of self and others in the community. Health insurance provided after 6 months, but not travel costs.

Orientation course available during placement

Recruitment all year

CAMPHILL VILLAGE TRUST

The Secretary, Camphill Village Trust, Delrow House, Hilfield Lane, Aldenham, Watford, Hertfordshire WD2 8DJ

✆ Watford (01923) 856006   ▭ (01923) 858035

Throughout the UK; possibility of some placements abroad

A charity founded in 1955; aims to provide a new and constructive way of life for mentally handicapped adults, assisting them to individual independence and social adjustment within the communities of the Trust. It guides them towards open employment while helping them to achieve full integration within society by providing a home, work, further education and general care. The centres are based on Rudolf Steiner principles.

Volunteers are needed to work alongside the residents in every aspect of communal life at centres where the handicapped can establish themselves, work and lead a normal family life in a social background. There are three Villages offering employment, two town houses for those in open employment, a college, and centres for agriculture, horticulture and assessment. Volunteers work in gardens and farms run on organic principles, in craft workshops, bakeries, laundries and printing presses, and participate in the general life and chores of the community. Special emphasis is placed on social, cultural and recreational life.

Ages 20+. Applicants should have an interest and understanding in work with the mentally handicapped and be prepared to live in the same manner as the residents. Experience not essential, but an advantage. All nationalities considered. Good command of English necessary.

One year minimum, if possible

Board, lodging, and a small amount of pocket money provided; 1 day off per week

Recruitment all year

CAMPHILL VILLAGE USA, INC

Associate Director, Camphill Village USA, Inc, Copake, New York 12516, United States

℡ (00 1 518) 329 4851/7924

New York State, United States

A community of 220 people, about half of whom are adults with mental disabilities. Situated on wooded hills and farmland 110 miles north of New York City, the Village includes a farm, a large garden, workshops, a store and 17 houses, each shared by 4-6 adults with disabilities and 2-4 co-workers.

Volunteers are required to live and work as co-workers within the community, taking part in work on the land, household chores, crafts, worship and cultural activities. 15-20 volunteers are recruited each year.

Ages 18+. No previous experience or qualifications necessary. Volunteers should have an open mind and a willingness to join in and experience community life. **PH** depending on extent of ability.

Six months minimum

Co-workers are provided with board and lodging in a village house, plus $50 per month pocket money. Those staying 12 months receive $300 towards a 3 week vacation. Health insurance provided, but not travel costs.

5-8 hours per week orientation course provided

Recruitment all year, although to participate in training programme, volunteers should plan to join in mid September

CASA DE LOS AMIGOS

R Sellick, Casa de Los Amigos, Ignacio Mariscal No 132, CP 06030, Mexico DF

℡ (00 52 5) 705 064 60521   🖷 (00 52 5) 705 0771
✉ amigos@laneta.apc.org

Mexico City

Established as a centre for human rights and social welfare by Mexico City Quakers in 1956. The Service and Education Project (SEP) provides support to community organisations in Mexico City. The projects focus on urbanisation, development issues, the environment and US/Mexico relations.

Placements available for volunteers to work with community organisations in the fields of community care; youth work; women and children; health education; and homelessness. Work includes field trips, guest lectures and study themes. Twelve positions offered annually.

Ages 18+. Good spoken Spanish required. Previous volunteer experience preferred.

Placements available all year, 6-24 months. 35 hour, 5 day week. Accommodation can be arranged in the guest house. No travel or insurance expenses provided.

Apply at least 4 weeks before planned arrival. Registration fee US$50, US$25 per month support fee.

CENTRO STUDI TERZO MONDO

The Director, Centro Studi Terzo Mondo, via G B Morgagni 29, 20129 Milan, Italy

℗ Milan (00 39 2) 29409041

Angola, Chad, Ethiopia, Mozambique, Somalia; India; Indonesia; Brazil, Ecuador, Peru

Founded in 1962, the centre has a wide-ranging involvement with the Third World, which includes arranging development projects, organising courses, initiating studies and research, and issuing documentation, books and journals. Also recruits volunteers for other Italian organisations employing volunteers overseas.

Volunteers are needed to work as teachers, in the medical and social services, in community work, and to organise integrated projects. Recruits 25 volunteers annually.

Ages 18+. Applicants should be reliable and have a serious commitment to voluntary work. Qualifications not always necessary but often desirable, depending on the post. All nationalities considered.

Open ended commitment

Board and accommodation depends on the country, but usually provided in private house. US$100 per week pocket money and insurance provided. 36 hour week. Travel costs are met for periods of at least 6 months service. Advice given to participants on obtaining sponsorship.

Compulsory orientation course organised for those without qualifications and experience. On return, advice/debriefing meetings organised every two months.

Recruitment all year

THE CHILDREN'S TRUST

Rachel Turner, Voluntary Services Organiser, The Children's Trust, Tadworth Court, Tadworth, Surrey KT20 5RU

© Burgh Heath (01737) 357171 ⬚ (01737) 373848

Tadworth, England

A children's hospital and residential home run by a consortium of charities

Placements available for those wishing to go into the caring profession, to work as volunteers on a residential summer scheme for profoundly disabled and exceptional needs children, who normally live at home. Work involves acting as a friend to the children, carrying out basic personal care, organising games, encouraging them to take an active part in daily activities, escorting them on outings and organising evening activities. Volunteers are part of an interdisciplinary team on individual planned programmes for the children under the supervision of teachers, therapists and senior care staff.

Ages 18+. Previous experience with children or handicapped children preferable, but not essential. Creative skills, handicraft or musical ability welcome. The work is very rewarding but can also be physically and emotionally tiring.

Mid July-early September; applicants are expected to stay the duration of the scheme. 6-12 months for residential school volunteers. 37½ hour week. Lodging and an allowance of £42 per week provided. Travel expenses within England can be reimbursed.

Apply by 31 March

CHURCHTOWN FARM

The Head of Care, Churchtown Farm, Lanlivery, Bodmin, Cornwall PL30 5BT

① Bodmin (01208) 872148   ▭ (01208) 873377

Cornwall, England

A centre for outdoor and environmental education opened by Scope in 1975 and specially designed for disabled people. The centre provides education and adventure courses for more than 1,500 people of all ages and abilities each year.

Voluntary assistants are required to perform various duties in and around the centre. These may include individual care, assisting outdoor pursuits instructors, conservation work and maintenance of the centre.

Ages 18+. No particular experience or qualifications necessary, although experience in outdoor education or of working with people with special needs an advantage. Applicants should be keen to work with disabled people in field studies and outdoor pursuits. **PH** must be able to assist others with special needs and require minimal assistance themselves.

2-12 months

Volunteers work approx 50 hours per week and receive £20 per week pocket money. Full board, dormitory accommodation provided.

Training course available

Recruitment all year

COMMUNITY SERVICE VOLUNTEERS

Community Service Volunteers, 237 Pentonville Road, London N1 9NJ

✆ 0171-278 6601 or Freephone 0800 374 991   ▭ 0171-833 0149
🌐 http://www.csv.org.uk

Throughout the UK

A national agency inviting all young people to experience the challenge and reward of helping those in need. For over 30 years it has seen the unique contribution volunteers make to the lives of those they help.

Over 3,000 volunteers are placed each year in 600 projects. Volunteers work with elderly people, physically handicapped children and adults, young people in care or in trouble and people leaving hospital. Volunteers are placed according to their interests, personality, experience and the needs of the project; work is usually with individuals or small groups, not in large institutions. Examples include independent living projects which enable individuals or families with personal difficulties or disabilities to live in their own home; volunteers help with domestic chores and personal care, and may accompany them to work, college, restaurants or cinemas. Volunteers also work in group homes for people who may have a learning difficulty, who are leaving care, or who are recovering from mental illness; volunteers help residents to lead their own lives as fully as possible by helping them with personal care and to shop, plan meals and enjoy leisure and social activities. Some placements are in hostels for homeless young people; volunteers help with administrative tasks and housework, and spend time befriending residents, talking and listening to them and helping them to find accommodation and employment or claim benefits.

Ages 16-35. Applicants should have enthusiasm, energy and a commitment to helping others. No academic qualifications or previous experience necessary. **B D PH**

4-12 months

Volunteers are placed away from their home area. Accommodation, full board, £23 weekly allowance and all out-of-pocket expenses provided. 40 hour week. Overseas volunteers pay £499 placement fee.

Placements reviewed after 1 month; CSV staff liaise with the volunteer and project organiser throughout the placement. One person on every project is assigned to the volunteer for support and regular supervision.

Recruitment all year; placements take 6-8 weeks to arrange

THE CORRYMEELA COMMUNITY

The Volunteer Coordinator, The Corrymeela Community, Ballycastle, County Antrim BT54 6QU

℡ Ballycastle (0126 57) 62626   ✉ (0126 57) 62770

Ballycastle, Northern Ireland

Founded in 1965, Corrymeela is an open village situated on the north Antrim coast, comprising a house, cottages and youth village, and supported by the Corrymeela Community, a group of people drawn from many different Christian traditions who work for reconciliation in Northern Ireland in many different conflict situations, and promote a concern for issues of peace and justice in the wider world. People under stress, such as those from problem areas, families of prisoners, the disabled and many others, go to Corrymeela for a break or holiday; conferences and other activities challenge participants to look critically at contemporary issues.

A limited number of volunteers needed to participate in the programme work of the residential centre, working with the groups who use the centre and being the link during their stay. They should expect to be involved in the practical aspects of running the establishment, assisting with catering arrangements, preparing accommodation, and working in the kitchen, laundry or reception. Work is with visiting groups of all ages and backgrounds.

Ages 18+. No qualifications or experience necessary. All nationalities considered. Applicants must be fit and adaptable to cope with the demands and pressures of community life and a very busy programme, and have a commitment to the process of reconciliation. They should also be open and prepared to give and receive a lot of themselves.

One year starting September, or 6 months starting March

Accommodation in shared private study bedrooms with all meals, £22 per week pocket money and insurance provided. Travel grant of £75 for volunteers from outside Ireland. No fixed hours. 6 days free per month; 1 week's holiday for every 3 months service.

Prospective volunteers should spend a few days at Corrymeela before applying. Weekly briefing and reflection programme with the full-time volunteer coordinator. Great care is taken in terms of staff support, external consultancy and pastoral access.

Apply December-March

CRISIS

Volunteer Coordinator, Crisis, 1st floor, Challenger House, 42 Adler Street, London E1 1EE

℗ 0171-377 0489   ☐ 0171-247 1525   @ crisis.uk@easynet.co.uk

London, England

A charity working for homeless people that runs four emergency schemes: WinterWatch shelters; Open Christmas service, offering support and vital services such as eye tests and dental treatment; FareShare, providing day centres and hostels with a regular supply of fresh, free food donated by shops and restaurants; and the Clothing Run, distributing clothes to help homeless people keep warm and retain their dignity. In addition, Crisis Open House is a national network of year-round shelters and a new network of rent guarantee schemes helps homeless people move into rented accommodation.

Wide range of voluntary positions available including church speakers to work in various churches; press and PR officers; computer input and administration assistants; finance volunteers; fundraising assistants; research, policy and information volunteers; school speakers to raise awareness; and cheque collectors. Volunteers also required to work on the emergency services outlined above.

Ages 18+. Qualifications and previous experience not essential; training provided, although experience on Word for Windows 6.0 useful for office-based positions. Some positions require a clean, current driving licence. All volunteers should have an interest in the issues of housing and homelessness, be flexible and have a willingness to help. In addition to general volunteers, projects like Open Christmas rely on skilled people such as electricians, chiropodists, doctors and hairdressers.

Opportunities available throughout the year; some projects require extra help at particular times of the year such as Christmas

Hours of work according to placement. All positions are voluntary but travel expenses are paid for any day on which 4 hours or more are worked. Full training is provided for all positions.

Contact Crisis for further information and an application form

DORFGEMEINSCHAFT
TENNENTAL

Dorfgemeinschaft Tennental, Sta Wegmannstrasse 1, 75392 Deckenpfronn, Germany

✆ (00 7056) 926-0   🖷 (00 7056) 926 110

Deckenpfronn, near Stuttgart, Germany

A village community for mentally handicapped people, founded in 1990

Volunteers are needed to live and work in the village with the disabled residents. Work includes helping on the farm and in the vegetable gardens, working in the woodwork shop and caring for the residents. Five positions available annually.

Ages 18+. No specific requirements but applicants should have a caring personality, be able to adapt to living in the community and believe in the work of the organisation. Volunteers must speak German or English. EEA nationals only.

Placements 3 months-3 years, all year round

Volunteers receive DM350 per month, plus insurance, accommodation in apartments and meals with social therapy families. Travel costs are not covered.

EDINBURGH CYRENIANS

The Project Manager, Edinburgh Cyrenians, 107A Ferry Road, Edinburgh EH6 4ET

℗/☐ 0131-555 3707

Edinburgh and West Lothian, Scotland

Set up in June 1968 to develop and provide services to homeless single people, the Edinburgh Cyrenian Trust runs a city community in central Edinburgh and a rural project on a small organic farm in West Lothian. Residents are a mix of young people referred by social workers, hospitals or other agencies.

Volunteers are required to live and work alongside residents and other volunteers, sharing the jobs involved in running a large household, with particular responsibility for managing household accounts, upholding the rules of the community, attending weekly meetings, forming helpful relationships with community members and offering assistance and support to residents. Community life is challenging, difficult and stressful, but can also be extremely rewarding. Some 22 volunteers are recruited annually.

Ages 18-28. Applicants should have personal commitment, open-mindedness, willingness to learn, a sense of responsibility, energy, enthusiasm and a sense of humour. No previous experience or qualifications necessary. All nationalities accepted; working knowledge of English essential. **B D PH** unsuitable for wheelchairs

6+ months

Volunteers work a 5 day week and receive full board accommodation in the community, with access to a flat away from the community on days off. £28 per week pocket money provided, plus £160 grant for 1 week's holiday after 3 months, £30 clothing allowance and £135 leaving grant after 6 months.

Regular training given and volunteers are supervised by non-residential social workers

Recruitment all year

FARM AFRICA

Fundraising Department, FARM Africa, 9-10 Southampton Place, Bloomsbury, London WC1A 2EA

℗ 0171-430 0440   ▭ 0171-430 0460   ▢ farmafricauk@gn.apc.org

Mainly London, but also other parts of the UK

FARM (Food and Agricultural Research Management) Africa is a registered charity founded in 1985 with the aim of helping small peasant farmers in Africa develop agricultural skills and techniques, increase food production and break the cycle of famine. Runs eight projects in East and South Africa.

Placements can be made for volunteers in the areas of public relations and fundraising

Ages 18+. No specific experience or qualifications needed, just enthusiasm and a real interest in Africa and some understanding of development issues. The ability to communicate the organisation's message on a variety of levels, particularly on the telephone, and to enjoy the work is also important. **B PH**

Placements scheduled to start in January/February; 3 months minimum

Hours negotiable. Employer's liability insurance cover and some travel expenses provided.

Ongoing recruitment, but applications in November/December preferred. One-to-one training given.

FELLOWSHIP OF RECONCILIATION TASK FORCE ON LATIN AMERICA & CARIBBEAN

Fellowship of Reconciliation Task Force on Latin America & Caribbean, 995 Market Street #801, San Francisco, CA 94103, United States

© San Francisco (00 1 415) 495 6334

Argentina, Bolivia, Brazil, Chile, Colombia, Mexico, Nicaragua, Panama, Paraguay, Peru

The Fellowship of Reconciliation is a national, inter-faith, pacifist organisation. In 1983 it founded the Fellowship of Reconciliation Task Force on Latin America & Caribbean which aims to strengthen communication and collaboration between North and Latin American non-violent movements; to support the network of North American groups working on Latin American and Caribbean issues; and to promote public education related to issues of peace and justice throughout the region.

Volunteer placements are arranged in negotiation with a host group. Work may involve translating publications and correspondence; peace education workshops; human rights documentation; or computer training, depending on host organisation.

Ages 21+. In most cases no experience necessary; some opportunities require experience in education and training. Volunteers must be fluent in Spanish or Portuguese, committed to non-violence, and open to cultural differences with a desire to serve and collaborate with others. All nationalities welcome, however only minimal orientation can be provided to those based outside North America. **B D PH** depending on abilities and facilities of host groups.

Three months minimum

$75 application fee covers the cost of administration and linking the volunteer with a host organisation. Volunteers must arrange and pay for their own travel and insurance. In most cases the host group finds appropriate accommodation for the volunteer, for which the volunteer has to pay. Advice available for participants on fundraising.

In some cases informal orientation sessions can be provided, alternatively volunteers may attend training sessions with other organisations.

Apply all year round

FÖRENINGEN STAFFANSGÅRDEN

The Director, Föreningen Staffansgården, Box 66, Furugatan 1, 82060 Delsbo, Sweden

✆ (00 358 653) 16850

Delsbo, 300 km north of Stockholm, Sweden

A Camphill Village for adults with mental handicaps. The community also has a farm, a garden, a bakery, six family houses, and workshops for weaving and woodwork.

Co-workers are required to live and work with mentally handicapped people, playing a full part in Village life including domestic tasks, crafts and farmwork

Ages 19+. No previous experience or qualifications necessary, but applicants must have a strong desire to share a period of their life with handicapped people. Applicants should be willing to learn Swedish; courses are provided. **B D PH**

Six months minimum; 1 year preferred

Co-workers receive board and lodging in a Village home shared with 10-15 other people, plus pocket money to cover their immediate needs. Accident and health insurance provided. Ticket home paid after six month stay.

Training seminars and courses organised in arts, therapy and the philosophy of anthroposophy

Recruitment all year

FRONTIERS FOUNDATION / OPERATION BEAVER

The Program Coordinator, Frontiers Foundation/Operation Beaver, 2615 Danforth Avenue, Suite 203, Toronto, Ontario, M4C 1L6, Canada

℡ Toronto (00 1 416) 690 3930 ▭ (00 1 416) 690 3934

Alberta, Manitoba, Ontario, Quebec, Northwest Territories and Yukon, Canada

Works in cooperation with requesting communities to fulfil their needs for basic housing. Volunteers from all over the world come to the programme to make practical efforts to reduce poverty and meet people from culturally diverse backgrounds.

Volunteers work on practical projects in cooperation with native and non-native peoples in rural communities. Construction projects involve building or renovating wood frame or log houses; recreation volunteers work in Alberta with local youth workers during the summer months; and educational projects take place in Northwest Territories and Yukon.

Ages 18+. Applicants should be hardworking, open-minded, flexible and culturally sensitive. They must also be able to live without television, flush toilets, and in some cases without running water or electricity. Volunteers with construction skills are given first priority, and previous voluntary experience is also an asset. Experience of working on camps or with children required for recreation projects and tutoring skills for Arctic educational projects.

12+ weeks; most volunteers arrive for the summer session, June-August. Educational projects take place January-June and September-December.

Salary not provided initially; modest living allowance paid after 12 week minimum period. Accommodation, food, local travel expenses and insurance provided. Travel to Canada and to the orientation site is the volunteer's responsibility.

Summer session volunteers are involved in an intensive 2 day orientation, while volunteers for other months participate in a less formal 1 day orientation.

Apply at least 3 months in advance; recruitment all year

GAP ACTIVITY PROJECTS (GAP) LIMITED

The Registrar, GAP Activity Projects Ltd, GAP House, 44 Queen's Road, Reading, Berkshire RG1 4BB

© (0118) 959 4914   ▭ (0118) 957 6634

Namibia, South Africa, Zambia; India; Germany, Hungary, Poland; Jordan; Japan, Malaysia, Vietnam; Ecuador, Mexico, Paraguay; Israel; United States, Canada, Fiji and the South Pacific

A charity founded in 1972 to give those with a year between leaving school and going on to further/higher education or vocational training the opportunity to undertake voluntary work in another country

Social work attachments are available in orphanages, homes for the elderly, hospitals, children's homes, or working with youth groups or physically handicapped people. Participants work as general assistants, providing help and care. Many of the projects can be physically and emotionally challenging.

Ages 18-19. UK nationals only. Applicants should be reliable, possess initiative and intelligence, and be prepared to work hard. Those working on German or Latin American projects must be able to speak the relevant language.

Most placements are for 6-9 months

Board and accommodation provided, and usually a small amount of pocket money. Volunteers must find their own travel and insurance costs, plus the placement fee of £440.

Candidates attend a briefing session before departure

Apply from September of last year at school or college; early application advisable. Interviews held from October.

GREAT GEORGES PROJECT

The Duty Officer, Great Georges Project, The Blackie, Great George Street, Liverpool L1 5EW

© 0151-709 5109

Liverpool, England

Founded in 1968, the Project, known locally as The Blackie, is a centre for experimental work in the arts, sports, games and education of today, housed in a former church in an area typical of the modern inner-city: multi-racial, relatively poor, with a high crime rate and a high energy level, but sometimes a lot of fun. The Project sets about its task of building bridges between the artist and the community with great enthusiasm, offering a wide range of cultural programmes, workshops and exhibitions, including sculpture, printing, photography, painting, writing, outdoor plays, carpentry, puppetry, playstructures, music, mime and dance. Open 7 days a week, 10.00-24.00, Sundays 12.00-24.00.

Volunteers needed to work with children/adults in projects undertaken at the Project and in the local community, with endless opportunities to learn and create. The general work of running the Project is shared as much as possible, with everyone doing some administration, fundraising, cleaning, caretaking, maintenance work, talking to visitors and playing games with children. Recruits 100-150 volunteers annually.

Ages 18+. Applicants should have a good sense of humour, stamina, a readiness to learn, and a willingness to work hard and share any skills they may have. Those who visit the Project are tough, intelligent, friendly and regard newcomers as a fair target for jokes, so the ability to exert discipline without being authoritarian is essential. No direct experience required. All nationalities considered. Good working knowledge of English needed. Volunteers will need to take sleeping bag, jeans, tough shoes and clothes.

1+ months. Volunteers are particularly needed at Christmas, Easter and during the summer.

Accommodation in shared rooms at staff house; long-term volunteers may have own room. Participants contribute £17.50 per week towards food and household expenses. Meals are vegetarian; cooking, shopping and cleaning on a rota basis. 12 hour day; 5½ day week. Wages generally paid after 6 months.

Orientation course includes a talk with films and a pack of literature

Recruitment all year

THE GUIDE ASSOCIATION

Guiding Services, The Guide Association, 17-19 Buckingham Palace Road, London SW1W 0PT

℗ 0171-834 6242   ☐ 0171-828 8317

India, Mexico, Switzerland, England (London)

The Guide Association of the United Kingdom, founded in 1910 by Robert Baden Powell, is a voluntary organisation for girls. It gives them the opportunity to follow any number of interests and at the same time learn self-reliance and self-respect. Guides share a commitment to a common standard set out in the Promise and Law.

Volunteer work is available in London and overseas at centres owned by the World Association of Girl Guides and Girl Scouts. Projects may include assisting the development of Guide Associations, training adult leaders or administration duties in connection with Guide House. The work is sometimes strenuous and the hours long. The Association also runs a scheme for short-term voluntary opportunities overseas. These last 3-26 weeks and include teaching English and health care work.

Ages 18+. Qualifications and experience required vary according to the position. Volunteers must be members of the Association. **B D PH** considered.

Length of placements variable

Board, accommodation and pocket money provision vary according to the position. Insurance provided in some cases. Travel costs usually paid by the volunteer. Advice is given to participants on obtaining sponsorship. Members are encouraged to write articles for the Guide magazines on their return.

Recruitment all year

HEALTH PROJECTS ABROAD

Volunteer Coordinator, Health Projects Abroad, PO Box 24, Bakewell, Derbyshire DE45 1ZW

℗ Great Longstone (01629) 640051   📠 (01629) 640054

Tanzania

The charity supports the development of access to health care facilities for people living in developing countries and gives young people from the UK the opportunity to participate in projects and learn firsthand about the realities of life in a developing country

Volunteers work alongside Tanzanian villagers, helping to complete locally initiated projects. They are usually involved in simple tasks such as assisting with the construction of dispensaries and renovation work at health centres and hospitals. Volunteers work with local people under the guidance of volunteer engineers.

Ages 18-28. Applicants must have enthusiasm and energy, be open minded and receptive to change, sensitive to the needs of the host community and able to work as part of a team. No specific skills, qualifications or experience required. **B D PH** All applicants considered on an individual basis.

Three months, beginning May, July and September. Includes 2 weeks travel time at the end of each project.

Each volunteer is required to raise £2,900 towards the cost of their own participation. This covers flights, accommodation, food, medical insurance, language training and support for the project. Advice is given on raising funds.

Applicants are selected at an assessment and briefing weekend. Two compulsory training weekends are held before departure; language training is provided on arrival in Tanzania and a follow-up weekend is held about 6-8 weeks after volunteers return.

Send for further details and an application form

INDEPENDENT LIVING ALTERNATIVES

Tracey Jannaway, Business Manager, Independent Living Alternatives, Ashford Offices, Ashford Passage, London NW2 6TP

✆/▭ 0181-450 4055

North and west London, and Essex, England

A non-profitmaking charity run by people with direct experience of disability, designed to promote independence to people disabled. Provides physical support to people who want to live in their own homes and helps them to take full control of their lives and live spontaneously.

Volunteers are needed to provide physical support in the form of partnership, on a full-time basis with a person disabled. Duties include washing, dressing, cooking and housework.

Ages 21+. Applicants must be able to drive, with a clean driving licence. Apart from this there are no particular qualifications except an open mind and the ability to be part of a semi-communal, flexible environment. **B D PH** depending on ability.

4 months minimum

Five day week. Accommodation and £58.99 per week, plus expenses, provided. Time off negotiable, with a minimum of 2 days off per week.

Training given on placement

Recruitment all year round

INDEPENDENT LIVING SCHEMES

Kenneth Smith, Independent Living Schemes, Lewisham Social Services, Louise House, Dartmouth Road, Forest Hill, London SE23 3HZ

0181-699 0111 ext 239   0181-291 1020
ken.smith@lewisham.gov.uk

Lewisham, south east London, England

Aims to enable severely disabled people (all wheelchair users) to lead the lifestyle of their choice, living in their own homes rather than in hospitals or residential care

Volunteer helpers carry out everyday tasks for the disabled person such as cooking, housework and shopping; assist with personal care including toiletting, bathing and lifting; and share social, community and leisure activities

Ages 18+. No experience necessary, just commonsense and a caring attitude. **B D PH** considered, depending on ability.

Six months minimum preferred

Rent-free accommodation sharing with other helpers is provided near the scheme. Household bills are met and volunteers receive a weekly allowance of £20 pocket money and £35 for food. In addition, £15 per month is provided for clothing and leisure. Travel expenses paid within the UK at beginning and end of placement. I week's paid leave after 4 months.

Training given on project. Supervision and advice available from ILS team social worker and support project worker.

Recruitment all year. Write or telephone for application form and information pack.

INDIAN VOLUNTEERS FOR COMMUNITY SERVICE

The General Secretary, Indian Volunteers for Community Service, 12 Eastleigh Avenue, South Harrow HA2 0UF

✆ 0181-864 4740

India

A registered charity founded in 1981 which involves young people in community service, providing them with the opportunity to discover and understand another culture and enabling them to perceive the causes of conflict and disparity in society. Provides orientation, advice and information on visiting rural areas in India and organises seminars and conferences on the issues of sustained development, aid and interdependence, especially in the context of the relationship between the Indian subcontinent and Britain.

Volunteers can help in rural development projects usually in the following areas: helping children in a school or a nursery; repairing small farm machinery in workshops; helping in a health centre; typing, compiling reports and newsletters; and teaching English to children and teachers.

Ages 18+. Applicants should have imagination and plenty of commonsense. They should be willing to learn from a different culture, have respect for it and value the experience. They must not be demanding or paternalistic, and should be prepared to work hard at anything to improve the quality of life. No qualifications, skills or experience are necessary. Any nationality may apply.

Placements vary; anything from 1 month to 1 year, departing September-March. No summer placements.

Basic shared accommodation and food provided on projects for £3 per day. Participants pay all their travel costs and personal expenses.

Compulsory interview and orientation organised before placements. Guidelines for preparation, advice on travel and health and meetings with returned volunteers are arranged for members only. Annual membership fee £15; life membership £50.

Recruitment all year

INNISFREE VILLAGE

The Volunteer Coordinator, Innisfree Village, 5505 Walnut Level Road, Crozet, Virginia 22932, United States

© (00 1 804) 823 5400

United States

Aims to provide a lifetime residential facility for adults with mental disabilities. The staff consists of volunteers who live and work together with the disabled co-workers in a natural and humanistic environment.

Acting as houseparents and co-workers, volunteers are needed to work on the 600 acre farm in the foothills of the Blue Ridge Mountains with the choice of working in the bakery, weavery, woodshop and garden. There are also two group homes in the nearby city of Charlottesville. Recruits 10-15 volunteers annually.

Ages 21+. Volunteers need energy, enthusiasm, patience, and a willingness to work with the differently abled. They must be in excellent health, and interested in the community process in a very rural setting. Volunteers must be college graduates or equivalent, preferably with some experience of working with mentally disabled, recently brain injured or emotionally ill people. Craft skills greatly appreciated. All nationalities considered. Fluent English required. Volunteers most obtain a B-1 Visitors Visa.

One year commitment; a limited number of short stays available

Volunteers have their own room and board in a house of 6-14 people. $160 per month spending money, $100 Christmas bonus, medical insurance and up to $250 for dental expenses provided. Travel costs are paid by the volunteer. Volunteers work a 5 day week, with 2 consecutive days free. Annual holiday entitlement of 15 days, with an additional holiday allowance of $30 per day.

The first month is a mandatory trial period with four orientation sessions covering a brief history of the village and its guidelines, and volunteers are encouraged to get to know the village as well as possible before settling down in one house. At the end of this period, the community evaluates and decides the best placement for the volunteer.

Recruitment all year

INTER - CULTURAL YOUTH EXCHANGE (ICYE - UK)

ICYE-UK, PO Box 11520, London SW6 7DT

©/☎ 0171-681 0983   @ icyeuk@gn.apc.org

Bolivia, Brazil, Colombia, Costa Rica, Honduras, Mexico, Uruguay; Ghana, Kenya, Nigeria; India, Japan, South Korea, Taiwan; New Zealand; Austria, Belgium, Denmark, Finland, France, Germany, Iceland, Italy, Norway, Poland, Switzerland

An international exchange organisation established in 1949 and made up of autonomous national committees. Aims to break down the barriers that exist between people of different cultures, faiths, ethnic groups and nationalities and to promote peace and justice and raise awareness of social and environmental issues at home and abroad. About 600 young people around the world take part every year.

The exchange programme offers the opportunity for young people to live in another country and to be involved in voluntary social work. Work includes projects dealing with drug rehabilitation, protection of street children, rural and health development, environmental education, childcare, women's groups, non-governmental organisations, museums and many more.

Ages 18-25 (for some countries up to 30). Applicants should be prepared to accept the challenges of living in a different environment amongst people from another culture. They should be mature and flexible, able to give and take. An interest in questions of peace, justice, development, ecology and the growing interdependence between nations and culture is a plus.

12 months starting end July. A very limited number of 6 month placements available, starting either July or January.

Participation fee covers travel, insurance, preparation, seminars in host country, pocket money and administration

Preparation before departure, orientation and language camp upon arrival, mid year and evaluation conferences while in host country and evaluation when back in the UK arranged

Recruitment starts in October/November the year before departure and goes on until April in the year of departure

INTERNATIONAL PARTNERSHIP FOR SERVICE-LEARNING

International Partnership for Service-Learning, 815 Second Avenue, Suite 315, New York NY 10017-4594, United States

© New York (00 1 212) 986 0989   (00 1 212) 986 5039
pslny@aol.com

United States (South Dakota), Mexico, Ecuador, Philippines, Jamaica; England, Scotland, Czech Republic, France; India, Israel

Founded in 1982, a not-for-profit organisation which provides international/intercultural programmes combining academic study and community service. The service makes the study immediate and relevant and the study relates to and supports the service.

Learning may be in the liberal arts, interdisciplinary and/or related to technical courses and career goals. Academic requirements may be fulfilled through the classroom and independent study. The service is related to the student's specific interests and skills, carried out under the direction of an established service agency. Recent programmes include serving in an Native Indian reservation community, and taking courses at South Dakota State University; and providing basic and needed care to the poor of Calcutta, studying the cultures of the nation and briefly visiting other towns and cities in India.

Ages 18+. Most participants are college/university undergraduates. No experience necessary; skills which can be brought to the service welcomed. Participants should be mature, responsible and have a sense of obligation to those being served. Applicants for France, Ecuador or Mexico should have studied the relevant language for at least one year. All nationalities welcome. **B D PH**

Placements generally during spring, summer and autumn or a full year; 3 week programme in India. Approx 15-20 hours per week, depending on the programme/project.

Costs vary from $4,400-$7,600 according to programme and usually cover most in-country expenses, full board accommodation with a family, support services and studies. Participants must arrange own insurance, travel expenses and spending money.

Orientation held on location at beginning of programme

INTERNATIONALER BUND

Internationaler Bund, Freier Träger der Jugend-, Sozial- und Bildungsarbeit eV, Burgstraße 106, 60389 Frankfurt am Main, Germany

© Frankfurt (00 49 69) 94 54 50   ☐ (00 49 69) 94 54 5280

Throughout Germany

An independent, non-profitmaking organisation whose objective is to enable people to integrate into the community, take on personal responsibility and contribute actively to the development of society. Also aims to stimulate people's willingness to participate in voluntary social service, and to develop and improve international understanding and cooperation.

Operates a Voluntary Social Year programme whereby young people work in various social facilities such as hospitals, old people's homes, sheltered workshops and psychiatric hospitals, assisting in all duties which a non-skilled helper is able to perform, such as helping patients to wash and dress themselves, feeding them and running errands.

Ages 18-25. No previous experience necessary, however applicants should have some knowledge of German.

6 or 12 months, beginning April (6 months) or September (12 months)

Participants receive approx DM200 per month pocket money and full board accommodation on site, with cash compensation during days off for meals not provided. 24 days leave allowed for 12 months' service. 40 hours per week, which may include morning/afternoon shifts and weekend duty.

Week-long briefing seminar held at beginning of service, where participants meet their group leaders and are assigned to their place of work. Further compulsory training courses are held throughout the period of service.

Recruitment all year

INVOLVEMENT VOLUNTEERS

The Director, Involvement Volunteers, PO Box 218, Port Melbourne, Victoria 3207, Australia

℡ Melbourne (00 61 3) 9646 9392 📠 (00 61 3) 9646 5504
📧 ivimel@iaccess.com.au

Australia, Fiji, Germany, Ghana, Greece, Kenya, Lebanon, Malaysia (Sabah), New Zealand, South Africa, Thailand, United States (California)

Through networked international volunteering, aims to assist people travelling overseas to participate as volunteers to gain experience while assisting community-based, not-for-profit organisations around the world

Placements are available to suit local needs which include assisting children with personal social problems and those from drug-affected families; the rehabilitation of retarded children; recreation for older adults; social welfare related training for volunteer organisations; and kerbside medical clinics for social outcasts

Ages to suit the placements. Relevant experience welcome but not always necessary for certain placements. Usually best for a pair of girls to provide mutual support in a foreign country. Understanding of spoken English essential, and local language an advantage.

6-12 weeks or more

Cost AU$460. Provides advice on placements, itinerary planning and arrangements. Board and accommodation varies according to placement and may be provided free of charge. Volunteers arrange their own visitor visa, international travel and insurance. In Australia, meeting on arrival, initial accommodation, introductions to banking and a communications base provided. Discounted internal travel, eco introductory trip and scuba diving instruction also available.

Apply at least 3 months in advance; more planning time recommended if possible

JOINT ASSISTANCE CENTRE

The Director, Joint Assistance Centre, G-17/3, Qutab Enclave I, Gurgaen 122002, India

Throughout India

A small voluntary group for disaster assistance working in close liaison with other groups throughout India who run voluntary projects of various kinds

Operate a learn-while-you-travel scheme whereby volunteers undertake administrative work at centres in Delhi or are placed on short stay workcamps with groups in other areas to help in environmental activities, agriculture, construction, community work, health and sanitation work, teaching first aid or preparation work for disasters. Specific projects are also organised including work on playschemes, organising fundraising campaigns and exhibitions to increase awareness, and teaching English in village schools near Delhi and Calcutta.

Ages 18+. Experience welcome but not essential. Applicants should have a personal faith in God, and an open mind towards new beliefs. They should be adaptable to difficult situations and have patience, tolerance, understanding and organisational skills. Conditions are very primitive, and the summers (May/June) are very hot. Only vegetarian food is allowed, and applicants must comply with the no alcohol/tobacco/drugs rule.

Minimum I month; 3-6 months commitment preferred

JAC believes that those fortunate enough to have the opportunities of higher education or travel abroad have benefited from the resources available in their society. Therefore each volunteer is required to make a contribution in order to participate in voluntary service, usually £75 per month. Self-catering accommodation provided; volunteers share in all housekeeping duties. Registration fee £15. No travel, insurance or pocket money provided. Volunteers must make their own arrangements for obtaining a visa. Travel within India paid if on JAC business.

No prior briefing arranged, but 2 day orientation on arrival provided for additional charge. Opportunities to take part in disaster management programmes and conferences. JAC can also put applicants in touch with former volunteers.

Apply at least 3 months in advance, enclosing 3 IRCs

KITH AND KIDS

Louise Palmer, Projects Administrator, Kith and Kids, c/o Irish Centre, Pretoria Road, London N17 8DX

℗ 0181-801 7432

London, England

Self-help group providing support for the families of children who have a physical or learning disability

Placements can be made for volunteers to take part in social training schemes, working on a 2:1 basis teaching disabled children and young adults, helping them with everyday skills and experiences in the community.

Ages 16+. No skills or qualifications needed. **PH** depending on ability.

Placements last two consecutive weeks in August or 1 week at Christmas and Easter

Hours 09.30-17.00 daily. No accommodation available; applicants should be based in or around London. Lunch, travel expenses within Greater London area and 3 days training before each project provided. Opportunity to go on a one week camping holiday in August.

LANKA JATHIKA SARVODAYA SHRAMADANA SANGAMAYA

The Executive Director, Lanka Jathika Sarvodaya Shramadana Sangamaya, Damsak Mandiraya, 98 Rawatawatte Road, Moratuwa, Sri Lanka

Sri Lanka

Founded in 1958, a non-governmental people's self-development movement covering nearly 8,000 villages. Provides a practical possibility of realising Mahatma Gandhi's concept of a world society where the wellbeing of all shall be ensured. Aims to create awareness among deprived communities and to mobilise latent human and material potential for the satisfaction of basic needs in a manner to ensure sustainable development and to develop strategies and implement action programmes for this concept.

Volunteers recruited in the fields of agriculture, appropriate technology, economic activities, house construction, energy conservation and the development of alternative energy sources. Opportunities also exist in the provision of preventive and curative health care including nursing, first aid, nutrition and feeding programmes, education and rehabilitation.

Ages 21+. A willingness to teach and to learn is the main consideration. Applicants should have an awareness of their responsibility to improve human conditions wherever needed and an ability to work in difficult circumstances. They should also have a commitment to the promotion of peace and international understanding, and to an ideal that leads to the equitable distribution of the world's resources according to need. Skills and experience vouched for by a recognised organisation or individual are required, but specialised skills are not a priority requirement and academic qualifications are optional. All nationalities considered.

Placements up to 6 months; extensions depending on performance

Board and lodging provided at a cost of Rs350 per day, but may be less in outstations. Volunteers are expected to meet their own travel, insurance and living expenses.

Compulsory orientation course organised. End of service evaluation provided, at which the volunteer's subsequent activities and placement in the home country is discussed.

Recruitment all year

THE LEONARD CHESHIRE FOUNDATION

Personnel Officer, The Leonard Cheshire Foundation, Leonard Cheshire House, 26-29 Maunsel Street, London SW1P 2QN

℡ 0171-828 1822

Throughout the UK

An international voluntary organisation founded in 1948, with some 300 services in 50 countries including over 120 in the UK. It has no boundaries of sex, creed or race, concerned only with the care of people with disabilities. The common aim of all Cheshire Homes and Services is to provide choice and opportunity for people with physical, mental and learning disabilities. Residents are encouraged to lead the most active life their disabilities permit and to participate in the running of the Home and decisions affecting it.

Volunteers are needed in many Homes to assist with the general care of residents who require help in personal matters, including washing, dressing, toileting and feeding, as well as with hobbies, letter writing, driving, going on outings or holidays and other recreational activities. Recruits some 100 volunteers annually.

Ages 18-30. Applicants must have an interest in and a desire to help people with disabilities; the work is hard and requires understanding and dedication. Previous experience useful but not essential. Preference generally given to those planning to take up medical or social work as a career. Volunteers must be adaptable, dedicated, hard working, punctual and willing to undertake a wide variety of tasks.

3-12 months

Volunteers work a 37 hour, 5 day week. Board, lodging and at least £28 per week pocket money provided. Travel costs paid by volunteers.

Recruitment all year; more jobs in summer months

LIFESTYLES INDEPENDENT LIVING PARTNERSHIP

ILS Manager, Lifestyles Independent Living Partnership, Woodside Lodge, Lark Hill Road, Worcester WR5 2EF

℗ Worcester (01905) 350686

Worcester, England

A local charity helping people with disabilities to maintain or gain independence in their everyday lives within their own homes and the community

Placements can be made for volunteers, to support individuals and families and help them with shopping, cooking, intimate personal care and housework, and sharing in leisure pursuits. Training provided where appropriate.

Ages 18+. No experience necessary, but applicants must be able to complete normal household duties. Good communication skills essential. EEA nationals only. **B D PH**

Placements scheduled all year, lasting 4-12 months

Hours vary, and can include sleep-overs, shift work and weekends. Weekly allowance of £51.50 plus a bonus paid upon successful completion of an agreed 4 or 6 month commitment. Participants have their own room in shared accommodation. Insurance and travel costs to and from placement within the UK provided.

Applications accepted throughout the year

LOCH ARTHUR VILLAGE COMMUNITY

Admissions Officer, Loch Arthur Village Community, Camphill Village Trust, Beeswing, Dumfries DG2 8JQ

℗ Kirkgunzeon (01387 76) 0687   ☐ (01387 76) 0286

Dumfriesshire, Scotland

A Camphill rural community providing a home, work, further education and general care for approx 30 handicapped adults. The Community consists of 6 houses, a farm and a 500-acre estate.

Volunteers are needed to live and work alongside residents in every aspect of life, including bathing, dressing and other personal tasks. Main areas of work are on the farm and in the garden, houses, workshops, bakery, weavery and creamery. Volunteers are also encouraged to take part in the Community's cultural, recreational and social activities.

Ages 18+. Volunteers should be caring, enthusiastic and willing to help wherever they are needed. No previous experience or qualifications necessary.

6-12 month commitment preferred. Some short-term placements available in summer, minimum stay 6 weeks.

Full board accommodation provided in the Community, plus pocket money

On-going instruction is given by experienced co-workers, plus formal introductory course sessions on a regular basis

Recruitment all year

L O T H L O R I E N   (R O K P A   T R U S T)

Project Manager, Lothlorien (Rokpa Trust), Corsock, Castle Douglas, Kirkcudbrightshire DG7 3DR

℗ Castle Douglas (01644) 440602

South west Scotland

Established in 1978, Lothlorien is a supportive community where those who are experiencing mental health problems can grow and develop their potential through living alongside people who are relatively well, in an atmosphere of friendship, acceptance and mutual support. It consists of a large log house with 14 bedrooms and communal living areas, set in an isolated rural area with 17 acres of grounds including organic vegetable gardens, woodland and outbuildings.

A volunteer placement offers the opportunity for personal growth and will be of particular interest to those considering a career in the helping professions. Volunteers must be prepared to work in the vegetable gardens, participate in domestic tasks and undertake maintenance work on the house and in the grounds. Four placements available.

Ages 21+. Volunteers are sought with a caring, flexible and gregarious attitude. No previous experience or qualifications are necessary, but those with special skills are encouraged to use them where appropriate and to involve other residents in their activities.

Six months minimum

Board and lodging provided, and volunteers receive £25 per week pocket money

Training and supervision provided by permanent staff

Recruitment all year

THE OCKENDEN VENTURE

The Personnel Officer, Ockenden Venture, Constitution Hill, Woking, Surrey GU22 7UU

✆ Woking (01483) 772012   ☎ (01483) 750774

United Kingdom

A registered charitable organisation, providing support for refugees, displaced people and the disadvantaged both at home and overseas. In the UK the Venture runs a reception centre for those referred to it that are in need of medical treatment, and a residential care home for those with severe handicaps.

Volunteers are recruited to care for a group of Vietnamese and Cambodian refugees with learning difficulties and/or a physical handicap. Volunteers are given the opportunity, through working as part of a team and using initiative, to learn about others and themselves in all types of situations. The house is run on non-institutional lines in order to create a home. Approx 8 placements per year but requirements vary according to the stage reached in the project.

Ages 18+. Applicants should have a genuine desire to help, a willingness to work hard, and be physically fit. Qualifications or experience not generally necessary. All nationalities welcome.

Preferably one year; although short-term appointments possible, especially during holiday periods. 5 day week operated on a shift system, based on 80 hours per fortnight.

Volunteers receive full board, lodging and £25 pocket money per week. Twenty three days holiday per year, pro rata for shorter periods.

Recruitment all year, most volunteers join in August/September

OXFAM

Oxfam, 274 Banbury Road, Oxford OX2 7DZ

✆ Oxford (01865) 313151   ▭ (01865) 313101

Headquarters in Oxford and regional offices throughout the UK

An international charity founded in 1942 to work with poor people regardless of race or religion in their struggle against hunger, disease, exploitation, and poverty. Employs around 550 people at headquarters.

60+ voluntary placements offered at the headquarters in Oxford in several areas including the in-house library, communications, information technology and routine secretarial and administration work. Self-contained projects involving a degree of elementary research occasionally available. Further placements available in London, Cambridge, Manchester, Glasgow, Edinburgh, Belfast and Dublin.

Ages 15+. No specific qualifications required. Those with language skills in Portuguese and Spanish helpful for work on the Africa and Latin America desks. Competence in word processing and basic computer skills an advantage. All nationalities welcome. **B D PH W**

Placements of 1-48 weeks, all year round. Hours and days worked negotiable. Public and employer's liability insurance, local fares and lunch allowance of up to £3 per day provided.

Applications must be submitted at least 4 weeks before placement start

Oxfam in the UK works with the following partner organisations: Oxfam America, 25 West Street, Boston MA 0211-1206, United States; Oxfam Belgique/België, 39 rue du Consail, Brussels 1050, Belgium; Oxfam Canada, Suite 300, 294 Albert Street, Ottawa, Ontario K1P 6E6, Canada; Community and Abroad, 156 George Street, Fitzroy, Victoria, Australia 3065; Oxfam Hong Kong, Ground Floor 3B, June Garden, 28 Tung Chau Street, Tai Kok Tsui, Kowloon, Hong Kong; Oxfam Quebec, 2330 rue Notre-Dame Ouest, Bureau 200, Montreal, Quebec H3J 1N4, Canada; Oxfam New Zealand, Room 101 La Gonda House, 203 Karangahapa Road, Auckland, New Zealand; NOVIB, Amaliastraat 7, 2514 JC The Hague, Netherlands.

THE PRINCE'S TRUST
VOLUNTEERS

The Prince's Trust Volunteers, 18 Park Square East, London NWI 4LH

© 0171-543 1234

Throughout the UK

A unique programme which provides young people from widely different backgrounds with the opportunity to come together in a team which works in the community. Enables participants, through meeting the challenge of working together and helping others, to grow in skills and self-confidence. Founded in 1990, directly inspired by the ideas of HRH The Prince of Wales, and managed locally through local authorities, youth and voluntary organisations, colleges and employers.

120 franchise outlets, each running several teams of 15 places each year. Involves individual placements and projects in which the whole team work together for their local community. At least one residential element, usually at an outdoor centre with a focus on team building; a second residential week involves working with disabled people or others in need. Some training in specific skills related to the projects is available including First Aid and Community Sports Leader Awards. At the end of the programme each volunteer receives a City and Guilds profile of achievement and a Prince's Trust Volunteers Certificate.

Open to those aged 16-25 who are employees, unemployed, in education or between education courses. Volunteers should be willing and able to mix with people with varied backgrounds and abilities, and prepared to work as a team. UK nationals only. **B D PH** welcome.

Sixty days; 12 weeks full-time or longer period part-time

Unemployed participants will continue to receive all benefits. Those in education may need to seek the support of the head of their college/school. Employed people must seek the support of their employer, who needs to agree to continue to pay their salary and the cost of the training programme. Teams help raise money for their own projects. Travel costs provided in the case of most unemployed volunteers. Initial team meeting and ongoing support from a trained leader.

Final team presentation and survey

Recruitment all year

THE PROJECT TRUST

The Director, The Project Trust, The Hebridean Centre, Isle of Coll, Argyll PA78 6TE

℅ Coll (01879) 230444   ✉ (01879) 230357
📠 101553.2560@compuserve.com

Botswana, Egypt, Namibia, South Africa, Uganda, Zimbabwe; China, Hong Kong, Indonesia, Japan, Malaysia, Sri Lanka, Thailand, Vietnam; Brazil, Chile, Cuba, Guyana, Honduras, Peru; Jordan

Founded in 1968, a non-sectarian educational trust. Aims to enable a new generation to experience life and work overseas, gaining some understanding of life outside Europe, particularly in the Third World, placing volunteers in a way which is of real benefit to the community.

Projects chosen to ensure volunteers are not taking work from local people. Opportunities include working with deprived, disabled or homeless children; and assisting in community development projects, in hospitals or with aid agencies. Recruits approx 220 volunteers annually.

Applicants must be at least 17.3 years, maximum 19 at time of going. They should have initiative, commonsense, flexibility, sensitivity and be fit and healthy to cope with the climate and conditions. Open to UK passport-holders in full-time education, taking 3 A levels or equivalent. **B D PH** where projects suitable.

One year, starting August/September

Volunteers live in the same type of accommodation as a local worker; food usually provided. Insurance, travel and pocket money paid. Leave at the discretion of the host country. Cost £3,175; volunteers must earn at least £150 by themselves and the rest through sponsorship.

Initial interviews held June-January at location close to the applicant's home; between September and January successful candidates attend 4 day selection course on Coll; cost deductible from sponsorship money. The island's few inhabitants play a major role in the selection and training of volunteers and this, plus the history of Coll, gives an invaluable insight into the conditions to be met overseas. Compulsory training course held July; candidates learn the rudiments of teaching and are briefed on their project. Two day debriefing on return.

Applications open 14 months before proposed date of departure

QUEST OVERSEAS

Michael Amphlet, Director, Quest Overseas, 25 Storey's Way, Cambridge CB3 0DP

© 0181-673 3313   ▭ (01223) 575514
□ michael@quest-overseas.co.uk   ⇲ http://www.quest-overseas.co.uk

Bolivia, Chile, Ecuador, Peru; Namibia, South Africa, Tanzania, Zambia; China

Formerly Volunteers Abroad, founded in 1992, Quest Overseas organises a unique combination of voluntary work projects and leadership training expeditions for teams of up to 12 gap year students

Quest South America involves 3 week intensive Spanish course in Ecuador, with private tutors for both beginners and advanced students; 6 weeks living and working with orphans in Peru; and 6 week expedition encompassing Bolivia, Chile and Peru.

Quest South Africa/Africa involves 6 month projects in South Africa, working as assistants with a wide variety of organisations and institutions, centred on Cape Town and Grahamstown; 6 week optional expedition encompassing Namibia, Tanzania and Zambia. Option also to undertake the expedition only.

The expedition and leadership training is demanding, challenging, adventurous, instructive and very rewarding

Ages 17/18+; applicants must be students between school and university, and should be responsible, motivated, enthusiastic and able to get on well with others.

January departure for all projects; African expedition starts mid July

Applicants pay all their own costs. South America £3,200 all-inclusive; South Africa £2,000 (Grahamstown), £2,800 (Cape Town), all-inclusive. African expedition £1,800 all-inclusive, but excluding flights if not already in Africa on South Africa project. Application fee £20.

Selection interview, followed by team meetings for successful applicants

Applications considered 3-18 months in advance of January departure; early application recommended

ST DAVID'S (AFRICA) TRUST GHANA PROJECT

St David's (Africa) Trust, Ghana Project, St David's House, Rectory Road, Crickhowell, Powys NP8 1DW

☎/📠 Crickhowell (01873) 810665   ✉ stdavids@gibnet.gi
🌐 http://www.gibnet.gi/~stdavids

Elmina, Ghana

An educational trust registered as a charity by the Charity Commissioners in Gibraltar, arranging voluntary opportunities for school leavers

Opportunities for volunteers, working in a mixed group of 6, to work at the Ahokotrum Rehabilitation Centre. The Centre was originally established to care for leprosy sufferers, but now includes a junior school for 190 children, a house for the elderly, a needlework/dressmaking school and a residential house for about 20 handicapped and orphaned children. Volunteers also help with simple English lessons for the girls at the needlework/dressmaking school.

Ages 18-25. Applicants should be year between students or postgraduates, in possession of a valid passport and in good health.

6 months, January-July

Cost £2,500, plus three donations of £250 each, includes travel, health insurance, private aircraft emergency insurance, board, lodging, all meals and a contribution to the work of the centre. The Trust offers advice on how to raise the cost of the visit and the donations required.

Application forms on request or download from the Web site

ST DAVID'S (AFRICA) TRUST
MOROCCO PROJECT

St David's (Africa) Trust, Morocco Project, St David's House, Rectory Road, Crickhowell, Powys NP8 1DW

℗/☎ Crickhowell (01873) 810665   ✉ stdavids@gibnet.gi
🌐 http://www.gibnet.gi/~stdavids

Taroudant, Morocco (Atlas Mountains)

An educational trust registered as a charity by the Charity Commissioners in Gibraltar, arranging voluntary opportunities for school leavers

Opportunities exist for year between students to volunteer for work and study in the mountain region surrounding the ancient walled city of Taroudant. The placement involves working with handicapped, blind and orphan children, and occasionally with animals. During the initial period of the stay on weekday mornings and afternoons there is the opportunity to take part in French and Arabic lessons. Volunteers will also be encouraged to help with simple English lessons given freely to selected young Moroccans during the week. There will also be guest speakers visiting to talk about Moroccan Islamic culture and history.

Ages 18-25. Applicants must be year between students or postgraduates and should have a working knowledge of French. All participants should be in possession of a valid passport and in good health.

Two programmes: mid September-beginning December, and beginning January-mid June

September-December programme costs £1,250 plus two donations of £250 each; January-June programme costs £2,500 plus three donations of £250 each. Costs include travel, health insurance, private aircraft emergency insurance, language tuition, board, lodging and all meals. Accommodation provided in an old, traditional-style house. The Trust offers advice on how to raise the cost of the visit and the donations required.

Application forms on request or download from the Web site

SERVICE PROTESTANT DE LA JEUNESSE - ANNÉE DIACONALE

Service Protestant de la Jeunesse, Année Diaconale, rue du Champ de Mars 5, 1050 Brussels, Belgium

✆ Brussels (00 32 2) 513 2401

Throughout Belgium

Youth office of the Protestant church in Belgium

Can arrange opportunities for volunteers to work in caring institutions throughout Belgium, including relief centres and homes for children, the elderly and people with disabilities. Approx 20 volunteers are placed each year.

Ages 18-25. Applicants must be physically and mentally fit, with a real desire to serve and care for others. All nationalities welcome; knowledge of French essential.

10-12 months, beginning early September

Volunteers work a 38 hour week in return for board, lodging, laundry, work accident insurance and BF4,000 per month pocket money. 12-15 days off in a year, depending on length of service. Volunteers arrange and pay for their own insurance and return travel to Belgium. Administration fee BF500 to be sent with completed application form.

Compulsory day and weekend orientation, reflection and evaluation sessions arranged, for which travel and accommodation costs are provided.

Recruitment all year

SHAD - SUPPORT & HOUSING ASSISTANCE FOR PEOPLE WITH DISABILITIES

Sue Denney, SHAD, Winkfield Resource Centre, 33 Winkfield Road, London N22 5RP

℗ 0181-365 8528

London, England

A scheme which enables people with physical disabilities to live in their own homes, with full control over their lives

Volunteers are required to assist physically disabled adults with all aspects of daily living, including personal care, cooking, housework and going out

Ages 18-30. Experience not essential. Limited number of overseas applications accepted; EU nationals only.

3+ months, all year

Volunteers work full-time with one person, as part of a team of 2-3 volunteers on a rota basis. Pocket money of £55 per week, plus fares and other expenses, separate accommodation and insurance provided. Four days off per fortnight plus regular long weekends.

Training provided

Recruitment all year

SHAD WANDSWORTH

SHAD Wandsworth, c/o The Nightingale Centre, Balham Road, London SW12 9DS

℡ 0181-675 6095

Wandsworth, southwest London, England

Funded by Wandsworth Borough Council, SHAD is committed to providing an opportunity for independent living to local people. Its success lies in its proven ability to offer independence, freedom of choice and self-determination to people with severe physical disabilities. Its ten disabled members all live their lives to the full in their own homes in the community.

Volunteers are needed to enable people with severe disabilities to live independently in their own homes. Volunteers provide the 'arms and legs' which enable SHAD members to get on with their own lives in a way which suits them.

Ages 18-30. No experience necessary, but volunteers should be physically fit. All nationalities welcome; good standard of English essential. **D PH** depending on ability.

Four months minimum

Volunteers work two to three 24 hour shifts per week on a rota basis. Accommodation provided. Pay £52 per week plus expenses. Overseas volunteers must pay own travel expenses from abroad.

Training provided by the disabled person with whom volunteers are working and manual handling training by a backcare professional

Apply 2 months before anticipated starting date

SIMON COMMUNITY
(IRELAND)

The Recruitment Coordinator, Simon Community (National Office), 28-30 Exchequer Street, Dublin 2, Ireland

✆ Dublin (00 353 1) 671 1606/671 1319   ✉ (00 353 1) 671 1098
✉ simonnat@indigo.ie

Cork, Dublin, Dundalk and Galway, Ireland

A voluntary body offering support and accommodation to the long-term homeless at emergency shelters and residential long-stay houses in Cork, Dublin, Dundalk and Galway

Volunteers are required to work full-time on a residential basis, living-in and sharing food with residents, taking responsibility for household chores and working to create an atmosphere of trust, acceptance and friendship by talking and listening, and befriending residents. Full-time work in Simon is demanding and involves a very full commitment to people who will be difficult and who will challenge the volunteer's motivation and feelings. It does not suit everyone, yet can be a very rewarding and enriching experience for those whom it does suit.

Ages 18+. Applicants should be mature, responsible individuals with an understanding of, and empathy for homeless people. Tolerance and an ability to get on with people and work as part of a team are also essential. No experience or qualifications necessary. All nationalities welcome, but excellent standard of spoken English essential; not suitable for those learning the language.

3+ months; first month is probationary period

Volunteers work 3 days on and 2 days off, with 2 weeks holiday entitlement every 3 months. Full board and lodging on the project provided, plus a flat away from the project on days off. Volunteers receive an allowance of IR£34 per week; insurance provided, but not travel costs.

Training on-site is given by project leaders; formal training courses in aspects such as first aid may also be provided

Recruitment all year

SIMON COMMUNITY
(LONDON)

Simon Community, PO Box 1187, London NW5 4HW

© 0171-485 6639

London and Kent, England

A voluntary community founded in 1963 which comprises of approx fifty homeless people and volunteers living together, operating a nightshelter and three residential houses in London. Their work is usually with the most vulnerable rough sleepers and involves visiting the homeless and responding to their needs, often by providing shelter or just a chat. Whilst living in the houses, residents and workers share the same lifestyle and take part equally in decision making, both in the house and in the community as a whole. Meals are eaten together and household chores are shared.

Volunteers required to participate in a range of duties including cooking and cleaning, street work, driving, sorting donated items, taking part in group meetings, administration, fundraising, campaigning, operating an outreach team and liaising with other organisations. These duties are varied and involve a great deal of responsibility and can be physically and emotionally demanding. Approximately 30 positions offered annually.

Ages 19+. Applicants should have enthusiasm, a sense of humour and a desire to work hard in a community to make a difference to the quality of people's lives. Good English essential.

Placements all year; minimum of 3 months

5½ day week with 40 hours off. Full board and lodging provided as well as travel within the community. £25 per week pocket money plus expenses.

SOCIETY OF VOLUNTARY ASSOCIATES

Society of Voluntary Associates, Head Office, 350 Kennington Road, London SE11 4LH

℡ 0171-793 0404   🖷 0171-735 4410

Throughout England and Wales

A national charity which has been promoting volunteer action in the penal field since 1975, working in partnership with the primary, statutory and voluntary agencies serving the criminal justice system. SOVA believes everybody is touched by crime and that members of the community have a contribution to make in preventing and reducing crime.

Volunteers are required to assist staff in managing community-based projects which recruit, select, train and support volunteers working with offenders, their families and young people at risk. The nature of the work depends on the volunteer's own interests and abilities.

Ages 18+. No experience necessary but applicants must have a strong interest in crime prevention and criminal justice. Placements are especially suitable for people interested in pursuing a career in social work or the probation service. All nationalities welcome. **B D PH** depending on nature and location of placement.

3 months-1 year

Hours worked by negotiation; generally 1 day per week. Volunteer employee public liability insurance provided. No wages, but expenses paid.

Full induction provided

Recruitment all year. Applicants should contact the Head Office, above, and will then be given information on the project nearest to where they live.

SUE RYDER FOUNDATION

The Administration Officer, Sue Ryder Foundation, Sue Ryder Home, Cavendish, Sudbury, Suffolk CO10 8AY

℗ Glemsford (01787) 280252

Throughout England and Scotland

A Christian-based charity founded in 1952 with over 20 homes for the sick, disabled and for cancer care. Seeks to render personal service to those in need and to give affection to those who are unloved, regardless of age, race or creed. The homes are a living memorial to the millions who gave their lives during two world wars in defence of human values, and to the countless others who are suffering and dying today as a result of persecution.

Volunteers are needed at headquarters, in certain homes and at the retreat house in Norfolk. Work includes helping with patients, routine office work, assisting in the kitchen, garden, museum, coffee and gift shop, general maintenance and other essential work arising. Experienced volunteers also needed for secretarial work and nursing.

Ages 16+. Applicants should be flexible and adaptable. Qualifications or experience not essential, but an advantage; preference given to students or graduates. Doctor's certificate required. EEA nationals only; Polish and Czech nationals may apply through the Foundation's representative in their country. Good standard of English required.

Two months minimum placement

Board, lodging and £15 per week pocket money provided

Two week trial period. On-the-job instruction provided.

Recruitment all year; larger number of volunteers required in summer

SURVIVAL

Survival, 11-15 Emerald Street, London WC1N 3QL

℗ 0171-242 1441   ☐ 0171-242 1771   ☐ survival@gn.apc.org
🌐 http://www.survival.org.uk

London, England

A worldwide organisation supporting tribal peoples. It stands for their right to decide their own future and helps them protect their lives, lands and human rights.

20-40 volunteers are needed each year to help with general clerical work in the London office. This may involve accounts/book keeping, fundraising, picture library administration, helping on research projects, data entry, library administration, press and publicity work.

Ages 16+. Volunteers are allocated work according to their experience, skills and abilities. They should be conscientious, hard working and reliable, with an interest in the work of Survival.

Three months minimum commitment, working at least one day a week, preferred

Work is unpaid, but travel costs within the London area are reimbursed

Applications accepted throughout the year

TOURISM CONCERN

Tourism Concern, Southlands College, Wimbledon Parkside, London SW19 5NN

© 0181-944 0464   📠 0181-944 6583

South London, England

A membership network set up in 1989 to bring together people with an active concern for tourism's impact on community and environment, both in the UK and worldwide. Aims to raise the issues of the impacts of tourism on people at the receiving end, especially in Third World countries.

A number of volunteers are needed to work in the London office, helping with tasks such as library work, wordprocessing, graphics, design, translation and fundraising

Age 18+. Fluent English essential; knowledge of other languages useful. Volunteers should have a keen interest in tourism issues and in working for an organisation that campaigns for just, participatory and sustainable tourism. In general, they will need to be fairly well travelled in order to have a good awareness of the issues. They must have skills relevant to the work involved. All nationalities welcome

Flexible hours, 5/6 day week. Work is unpaid but travel costs within England provided. Applicants must arrange their own insurance and accommodation.

WINANT CLAYTON
VOLUNTEERS ASSOCIATION

The Coordinator, Winant Clayton Volunteers Association, Davenant Centre, 179 Whitechapel Road, London E1 1DU

℡ 0171-375 0547

Throughout the United States, and in the UK for US citizens

A community service exchange scheme operating since 1959 (American volunteers have been coming to the UK since 1948), which aims to offer assistance to city projects in the eastern states and provides insights into a different culture

The scheme sends about 20 volunteers each year to the United States to work on a variety of community projects; simultaneously a group of Americans travel to the UK to undertake similar work. Projects include assisting at psychiatric rehabilitation centres and homes for emotionally disturbed children, working with the elderly and housebound, on AIDS projects, and in day camps/centres for deprived inner-city teenagers/children.

Age 19+ . Applicants are not expected to be experts but need to show a genuine interest in people, have a sense of humour, be open minded and flexible enough to adapt to the unexpected. Experience of working with children, youth and community or other voluntary social work preferred. Volunteers are matched with placements so that existing skills are utilised and new ones are developed. The scheme is open to UK/US residents only. **B D PH W** depending on ability.

Placements last 3 months, June-September

5 day week; hours comparable to full-time staff. Board, accommodation and pocket money provided. Participants pay travel and insurance costs; small grants may be available. Orientation course held in April.

Applications should be submitted by mid January. Interviews held during February, and successful candidates are informed by 1 March. Registration fee £12. Applicants in the US should contact Winant Clayton Volunteers, St Bartholomew's, 109 East 50th Street, New York NY10022 ℡ (212) 7511616 ext 271.

YOUTH ACTION FOR PEACE

Youth Action for Peace (YAP), Methold House, North Street, Worthing BN11 1DU

✆ Worthing (01903) 528619   ▭ (01903) 528611

Worldwide

Coordinates international youth exchanges and organises international seminars and training courses. The international secretariat is in Brussels and the movement operates through a network of national branches and partner organisations in Europe, the Middle East, North Africa and South America. The range of projects is varied and all of them aim to support local communities and to encourage young people to be more aware of other cultures.

Projects include working with disabled children, the homeless, the environment and adult education. The purpose of the Long Term Volunteer programme is to integrate volunteers into a local community project, giving them the opportunity to learn a new language and to discover a region. In exchange, the volunteers help the project in its management and in organising local action. Opportunities for participants to work in one of the national offices and also to participate in one of the international activities.

Ages 18-30; upper limit of 25 for some projects. No experience or qualifications necessary. Participants should be motivated to work with an international team of young people, be adaptable and responsible. All nationalities welcome. **B D PH W**

6 or 9 month placements

February-March. 30-35 hour week. Board, accommodation, pocket money and 75% travel reimbursement provided. No travel arrangements made. Volunteers advised to take out their own insurance. Application fee £45.

Orientation course provided for those going to the Middle East, Nagrehb and Eastern Europe. Volunteers requested to write a report on their project.

Selection takes place in May/June

Say L O to L A when you have a home exchange with a family in the US. Swap John for Jean-Pierre on a 2 week Anglo-French exchange. And make your own Soviet union when you stay with a family in Moscow. **HOME FROM HOME** has hundreds of opportunities and a wealth of information to help you discover a different way of life.

If you are fed up with being packaged on holiday; if you want to improve your language skills and make lasting friendships; if exams are looming and your vocabulary is a bit limited; if you really want to get to know a country, its language and culture, then the Central Bureau guide **HOME FROM HOME** will provide you with all the information needed to discover a different way of life in a way not possible when visiting as a mere tourist.

Being welcomed into the home of a foreign family offers an excellent opportunity to immerse yourself in another culture. All the essential advice and information needed to arrange a successful and enjoyable homestay, exchange, term stay or home exchange is in **HOME FROM HOME**, which details over 100 bona fide organisations arranging stays and exchanges in 50 countries worldwide. Each organisation is profiled, giving information on its aims and activities; an important factor is to have the most compatible host family, so full details of matching are provided. Information is also given on those organisations that can arrange language courses during the homestay or exchange.

Most host families are only too happy to include visitors in their activities, but where additional leisure or sport activities are available, **HOME FROM HOME** provides details on those too. The full costs of the stay or programme are given, including any agency fee, meals, travel and insurance. Where additional costs are involved, for example escorted travel or tuition fees, these are also indicated.

As well as full information on each homestay or exchange, **HOME FROM HOME** also gives practical advice on health, insurance requirements, visas, passports, travel, dealing with emergencies and guidelines for visitors as well as host families.

HOME FROM HOME has opportunities for those aged 8+; from 1 day to a whole year; from Austria to Uruguay; from Britain to Japan; from staying with a French family for two weeks to spending a year in school in Canada; from swapping your home in Britain for a holiday in one in the US. For further information on the Bureau's publications and programmes contact the Information Desk on © 0171-389 4004.

HOME FROM HOME is published biannually   Third edition   ISBN 0 900087 99 4   £8.99

YOUTH WORK/
CHILDCARE

Many opportunities exist in a year between to work with children and teenagers outside their family environment, at clubs, playschemes and special centres both in Britain and abroad. The work may include caring for children with disabilities, learning difficulties, emotional or social problems. The opportunities included in this section all last for at least five months. Many short-term opportunities are available during school summer holidays on playschemes or at holiday centres for disadvantaged children. For further details check out the Children's Projects and Community Work sections in the Central Bureau's annual guide **Working Holidays**. Organisations recruiting volunteers to work with children and teenagers are looking especially for mature, responsible individuals, usually over the age of 18, preferably with formal or informal experience of similar work. The 1989 Children Act requires all those working in Britain with children under 8 to submit their details for police screening.

Are you genuinely fond of children? This could seem an obvious question, but you may well be living and working with them for 24 hours a day, which can be very demanding. As well as a real liking for kids this requires immense physical and mental energy, patience, and the ability to work hard. Can you exert discipline without being dictatorial? Can you think up enough games and activities to avoid boredom and unruly behaviour? Can you handle having the mickey taken out of your accent, clothes or hairstyle? Do you have the patience and care to help handicapped children to dress, feed themselves or go to the toilet? Can you deal firmly with tantrums, arbitrate between squabblers, comfort someone who is hurt or homesick? These questions should be considered carefully before you commit yourself to working with children. But don't paint yourself too bleak a picture - the work may be challenging and exhausting but is also tremendously exhilarating. Helping young people discover and develop creative and social skills can prove to be a uniquely rewarding experience.

Working as an au pair is a practical and economic way to spend some time learning the language and experiencing the way of life in another country. Although au pair positions in most countries are now open to both sexes, many families stick to the traditional female au pair and as agencies recruit accordingly, male applicants will find opportunities more limited. The term *au pair* means *on equal terms*, and this means an au pair should be treated as a member of a family and not as a servant or domestic. In return for board, lodging and pocket money you will be expected to help with light household duties including simple cooking and the care of any children, for a maximum of 30 hours per week. This should allow you sufficient time to meet friends, go sightseeing and take a part-time course in the language. Unfortunately, there is no absolute guarantee that these conditions will be met as arrangements depend almost totally on goodwill and cooperation between the host family and the au pair, so you should be aware of this and make sure terms and conditions are firmly established before accepting a post. The agency or its representative should be able to intervene if problems arise and arrangements break down for any reason, but remember that a good working relationship will require goodwill and tolerance on both sides. Au pair positions are open to those aged 17-27/30; stays are usually for a minimum of six months. There may be a limited number of summer stays of 2/3 months, depending on the country. The work involves general household chores such as ironing, bedmaking, dusting, vacuuming, sewing, washing up, preparing simple meals and taking the children to and from school, plus general childcare duties. A typical working day is of 5/6 hours, with 3/4 evenings babysitting in a 6 day week. The remainder of the evenings, 1 full day and 3 afternoons per week are usually free. In addition to board and lodging approx £30-£35 per week pocket money is provided. There is usually an agency service charge, and applicants are responsible for their travel and insurance costs, although most agencies can provide information and advice. In some cases, normally after a stay of 12 months or more, the host family will pay a single or return fare. As a general rule, those wishing to work as au pairs should enjoy working with children, have experience of doing housework and at least a basic knowledge of the relevant language.

Agencies in the UK may charge up to a maximum of £40 for finding an au pair position provided that they use an agent abroad as an intermediary and they are not receiving any payment from the host family. This, however, does not apply to au pair programmes in the United States, see below. The fee is payable only after the applicant has been offered and accepted a position. The au pair agency should ensure that the correct arrangements are made for entry into the chosen country; however it is wise to check these requirements yourself with the relevant consulate. Make sure you know who is responsible for making travel arrangements and paying the fares; usually agencies will give advice on travel, but applicants make their own arrangements and pay the costs. It is essential to have sufficient funds or insurance to pay the fare home in case of emergency. Before leaving be sure you have a valid passport, a visa/work permit as necessary, and a letter of invitation from the host family, setting out details of the arrangements that have been made, including details of pocket money and any contributions that may be payable to national insurance or other schemes in the destination country.

The au pair programme in the United States is open to 18-26 year olds with practical child care experience, a full driving licence, an acceptable level of spoken English and the ability to commit to a full year. Character and childcare references and a medical certificate are required. Most families prefer non-smokers. Au pairs work for a maximum of 45 hours a week with at least 1½ days off each week and a whole weekend each month. Work is centred around the children and includes active duties such as feeding and playing and passive supervision such as babysitting. Benefits include return flights, $128.25 weekly payment (which is expected to increase to $139.05 per week from 1 October 1997, subject to Congress approval), $500 tuition allowance, two weeks paid vacation and an optional 13th month to travel throughout the US. Applicants are interviewed and, if accepted, matched according to interests and experience with a selected host family and issued with a J-1 Exchange Visitor Visa authorised by the US Government. A short orientation programme is held on arrival and au pairs have access to a local representative during the length of their stay. Agencies will also require a good faith deposit of around £350 which is refunded on completion of the programme.

Some agencies can also arrange positions in Australia and Canada. However, these tend only to be open to those with extensive childcare experience and/or qualifications. There is also a growing demand for English-speaking au pairs to teach English informally to both children and parents of the host family. This is particularly the case in Scandinavia, Greece, Spain, Israel and in East/ Central European countries.

Au pair posts should not be confused with regular domestic employment, posts as nannies or mother's helps, or posts advertised as demi pair or au pair plus, which are covered by different employment and entry regulations.

Jane Madsen spent a year in America, on an au pair placement. Here she looks back on the time she had:

I left college at 18 and had big decisions to make: what did I want from life and how was I going to go about it? I had long talks with my tutors and parents and the outcome was that my mind was set on going to America.

Everyone was surprised and bet me that I wouldn't go through with it. Because my friends said such negative things it just made me more

determined to make it work and prove everyone wrong.

I contacted Students Abroad and a day after, my application had been given out to prospective families. I received a phone-call from a family living in Salt Lake City, Utah. They sounded fantastic and had three children. I accepted their offer and 10 days later the big day dawned. When the plane landed at Salt Lake City Airport my head spun with feelings of anticipation and excitement as I thought about my new family, my new job, and a different way of life.

My first few days were spent getting to know the children as well as the new area I now lived in. Driving on the right hand side of the road wasn't as tricky as I thought it would be. After a week my family took me for my first ski lesson which was very exciting even if I did spend more time sat in the snow than on my feet! The more I settled in the easier it became and I really enjoyed my work. Then the dreaded homesickness came. I had been in Utah six weeks by now and the following weeks were very testing. But the homesickness went and I really felt a part of the family and was included in everything they did. Before I knew it summer was here, and I got to do some fun things such as hiking along Robber's Roost Canyon in Southern Utah with friends or going to the horse races in Wyoming for a day. I felt proud of myself for exploring different States, each one with their own laws, like visiting a different country each time.

Christmas Day arrived and it was the first white Christmas I remember seeing. The children spent the day playing with their toys and in the afternoon we went to Temple Square to see the lights before eating our Christmas dinner. February was here before I knew it. Saying goodbye was heartbreaking and I cried so much I could have created the next Salt Lake! The family were absolutely wonderful to me and made me feel such a part of their life. I'm glad and feel honoured that they chose me as their au pair. Spending a year in a different country has taught me a lot and it's an experience that will play a big part in my future life and career.

The agencies listed below are just some of the many operating in Britain. The countries in which they make au pair placements are given in *italics*. A wider selection together with comprehensive details on the regulations governing au pair and other childcare posts can be found in **WORKING HOLIDAYS**, the Central Bureau's complete international guide to seasonal job opportunities, available through good bookshops or direct from the Central Bureau; © 0171-389 4880 for further information.

Academy Au Pair & Nanny Agency 42 Cedarhurst Drive, Eltham, London SE9 5LP
© 0181-294 1191
Australia, Austria, Belgium, Canada, Denmark, France, Germany, Italy, the Netherlands, Spain

Au Pair in America 37 Queens Gate, London SW7 5HR © 0171-581 7322 ⍐ 0171-581 7384
United States

Avalon Au Pairs 7 Highway, Crowthorne, Berkshire RG45 6HE
©/⍐ Crowthorne (01344) 778246
⎙ aupair.surrey@mcmail.com

🏳 http://www.yell.co.uk/sites/aupair
Various European countries

Bunters Au Pair & Domestic Agency 8 Fern Lea Drive, Macclesfield, Cheshire SK11 8PQ
© Macclesfield (01625) 614534
⍐ (01625) 617030
Austria, Belgium, France, Germany, Italy, Spain

Edgware Au Pair Agency 19 Manor Park Crescent, Edgware, Middlesex HA8 7NH © 0181-952 5522 ⍐ 0181-951 5219/1005
United States

Helping Hands Au Pair & Domestic Agency 39 Rutland Avenue, Thorpe Bay, Essex SS1 2XJ
© Southend-on-Sea (01702) 602067
Austria, Belgium, Denmark, France, Germany, Italy, Netherlands, Norway, Spain, Switzerland

International Catholic Society For Girls St Patrick's International Centre, 24 Great Chapel Street, London W1V 3AF © 0171-734 2156
⍐ 0171-287 6282
Austria, Belgium, France, Germany

Jolaine Agency 18 Escot Way, Barnet, Hertfordshire EN5 3AN
© 0181-449 1334 ⍐ 0181-449 9183
Belgium, France, Germany, Italy, Spain, Turkey

Langtrain International Torquay Road, Foxrock, Dublin 18, Ireland
© Dublin (00 353 1) 289 3876
Austria, Belgium, Canada, Denmark, France, Germany, Ireland, Italy, Spain, Switzerland

Mondial Agency 32 Links Road, West Wickham, Kent BR4 0QW
© 0181-777 0510
Austria, France, Spain

Mum's Army 10 Hither Green Lane, Abbey Park, Redditch B98 9BW
✆ Redditch (01527) 61661
℻ (01527) 596056
France, Germany, Italy, Netherlands, Spain

Nannies Now Avondale House 63 Sydney Road, Haywards Heath, West Sussex RH16 1QD ✆ Haywards Heath (01444) 453566 ℻ (01444) 440445
Australia, Finland, United States

Problems Unlimited Agency
24 St Luke's Road, Old Windsor, Berkshire SL4 2QQ ✆ Windsor (01753) 830101 ℻ (01753) 831194
Belgium, France, Germany, Netherlands, Spain

Solihull Au Pair & Nanny Agency
1565 Stratford Road, Hall Green, Birmingham B28 9JA ✆ 0121-733 6444
℻ 0121-733 6555
Denmark, Finland, Greece, Switzerland Turkey

South Eastern Au Pair Bureau
39 Rutland Avenue, Southend-on-Sea, Essex SS1 2XJ ✆ Southend (01702) 601911 ℻ (01702) 462857
Denmark, Norway

Students Abroad 3 Kneller Road, New Malden, Surrey KT3 5ND
✆ 0181-330 0777 ℻ 0181-330 0345
Austria, Belgium, Canada, France, Germany, Greece, Israel, Italy, the Netherlands, Spain, Switzerland, Turkey, United States

Universal Care Chester House, 9 Windsor End, Beaconsfield, Buckinghamshire HP9 2JJ
✆ Beaconsfield (01494) 678811
Austria, Belgium, Denmark, France, Germany, Italy, Spain, Switzerland

Adventure & Computer Holidays Ltd

AFS/Intercultural Education Programmes

Beannachar Ltd

British Forces Germany

Camphill Am Bodensee

Camphill Rudolf Steiner Schools

Camphill Special School - Beaver Run

Friends of Israel Educational Trust

Nansen Internasjonale Center

Oxford Kilburn (OK) Club

Schools Appointment Service

SPW

Theatrino

ADVENTURE AND COMPUTER HOLIDAYS LTD

Adventure and Computer Holidays Ltd, PO Box 183, Dorking, Surrey RH5 6FA

©/☞ Abinger (01306) 730716

Surrey and Cornwall

Established in 1983 by a qualified teacher, school governor and member of the British Activity Holiday Association's Safety Committee. Organises activities and events for children aged 4-14, including residential adventure holidays, day camps, weekly clubs and children's parties.

Opportunities for camp leaders and activity instructors to work on day camps near Dorking in Surrey or on residential holidays in Cornwall

Ages 20+ for day camps; 21+ for residential holidays. Residential holiday staff should also have a clean driving licence. Experience of working with children necessary for all positions. UK nationals only.

Positions available during half terms and school holidays, with a few additional residential positions available April-September

Day camp staff must find accommodation for themselves within easy reach of the camp or in London; daily transport to the camp from London is provided. Accommodation provided if required for residential staff in single or twin rooms. Salary £130 per week for day camp staff, plus £30 for those accompanying children on the London coach; £160 per week for residential holiday staff.

Orientation course organised

Write for an application form

AFS / INTERCULTURAL
EDUCATION PROGRAMMES

The National Director, AFS/IEP, Arden House, Wellington Street, Bingley, West Yorkshire BD16 2NB

✆ Bingley (01274) 560677   ✉ (01274) 567675

A wide range of countries in Latin America, Africa and Asia

AFS is an international, voluntary non-profitmaking organisation represented in 55 countries. It has operated in the UK since 1947 and is a registered charity. Provides intercultural learning opportunities to help people develop the knowledge, skills and understanding needed to create a more just and peaceful world. The only organisation of its kind to receive a citation from the United Nations in recognition of its work for world youth.

Opportunities to spend 6 months abroad living with a volunteer host family whilst working alongside local people on community social projects for underprivileged children and young people, gaining another language and an insider's appreciation of the culture

Ages 18-29. Applicants should be flexible, adaptable and interested in other cultures and ways of life. It is not a requirement to speak the language of the intended country before departure.

6 months departing in January/February or July

Cost £2,750. All participants are given advice and support on doing their own fundraising. The fee covers travel to and from the host country, expenses involving the project, medical insurance, orientation courses and ongoing support from volunteers and staff in the host country and in the UK.

Orientation courses held before departure to help participants prepare for the experience, and at regular intervals during the 6 months. Intensive language training provided during the first month.

Applications accepted up to 18 months in advance of departure. Prefer to receive applications at least 6 months before departure, but can occasionally accept late applicants.

BEANNACHAR LTD

Elisabeth Phethean, Housemother, Beannachar Ltd, Banchory-Devenick, Aberdeen AB12 5YL

℗ Aberdeen (01224) 861825/868605/861200/869138

Outskirts of Aberdeen, Scotland

A Camphill community for further education and training, with the aims of providing meaningful work and a home for young adults in the 17-30 age range who have varying degrees of handicap or disturbance

Volunteers are required to help care for students and work with them on a communal basis. Work involves gardening, cooking, building, cleaning, looking after animals, laundry, weaving and woodwork. Volunteers are also expected to participate in other community activities such as folk dancing, drama, festivals, walking, swimming, games and outings.

Ages 19+. Volunteers should be enthusiastic, caring and willing to learn. No previous experience or qualifications necessary. **B D PH**

6-12+ months

Volunteers work a 6 day week and receive £25 per week pocket money, plus full board and lodging in the community. Students and staff live together in three large family units. Four weeks holiday for those working a full year.

Volunteers are invited to join an introductory course and attend occasional evening lectures

Recruitment all year

BRITISH FORCES GERMANY

Ms Pamela Bolton, Chief Youth Service Officer, BFG Youth Service, GI UKSC(G), BFPO 140

℗ (00 49) 2161 47 3176

Northern Germany: Bruggen, Gutersloh, Hameln, Krefeld, Osnabrück, Paderborn, Rheindahlen and Wildenrath (locations may change as a result of reduction of British Forces)

The BFG Youth Service was established in 1969 and provides an organisation and structure for all youth provision in those parts of northern Germany in which British Forces are stationed

Operates a Trainee Youth Worker Scheme to recruit workers for youth clubs. Particularly suitable for mature young adults wishing to gain full-time professional training, and for newly-qualified youth workers, for whom the work will serve as their Youth Service Probationary year. Work involves being responsible, under professional supervision, for the management of youth clubs with a mixed membership of 100-300 children aged 10-16.

Ages 18-25. Applicants should be socially mature, persuasive and outgoing, capable of working on their own initiative but also with committees and other adults. UK nationals only. Applicants must be single or unaccompanied, and have experience of working with young people. Knowledge of German welcome but not essential.

Twelve months, beginning August/September

Honorarium, accommodation and food allowance provided. Trainee youth workers are entitled to 5 weeks annual leave and the use of certain BFG facilities. Hours of work similar to those of youth workers in Britain, including evening sessions and weekend work.

Recruitment usually takes place in late spring

CAMPHILL AM BODENSEE

Sekretariat, Camphill am Bodensee, Heimsonderschule Brachenreuthe, 88662 Überlingen-Bodensee, Germany

✆ (00 49 7551) 80070   ☎ (00 49 7551) 800750

Near Überlingen, Germany

A residential school for mentally handicapped children, based near Lake Constance. The school cares for 80 children aged 4-17, and consists of 10 house communities, a therapy building, a community hall, a garden and a farm. Emphasis is placed on catering for the needs and problems of autistic children. The work is based on the teachings of Rudolf Steiner, and aims to help the children achieve individual independence within the Camphill Trust communities.

Volunteers are required to live and work with the children, helping out in classes and with bathing, dressing and other personal tasks. Volunteers are also encouraged to participate in the cultural, recreational and social aspects of community life.

Ages 19+. No previous experience or qualifications necessary. Volunteers should be caring, enthusiastic and willing to help wherever they are needed. Basic knowledge of German necessary.

6-12+ months, usually starting mid August

Volunteers work a 6 day week, and have 5 weeks holiday in a year. Full board single/double room accommodation, insurance and DM350 per month pocket money and social security provided. Volunteers pay their own travel expenses.

Those staying for a year have the opportunity to take part in a training course in curative education

Recruitment all year

CAMPHILL RUDOLF STEINER SCHOOLS

Central Office, Camphill Rudolf Steiner Schools, Murtle Estate, Bieldside, Aberdeen AB1 9EP

✆ Aberdeen (01224) 867935   ✉ (01224) 868420

Outside Aberdeen, Scotland

Founded in 1939 by the late Dr Karl König, the Camphill schools offer residential schooling and therapy, based on the teachings of Rudolf Steiner, for children and young adults in need of special care. Co-workers and their families live with the 111 pupils in 19 separate house communities on the three small estates that comprise the schools' grounds.

Co-workers are required to live with children in family units, helping with the care of children and the running of the house and garden, and of the estate. There are 40-50 vacancies for volunteers each year.

Ages 20-40. No previous experience or qualifications required, but applicants should have an open mind and an interest in children, community life, curative education and anthroposophy.

Twelve months minimum, beginning August, late October, early January and late April

Co-workers receive board and lodging plus £25 per week pocket money. There is one day off each week, otherwise no separation between on and off duty. Volunteers from mainland Europe are given return fare after 1 year.

One year introductory course available and 3 year course in curative education

Recruitment all year

CAMPHILL SPECIAL SCHOOL - BEAVER RUN

Applications Group, Camphill Special School - Beaver Run, 1784 Fairview Road, Glenmoore, Pennsylvania 19343, United States

℗ (00 1 610) 469 9236   ▱ (00 1 610) 469 9758

Pennsylvania, United States

A children's village community of approx 150 people, of which nearly half are mentally handicapped children and adolescents living with houseparents, teachers and their own families

Volunteers are required to live and work together with mentally handicapped/disabled children and adolescents, and the families of long-term co-workers. They help to care for small groups of children, with responsibilities in the home and in the school.

Ages 20-35. Some previous experience of work with children with or without mental handicaps is desirable. Volunteers should be enthusiastic and keen to learn.

Six months minimum; one year placements, August-August, preferred

Volunteers accompany the day's schedule of the children and have time off in between, plus one full day per week. Children return home during vacation periods, and additional time off during these periods can be arranged. Board, lodging and insurance provided. Participants receive $130 monthly pocket money plus $500 bonus for summer vacation after 12 months' service. Travel costs not provided.

Foundation course available

Recruitment all year

FRIENDS OF ISRAEL
EDUCATIONAL TRUST

The Director, Friends of Israel Educational Trust, PO Box 7545, London NW2 2QZ

© 0171-435 6803   ☎ 0171-794 0291   ✉ foi_asg@msn.com

Israel

Founded in 1976, the Trust aims to promote in the UK a knowledge of Israel and its people via talks, lectures, presentations and working visits to Israel

The scheme annually offers 12 school leavers a chance to spend time in Israel. The programme involves working in youth centres as part of a community service programme in both rural and urban environments, working on a kibbutz and teaching in high schools. Participants take part in seminars, organised tours and independent travel.

Ages 18+. UK nationals only. Applicants should be open to new experiences and want to participate in the pioneering spirit of modern Israel. They should be prepared to undertake any tasks/challenges set. No experience necessary, but most applicants are post-A level, or equivalent, school leavers.

Five months, February-August

Travel, basic lodging, food in canteen or self-catering and basic insurance provided, plus back-up from specialists throughout the programme. Token amount of pocket money provided on the kibbutz. Approx 30 hour week.

Full debriefing given on return, with ongoing contact

Apply by 1 July. Applicants should explain in an essay of minimum 400 words their reasons for wishing to visit Israel, and enclose two references, one academic, one personal. Shortlisted candidates are interviewed.

NANSEN INTERNASJONALE CENTER

Recruitment Officer, Nansen Internasjonale Center, Barnegården Breivold, Nesset, 1433 Vinterbro, Norway

℗ (00 47 64) 94 67 15/91

Vinterbro, Norway

Aims to help teenagers with social problems at a relief and activity centre in a renovated farm 25 km south of Oslo. The work is based on total participation and involvement from voluntary staff, permanent staff and residents.

Volunteers work alongside permanent staff, and partake in all aspects of farm life and the daily welfare of teenagers, including looking after the farm animals, cleaning and cooking, creative work, hobbies and sports activities, planning short and long term projects and participating in tours. The work is physically and mentally demanding but rewarding. The staff is international; working languages are Norwegian and English.

Ages 22+. Applicants should be mature, practical, motivated, committed to working with children in need of care, and willing to take part in all activities. Experience useful but not essential. Driving licence essential.

12 months, starting any time of year

Long working hours on a rota basis, with approx 4 days free per fortnight and approx one week every second month. Board and lodging plus NKr500 per week pocket money provided. Volunteers arrange their own travel and insurance.

First 2 weeks are an induction period. Guidance seminar held twice yearly. Weekly guidance meeting held with permanent staff members.

Apply at least 4 months in advance as it takes 3 months for work permit clearance; enclose IRC for countries outside EU

OXFORD KILBURN (OK) CLUB

Oxford Kilburn (OK) Club, 45 Denmark Road, Kilburn, London NW6 5BP

✆/☎ 0171-624 6292

London, England

Established in 1958, originally as a boys club, the OK Club is a Christian-based organisation which works closely with the community of South Kilburn in London, visiting homes, schools and churches and running a variety of activities and groups throughout the year for families in the area. The three main age groups within the Club are Juniors (8-11 years), Inters (11-14 years) and Seniors (14+). The overall aim of the Club is to provide for the physical, educational, social, recreational and spiritual needs of the young people and their families. Also organises an extensive holiday programme, including day trips, camping weekends and adventure holidays in the UK and abroad.

Youth workers required to assist in the organisation and running of afternoon and youth clubs. Various administrative duties involved. Tasks include training the youngsters in life skills and social awareness, together with sports, games, art and crafts. Opportunities for travel in the UK and overseas. Three positions available annually.

Ages 18-25. Previous experience of working with children essential. Applicants should be committed Christians. All nationalities welcome. **B D PH** where work allows

Placements begin in September and last one year

40 hour week. Salary £100 per month plus board, accommodation, insurance and travel. On-the-job training provided.

SCHOOLS APPOINTMENT SERVICE

Schools Appointment Service, 23 Peters Close, Prestwood, Buckinghamshire HP16 9ET

℗ Great Missenden (01494) 863027 ▱ (01494) 864122

Mainly in the UK

A recruitment service set up in 1994 which places non-teaching residential staff in independent schools to help organise activities and to assist with the care and welfare of pupils.

Offers up to 36 placements per year as assistants to matrons and housemasters/mistresses and as boarding, games and nursery assistants. Tasks may include supervising the children's morning routine and helping with homework; participating in after-school clubs, games and evening activities; supervising domestic staff, mending and sorting children's laundry; assisting the matron with the care of children's minor ailments; accompanying children on visits and excursions; helping with music, art, drama, cookery and sports lessons; and undertaking remedial work with special needs pupils and teaching in the kindergarten or nursery class.

Ages 18-22+. Applicants should have completed A levels or equivalent, or have just graduated. Driving licence, first aid qualifications, crafts and sports skills useful. Experience of boarding school life preferable but not essential. Applicants should be reliable, active, energetic, team-spirited and keen to gain experience of childcare prior to a medical/teaching career. All nationalities welcome.

Placements last up to one academic year

45-55 hours per week. Night duties and off-duty times are organised on a rota basis. Salary £60-£120 per week with board, accommodation and interview expenses usually provided.

Write for an application form

S P W

Jim Cogan, Director, SPW, 17 Dean's Yard, London SW1P 3PB

✆ 0171-222 0138/976 8070   ✉ 0171-233 0008/963 1006

Southern India

An educational charity set up in 1985 to organise placements for young people wanting to work in developing countries. Its main purpose is to provide those on a year between with challenging experiences outside formal education and focus their efforts on developing countries where educational and social services are poor.

Placements involve working with children at institutions in south India including orphanages, homes for retarded children, and rehabilitation centres for children with polio. Secondments are in pairs, ideally of two close friends of the same sex.

Ages 18-25. Applicants are usually taking a year out before, during or after going into further education and are expected to have/to be about to gain high A level (or equivalent) grades and have a real commitment. Flexibility and openness to other cultures essential, as is resourcefulness to cope with living in spartan conditions. Applicants must be fluent in English and be strongly supported by individual and institutional references. **D PH** where practicable.

6 months, beginning September or January

Cost approx £2,250, of which £1,000 covers expenses such as travel, insurance, inoculations, £750 sponsorship which provides basic living allowance, training and administration overseas, and £500 sponsorship for a local volunteer. All volunteers are asked to raise extra money to contribute towards the mini-projects which they carry out whilst overseas. Optional school sponsorship scheme through which schools agree to provide financial support for their participating students.

Obligatory pre-departure and in-country training sessions, including basic local language learning

Early application advised

THEATRINO

Theatrino, via Roma 54, 18038 San Remo, Italy

© (00 39 184) 50 60 70

Throughout Italy

A theatre company involved with teaching English to Italian children

Young actors required to help children and teenagers improve their English through sketches varying from slapstick and magic to short Shakespearean extracts. Tours can be tiring but offer rewarding opportunities to work in Italian primary and secondary schools.

Ages 19+. Applicants should have English as their mother tongue, experience of working in theatre for education and a genuine interest in children. Knowledge of Italian useful.

Placements last for 2-3 months during the summer or 5 months during the winter. Salary £500 per month. Accommodation, insurance and transport provided.

Looking to travel the world on a shoestring? Keen to experience more of a country than discos and high-rise hotels? In need of something special to spice up your cv? Our free **TEN WAYS** posters have dozens of ideas to help you do some thing a little different.

If, for you, going abroad means more than lounging about on a lilo, **TEN WAYS TO DISCOVER THE WORLD** can help you to get fully immersed into the local lifestyle. It has lots of ideas for meeting local people and living, studying and working abroad so that you can experience a different culture firsthand. You'll even get a chance to practise your language skills too. This poster offers options for anyone aged 8-80, including homestays and exchanges, home swaps and penfriends.

There are three posters available, each focusing on a different aspect of travel and each giving - yes you've guessed it - ten ideas for spending time abroad. As well as information on the types of opportunities available, the posters include feedback from those who have already taken up the challenge, and helpful advice on what to do next.

So your ideas are flowing, but your cash isn't - well **TEN WAYS TO WORK & TRAVEL** will give you some interesting options for short-term work around the world so that you can finance your travels. Not only is seasonal work an ideal way of earning some extra money, but it also gives you the chance to try out something completely different, develop some practical skills and meet new friends. If you're looking to do something really worthwhile with your time, then the section on volunteering will give you a range of inexpensive alternatives. And if jetting off around the world isn't for you, there's a section of finding worthwhile work a little closer to home.

After taking a year out you'll be bursting with enthusiasm and eager to persuade others to do the same, so why not tempt them with a copy of **TEN WAYS TO FILL THE GAP**. This eye-catching poster is bound to get even the most lethargic thinking beyond their exams.

TEN WAYS posters are free, so if you'd like a set, simply send an A4 SAE (or 2 IRCs and an addressed envelope if overseas), to 10 Ways, Publications Unit, Central Bureau for Educational Visits & Exchanges, 10 Spring Gardens, London SW1A 2BN. Bulk orders for schools, colleges and careers offices are available for a nominal charge.

CHRISTIAN SERVICE

The organisations in this section recruit volunteers for projects based both in Britain and abroad. Opportunities may involve social service, assisting with the work of churches in their local communities, evangelical outreach work, or a combination of all of these.

In general, applicants must have a Christian commitment or at least be thinking seriously about their faith. Most agencies will not pry too deeply into an applicant's beliefs as long as it is clear they are happy to share their Christian faith with others. In some cases, however, applicants must be referred by their local church. Volunteers who do not have a Christian faith are likely to find difficulties in relating to the people and community with whom they are working, and are better advised to apply through other agencies, such as those covered in the **COMMUNITY & SOCIAL SERVICE** section.

You will need to think carefully about why you feel called upon to do Christian service. Perhaps you want to bear witness to your faith and share it with others. You may be looking for a chance to find out more about your own personal beliefs. You may want to try yourself out for a limited period to see whether you have a calling for a lifetime of Christian service. You may want to discover how Christians live in other countries, or in other parts of Britain, and work in solidarity with them. Or you may feel more motivated to perform a social service by improving conditions for God's people in need. Roger Taylor, Director of the Time For God Scheme says that applicants are always asked at interview why they want to work as a volunteer:

Many young people want a break from study, or some further experience to

test out a future career in youth or social work. Some are unemployed and for them the year will hopefully act as a stepping stone to future work. Most could fulfil these goals in other kinds of voluntary work, but they also want to serve God and to put their faith into practice.

Mark had been working in a personnel department since leaving school when he applied to Time For God. Working as a volunteer was a chance to express his Christian faith and give something back. He worked in a residential YMCA in London and then went on to train to become a youth and community worker, a career decision made directly as a result of his Time For God experience:

The experience opened my mind, I can accept and understand people better now. My faith in Christ has grown much stronger.

Jane, now a RE teacher in an inner city area, looks back on her Time For God experience, where she worked with two other volunteers at a church-based community centre:

Coming to terms with the fact that other volunteers' faith was in some ways very different to my own led to confrontation at times, but also a willingness to step back from views which hadn't been subject to enough reflection, and to respect other traditions and cultures.

She had intended to study chemistry at university but changed to theology and says the changes in her career plans were good because the previous ones were based on limited self-awareness and were unrealistic. These accounts show what an influential impact a Time For God year has on life, work and faith. Roger

Taylor feels that there are two particular features of the year which help to give this impact:

The first is that most volunteers will experience some form of culture shock during the year. This may occur in moving from an urban to rural setting or vice versa, or in living among people of different ethnic backgrounds. This means that to some extent volunteers are vulnerable to their surroundings. They go into an area without the trappings of a particular professional skill and go there to **be** as well as to **do** things. The second is that Time For God offers a network of support and training to help ensure that the experience is fulfilling and challenging but not overwhelming. Time For God itself offers residential training courses at the beginning, middle and end of service, and at least one visit from staff to each volunteer. The training provides opportunities to meet other volunteers, share experiences and develop skills. All the training events have worship as an important focus for experience. For some, training events are the most overtly Christian aspects of the year. They may be placed in a residential care home or community centre where only one or two other staff would describe themselves as Christians, or they may spend their time entirely in a Christian community. When placing volunteers we take their preference very seriously because for some it provides a welcome break from church activities, while for others it is an important chance to be with other Christians.

As the scheme's Director, for me the most important part of Time For God is the benefit it has for young people. The work they do in placements is extremely valuable, whether that be with people who have learning difficulties, homeless people or children at an after-school club. It will have lasting benefits in itself, but the majority of volunteers leave feeling they have gained far more than they have given. By experiencing life in a different area, volunteers have widened the context of their faith. Volunteers have met and lived with those who are very different from them and yet have felt accepted and accepting. In the future, even in a small way, they can break this mould.

Careforce, an agency that serves evangelical churches and Christian organisations by placing volunteers where help is most needed and appreciated, feels that a year spent in Christian service gives those involved a chance to grow, to experience new situations, to develop and discover gifts and ultimately to find rewards, satisfaction and great enjoyment. Through Careforce, Chris Pickford worked on a residential rehabilitation project for alcoholics and drug addicts at the Bethany Christian Trust in Edinburgh:

I was thrown in at the deep end, asked to do tasks I'd never done before in an environment that couldn't have been much more foreign to me. For example, being in charge of a work programme, trying to get older guys (many of whom haven't worked for years or never at all) to paint, do gardening, clean, put up shelves etc. It was an interesting experience - especially with my lack of DIY ability! This year has not just been good to fill out my cv, but having the opportunity to get to know guys with very different life experiences has been invaluable for me as a person and for my faith. I have changed a lot and have been shown so much about myself - things I do for self-protection and to please other people rather than God. Also how quick I am to judge others and look on the outside and how wrong that can be. It has been an amazing year. I would encourage anyone to do a year with Careforce. Be prepared for a few jolts to your comfort zones but be excited at the certainty of seeing God at work - in yourself as well as in those around you.

The Brethren Volunteer Service, a Christian service programme dedicated to serving basic human needs, surveyed 200 of its past volunteers to find out the impact on their lives of a period of service. A volunteer service experience is highly individual and unique, and such an experience is difficult to evaluate or put on paper. Nevertheless, over 80% of the respondents claimed that the period of Christian service had given them a better understanding of themselves, helping them to re-examine their opinions and ideas, and strengthening their commitment to serve others. Virtually all were united in their opinion that the time spent in Christian service had set a direction for their life by helping to simplify their lifestyle, increasing their awareness of others' needs and clarifying their values. Apart from the personally enriching experiences gained in a period of service, there is the benefit to those you have served. A pastor on a project in Argentina, organised under the auspices of Latin Link, wrote to each of the team's home churches:

I think that you unknown brothers so far away will rejoice to hear about the fruits borne by the young people you sent to our country - fruits of love, kindness, patience and hard work. Besides, they left many doors open to reach people outside the church by their public testimonies through radio, television and the press.

Baptist Missionary Society

Brethren Volunteer Service

Careforce

Christian Foundation for Children & Aging

Christian Literature Crusade

The Church's Ministry Among Jewish People

Frontline Teams Abroad

Frontline Teams UK

Habitat for Humanity Inc

Hothorpe Hall

Interserve

Latin Link

The Leprosy Mission

Mid Africa Mission

The Missions to Seamen

Operation Mobilisation

Scottish Churches World Exchange

South American Mission Society

The Time For God Scheme

The United Society for the Propagation of the Gospel

Wycliffe Bible Translators

Youth for Christ

BAPTIST MISSIONARY SOCIETY

Baptist Missionary Society, PO Box 49, Baptist House, 129 Broadway, Didcot, Oxfordshire OX11 8XA

✆ Didcot (01235) 512077   ☎ (01235) 511265
✉ 100626.1577@compuserve.com

Zimbabwe; Bangladesh, India, Nepal, Sri Lanka; Albania, Belgium, France, Italy, Malta; Thailand; Brazil, El Salvador, Jamaica, Trinidad; additional countries are being introduced all the time

An organisation enabling British Baptists to make the Gospel of Jesus Christ known throughout the world

Volunteers required to take part in the 28:19 Action Team Programme and become involved in a wide variety of activities, from evangelical events to teaching, social care, youth work and tasks such as painting churches. In this way team members demonstrate the Gospel message in a practical way, helping people in other countries to discover the love of Jesus for themselves. Three different types of teams are in operation: Overseas Action Teams work alongside BMS missionaries or partner churches in other countries before returning to the UK to share their experiences with Baptist churches and encourage others to get involved in world mission; UK Action Teams, where people from overseas come to the UK and work alongside Baptist churches; and Summer Action Teams where time can be spent overseas and in the UK.

Ages 18-25. Applicants must be committed Christians seeking to serve God in an overseas mission. All nationalities welcome. **B D PH**

Overseas Action Team and UK Action Team years run September-July. The Summer Action Team lasts 2-6 weeks, July/August.

Team members must raise a contribution towards the cost of training, travel, food and accommodation; £2,500 for the Overseas Team, £1,500 for the UK Action Team, and £250-£500 for the Summer Team

Participants must successfully complete a 5 week intensive training course at the start of the programme

Recruitment all year; write for an application form

BRETHREN VOLUNTEER SERVICE

The Recruitment Office, Brethren Volunteer Service, 1451 Dundee Avenue, Elgin, Illinois 60120-1694, United States

℃ (00 1 847) 742 5100   (00 1 847) 742 6103

Primarily in the United States, but for US and Canadian citizens also in Haiti, Puerto Rico, Virgin Islands; Czech Republic, France, Germany, Ireland, Netherlands, Northern Ireland, Poland, Switzerland; China, Japan, Korea; El Salvador, Honduras, Nicaragua; and Israel

A Christian service programme founded in 1948, advocating justice, peacemaking, serving basic human needs, and working for the environment. Characterised by the spirit of sharing God's love through acts of service, and reflects the heritage of reconciliation and service of the Church of the Brethren, its sponsoring denomination.

Over 150 projects, some dealing with immediate needs, others working towards changing unjust systems. Recent projects have needed agricultural workers, environmentalists, maintenance experts, construction supervisors, craft workers, medical personnel, social/youth workers, community organisers, peace/prison reform organisers, refugee resettlement coordinators, teachers and administrators.

Ages 20+; 18+, US and Canadian nationals. Applicants should be willing to act on their commitments and values, offering their time and talents to work that is difficult and demanding. They are expected to study and examine the Christian faith, be open to personal growth and willing to share in the lives of others. High school education or equivalent required. Those with relevant skills and experience especially needed; also the less experienced if they bring a willingness to grow and a desire to learn. All nationalities considered. **B D PH**

One year minimum for United States; two years service other countries

Participants meet their own costs to orientation in the US; thereafter BVS provides most travel, medical insurance and $45 per month allowance. Board and lodging provided in apartments/houses or occasionally with a family. Application fee.

Three week orientation begins term of service, when assignments are made as a mutual decision between BVS and volunteer. There may be a waiting time between orientation and placement with interim assignment arranged. Debriefing provided during in-service retreat.

Applications accepted all year round

CAREFORCE

Ian Prior, Director, Careforce, 577 Kingston Road, London SW20 8SA

© 0181-543 8671   ✉ 0181-540 0113

Throughout the UK and Ireland

Careforce was founded by the Church Pastoral Aid Society, Crusaders, the Scripture Union and the Universities and Colleges Christian Fellowship. It exists primarily to serve churches and Christian organisations throughout Britain and Ireland by placing young volunteers in situations where practical help is most needed.

Volunteers work in evangelical churches, mainly in the inner-city, or with evangelical Christian organisations caring for people in need.
The work involves practical caring within churches; outreach and evangelism; youth work; serving people who are homeless, have alcohol/drug related problems, are from families facing difficulty, have learning difficulties, have a physical disability, or are elderly.
Over 100 volunteers were in post for the 1996/1997 period.

Ages 18-25. Mainly UK and Irish nationals, with some applications accepted from overseas. Applicants should be committed Christians, willing to be placed where they are most needed, to serve and to learn. No previous experience or qualifications necessary.

11-12 months, beginning September

Volunteers work approx 40 hours per week. Full board and lodging with a family, in a flat or residential home provided, plus insurance cover. Volunteers receive £27 per week pocket money.

Two 2-day training conferences held, one in October and one in February, plus regular visits from Careforce staff

Interviews for the following September are held from January onwards. Early application appreciated.

CHRISTIAN FOUNDATION FOR CHILDREN AND AGING

Director of Voluntary Service, Christian Foundation for Children and Aging, One Elmwood Avenue, Kansas City, Kansas 66103, United States

© (00 1 913) 384 6500/(00 1 800) 875 6564   (00 1 913) 384 2211

Madagascar; India; Haiti; Philippines; Bolivia, Brazil, Chile, Colombia, Costa Rica, El Salvador, Guatemala, Honduras, Mexico, Nicaragua, Peru, Venezuela;

Founded in 1981 by former missionaries and lay volunteers, a non-profitmaking, interdenominational organisation dedicated to help overcome hunger, disease, loneliness and suffering by caring for homeless, orphaned, crippled and abandoned children, refugees and the aged. Provides shelter, medicine, education, vocational and nutritional training, and pastoral and social service regardless of age, race or creed.

Volunteers needed include childcare centre workers, healthcare instructors, nurses, nutritionists, social/community workers, craft workers, teachers, recreation organisers, house parents, group home staff, secretaries and translators. Support given includes health centres and schools for the poor and handicapped, children's clinics and centres, the training of mothers in vegetable production and for income-producing trades and educational programmes. Recruit approx 100 volunteers annually.

Ages 21+. Applicants should be motivated by gospel values and a Christian love which calls them to serve the poor, recognising their dignity and working with them towards self-sufficiency. Some professional skills preferred, although direct experience not necessary. Spanish or Portuguese language skills required for most placements. As part of the screening process, candidates are invited to Kansas City for a discernment period. Applicants will need to cover travel expenses for this. This does not imply that a commitment has been to serve together; rather it is an opportunity for CFCA and the volunteer to find out more about each other before a decision is made. **B D PH**

One year minimum

Board and lodging provided on site. Travel, insurance and pocket money provided by the volunteer.

Orientation provided in Kansas City

Recruitment all year

CHRISTIAN LITERATURE CRUSADE

Christian Literature Crusade, 201 Church Road, Upper Norwood, London SE19 2PT

Address for applications: Candidates Secretary, 51 The Dean, Alresford, Hampshire SO24 9BJ

© 0181-771 7768 ✆ 0181-653 0851

Throughout the UK and overseas, particularly France and Spain

A missionary society of people from many backgrounds, denominations and nationalities who are dedicated to serving God. Founded in 1941, it now has over 700 workers operating in 150 centres and 40 mobile units in around 45 countries. Distributes literature in over 70 languages and seeks to make evangelical literature available to everyone.

Opportunities for short-term volunteer workers as book-keepers, computer operators, secretaries, packers, printers, mobile workers, retail and warehouse personnel for home and overseas, in city centre bookshops, warehouses, offices and print shops

Ages 18+. Applicants must be committed Christians. Knowledge of French or Spanish useful. Previous training in literature is not necessary, though some experience in business is an advantage. Bible college training is recommended as a useful preparation for the placement. All nationalities welcome.

6-24 months

Volunteers work full-time. Accommodation provided for short-term workers living away from home. Day-to-day travelling expenses provided.

THE CHURCH'S MINISTRY AMONG JEWISH PEOPLE

Israel Volunteers, CMJ, 30C Clarence Road, St Albans, Hertfordshire AL1 4JJ

St Albans (01727) 833114   (01727) 848312
100731.2227@compuserve.com

Israel

Founded in 1809 within the Church of England, aims to take the gospel to the Jewish people, to support and encourage Jewish believers and to teach the Church about its Jewish roots

Volunteers are required to work at its three centres based in the Old City of Jerusalem, on Mount Carmel near Haifa and in downtown Tel Aviv. Each centre acts as a place of worship, a meeting place and a hostel. The work is mainly domestic and maintenance, with some reception duties.

Ages 18+. Applicants must be fully committed Christians involved in their local church, in good physical and mental health. They will need to prepare themselves for the cultural differences they will face.
B D PH considered

3-9+ months

Volunteers are provided with full board accommodation in shared bedrooms, and pocket money to meet their needs. They are allowed one day off per week, and holiday time is accrued according to length of stay. Volunteers pay their own travel costs and medical insurance, although home churches may help out with this.

Short orientation course held where possible before beginning of placement

Recruitment all year

FRONTLINE TEAMS ABROAD

Overseas Administrator, Oasis Trust, 87 Blackfriars Road, London SE1 8HA

✆ 0171-928 9422   📠 0171-928 6770
✉ 100620.3640@compuserve.com   🌐 http://www.u-net.com/oasis

France, Germany

The Oasis Trust is a Christian organisation established in 1986, which works alongside churches in the UK, mainland Europe, Asia, South America and Africa and is involved in a wide range of activities from running hostels for homeless young people to producing television programmes

Frontline Teams Abroad enables participants to live and work in France or Germany as part of a team attached to a local church. Previous projects have included helping out in drop-in cafés, building work and helping to run drama and music projects. Projects in Germany take place in a small church in East Berlin, where participants support *Lebensladen* - youth groups; participants may also be involved with drama projects, administration and evangelism.

Ages 18-40. Applicants must be committed Christians, with a desire to learn from the Christians in the country in which they will be serving. Conversational ability in French or German respectively required. All nationalities welcome. **B D PH W** depending on work.

6-9 month placement, September-April

5 day week with one day training. Cost £2,500-£2,990, depending on country and length of project, includes UK and overseas training, board and lodging, travel, insurance, visas and flights.

Compulsory 2½ week training course held in the UK

Write for an application form

FRONTLINE TEAMS UK

Frontline Project Manager, Oasis Trust, 87 Blackfriars Road, London SE1 8HA

℡ 0171-928 9422   📠 0171-928 6770
✉ 100620.3640@compuserve.com   🔗 http://www.u-net.com/oasis

London, West Midlands, North East England

The Oasis Trust is a Christian organisation established in 1986, which works alongside churches in the UK, mainland Europe, Asia, South America and Africa and is involved in a wide range of activities from running hostels for homeless young people to producing television programmes.

Opportunities to be part of a church-based team, working on projects with children, schools and the elderly and in social care work. Participants attend weekly training days, with workshops on topics such as addictions, AIDS/HIV issues and the Gospel and the media, and have the opportunity of spending one week working in a completely different environment, for example, working alongside a prison chaplain or joining an evangelistic mission. A special interest option allows participants to spend 50% of their time developing a specialism such as drama, music or worship; this option is ideal for those who want to take a year out to pursue a particular line of interest.

Ages 18-30. Applicants should be committed Christians.
All nationalities welcome. **B D PH W** where work allows

Mid September-mid July

Cost £2,500 for the year which covers all training, support and pastoral care, pocket money, accommodation and food

Participants attend a week-long induction course giving an in-depth look at the basic theory and practice of evangelism and teamwork

HABITAT FOR HUMANITY INC

Kathyie A Doyle, Habitat for Humanity Inc, 121 Habitat Street, Americus, Georgia 31709-3498, United States

℗ (00 1 912) 924 6935   ▱ (00 1 912) 924 6541

Over 1,200 active affiliates located in the United States and in more than 40 nations worldwide

A non-profit, ecumenical Christian housing ministry working in partnership with people in need to build and renovate decent, affordable housing. The houses are then sold to those in need at no profit and with no interest charged on the mortgage. Habitat seeks to build lives as well as houses; to date has provided shelter to 250,000 people worldwide. Through the houses they build, hope is restored and lives are changed and the devastating cycle of poverty is broken.

Several hundred volunteers recruited to work on projects in North America, especially at international headquarters in Georgia. Positions include construction, administration, childcare, photography, fundraising, data entry, graphic arts, secretarial and information systems. Approx 100 volunteers are needed for three year terms on international projects.

Ages 16+, North America; ages 21+, international projects. Applicants can be single or married with dependants. Knowledge of a foreign language helpful but not essential. International volunteers should have a Christian commitment. For International Partner positions, some college community development or managerial experience required.

3-12 months in North America; 3 year programme overseas

Accommodation, food and insurance provided at headquarters. Benefits also include paid utilities, laundry facilities, cleaning supplies and childcare. Travel not provided, except for volunteers assigned to overseas affiliates.

Compulsory orientation course

Ongoing recruitment

HOTHORPE HALL

Sheila Dunning, Hothorpe Hall, Christian Conference Centre, Theddingworth, Leicestershire LE17 6QX

Market Harborough (01858) 880257 ⎘ (01858) 880979

Leicestershire/Northamptonshire, England

An 18th century manor house set in 5 hectares of gardens and woodlands, and surrounded by countryside. Provides full board accommodation and conference facilities for groups of up to 150 people of many different denominations and backgrounds, but mainly from churches, schools and charitable organisations.

Volunteer helpers are needed to help look after guests and maintain facilities. Mainly domestic duties. Up to 50 workers recruited annually.

Ages 18+ but no particular qualifications or experience required, except Christian commitment. Good spoken English essential.

Minimum 4 weeks, maximum 6 months

Wages £21 per week. Meals and accommodation (usually shared) provided. Volunteers pay their own travel expenses.

Recruitment at any time; write for an application form

INTERSERVE

Andy Morgan, On Track Coordinator, Interserve, 325 Kennington Road, London SE11 4QH

℗ 0171-735 8227   ▭ 0171-587 5362
▭ 100014.2566@compuserve.com

India, Nepal and Pakistan; some opportunities in other countries

A member society of the Evangelical Missionary Alliance, Interserve is an international evangelical mission with over 400 partners in a wide range of ministry in south Asia and the Middle East, along with several serving among Asian ethnic groups in Britain.

Volunteers serve local Christian groups, teaching English, working with computers, administration and caring for children. There are opportunities to learn about missionary work.

Ages 18+. UK residents only. Applicants must be committed Christians who are involved with their local church/school Christian Union. They should have a good general education to A level standard or equivalent.

Approx 6-8 months

Volunteers work an average of 30 hours per week, and stay with Christian families or in a hostel. They are responsible for all travel and insurance costs, as well as board and lodging costs and personal expenses whilst on placement.

Compulsory orientation course provided before departure, and personal interview and follow-up at end of placement. All placements are supervised by long-term staff on location.

Apply as soon as possible, places are limited

LATIN LINK

Simon Walsh, Short-Term Experience Projects (STEP), Latin Link, 325 Kennington Road, London SE11 4QE

© 0171-207 5880 ⊞ 0171-207 5885

Argentina, Bolivia, Brazil, Ecuador, Nicaragua, Peru

A fellowship of personnel in Latin America and Europe, who, alongside their supporters and supporting churches, are committed to demonstrating the interdependence of the worldwide church, encouraging cross-cultural mission and channelling resources to and from Latin America for the benefit of the church worldwide

STEP offer the chance to live and work alongside a Latin American church community and help out in a basic building programme. In 1996 over 200 volunteers worked on 18 projects, building orphanages, classrooms for local schools and church community centres amongst other things. There is also time to get involved in evangelistic activities and general church work.

Ages 18-35; older applicants with special skills welcomed. Applicants must have a Christian commitment and a willingness to work as a team with Latin Americans. No previous experience or qualifications necessary; skills in music or drama, knowledge of Spanish or Portuguese, medical qualifications and practical skills useful. **B D PH** depending on ability.

Spring teams: 4 months, mid March-mid July; summer teams: 7 weeks, mid July-September. Spring team members have the option of staying on to join a summer team project.

Participants are responsible for all travel and living expenses during the project; approx £1,590 for spring projects, £1,295 for summer projects, covers travel, food, accommodation, insurance and pocket money, orientation and debriefing, first aid equipment, life jackets and mosquito nets (where necessary). Advice given on fundraising. Accommodation is self-catering, and the same as that available to local people.

Compulsory orientation course held before departure, and reunion conference held in autumn/early winter. Language tapes provided, health information and lecture, and training manual on cross-cultural mission. Leaders provided with extra training.

Full details of projects available 3 months before teams are scheduled to depart. Summer applicants interviewed February-April of same year. Spring applicants interviewed October/November of previous year.

THE LEPROSY MISSION

Personnel Officer, The Leprosy Mission, 80 Windmill Road, Brentford, Middlesex TW8 0QH

℆ 0181-569 7292   ✉ 0181-569 7808   ✉ tlmint@cityscape.co.uk

India, Nepal, Thailand

A medical missionary society whose main object is to minister in the name of Christ to the physical, mental and spiritual needs of leprosy sufferers, to assist in their rehabilitation and to work towards the eradication of leprosy

The Mission sponsors a limited number of selected medical students to spend an elective period in one of its centres. Students work under the supervision of a medical superintendent, and, as well as gaining an introduction to the treatment of leprosy and the opportunity to observe a general hospital in a tropical setting, they are also encouraged to engage in a special study or project.

Volunteers should be elective medical students in their fourth and final year of studies with suitable training and experience, and who have completed at least I full clinical year. They should have a Christian commitment in one of the Protestant denominations, and be considering work in the Third World after qualifying. Letters of recommendation are required from the minister or elder of their church and from the dean of their medical faculty.

8+ weeks

Board and lodging provided. Volunteers pay their own travel expenses

Volunteers are expected to write a report on their period overseas after returning

Applications should be submitted at least 9 months in advance

MID AFRICA MINISTRY

Mid Africa Ministry, Partnership House, 157 Waterloo Road, London SE1 8UU

© 0171-261 1370　☐ 0171-401 2910　☐ mam@john316.com

Rwanda, Burundi, eastern Zaire and southwest Uganda

A missionary society serving the Anglican Church in Africa; involved in medical, educational and development church work

Volunteers required to teach in primary and secondary schools or work in hospitals and clinics; some administration posts also available. Participants will be expected to be involved in the life and worship of the local Anglican Church overseas.

Ages 18+. Applicants should have A levels, or equivalent, or vocational qualifications for teaching, and medical qualifications for medical work. Knowledge of French required for francophone countries. Volunteers should be flexible and open-minded, appreciating the culture of the local people. All nationalities welcome if based in, or have easy accessibility to, the UK.

6-12 months. Teaching posts require one academic year commitment and commence September or January. Other posts are variable throughout the year.

Volunteers fund their own stay. Basic accommodation provided, usually with limited provisions. Occasionally the parent teacher associations in the host schools provide pocket money. Participants are required to have medical and travel insurance cover.

THE MISSIONS TO SEAMEN

The Ministry Secretary, The Missions to Seamen, St Michael Paternoster Royal, College Hill, London EC4R 2RL

© 0171-248 5202

Has seafarers' centres at over 100 ports in Britain and around the world, including Brisbane, Dampier, Dunkerque, Fremantle, Hull, Immingham, Kobe, Liverpool, Marseille, Mombasa, New Orleans, Port Hedland, Rotterdam, Seaham, Singapore, Southampton and Yokohama

An Anglican missionary society founded in 1856, caring for the spiritual and material welfare of seafarers around the globe. The Mission helps to combat isolation, exploitation and the dangers of the sea, working for improvements in conditions, education and welfare, serving seafarers of every race, colour and creed, offering a ministry of word, sacrament, counselling care and Christian welcome. The most important feature is the visit of the chaplain and staff to ships on arrival in port.

There is a volunteer service scheme for chaplain's assistants, providing an opportunity to be involved in practical Christian service within the shipping industry. Work is varied and involves visiting ships, conducting sightseeing tours, arranging sporting events, visiting hospitals, and helping with worship. Serving in the seafarers' centres can include bar and shop work, arranging video shows, telephone calls, gardening and cleaning. Recruits approx 18 volunteers annually.

Ages 21-26. Applicants should be sympathetic and understanding, good at quickly establishing relationships, prepared to befriend people of all nationalities and must have an interest in this particular form of ministry. No specific experience necessary, but the possession of a clean driving licence is required. Applicants must be members of a Christian denomination and prepared to participate fully in Anglican ministry and worship, and will need three suitable references.

One year, starting September

Board and lodging, travel costs, medical/accident insurance, pocket money of approx £35 per week and 3 weeks holiday per year provided

Completed applications should ideally be sent before the end of March

OPERATION MOBILISATION

Operation Mobilisation, The Quinta, Weston Rhyn, Owestry, Shropshire SY10 7LT

© Chirk (01691) 773388 ☐ (01691) 778378 ☐ info@uk.om.org
🕭 http://www.om.org

Worldwide

A major international mission agency established in 1963, which now has 3,000 workers in 80 nations and two ministry ships, *Logos II* and *Doulos*. More than 100,000 people have now served with the organisation in both shorter and longer term mission programmes.

Volunteers required for three different project teams: Action Evangelical Teams are involved in evangelising, especially among the unreached in the Middle East, South and Central Asia and Europe through creative outreach, helping to plant churches, tent making and ships ministry. Special Ministry Teams are involved in serving people in special need by combining evangelism with practical help through work among the poor, relief and development work. Vital Support Teams are involved in increasing the effectiveness of a global ministry by joining a home office resourcing team and serving through administration and secretarial work, financial development and accountancy, technical services, media and graphics, recruiting and pastoral care.

Ages 17+. Applicants need to be evangelical Christians, have a willingness to serve others and speak good English. All nationalities welcome.

1 year placement, commencing January and August

35-40 hours per week. Accommodation provided on some projects. No insurance cover supplied. Volunteers can obtain support/ sponsorship, depending on the country, which varies between £300-£500 per month plus travel.

2-3 days training given at the UK office

SCOTTISH CHURCHES WORLD EXCHANGE

The Director, Scottish Churches World Exchange, 121 George Street, Edinburgh EH2 4YN

✆ 0131-225 8115

Africa, Asia, Central America, Europe and the Middle East

An agency of the Scottish Churches, managed by a committee of representatives or observers from most of the major Christian denominations

Placements are arranged with an overseas partner of one of the Scottish churches or agencies. Volunteers are placed according to their interests, skills and personality. Emphasis is placed on volunteers becoming part of the local church and community.

Ages 18+. Open only to candidates from Scottish churches, others in Scotland willing to work in a church-related post, and to members of the United Reform Church anywhere in the UK. Relevant skills and experience welcome but not essential.

6-18 months, beginning August/September

Food, accommodation and pocket money provided by the host partner and World Exchange. Volunteers are expected to try and raise at least £2,000 towards the cost of their placement, which represents about one third of the real cost.

Compulsory preparation courses consist of four days at Easter and a week in early summer. On return, volunteers have a medical check, debriefing, and are encouraged to attend a weekend conference for returned volunteers.

Preliminary interviews held October-February; final selection days January-March

SOUTH AMERICAN MISSION SOCIETY

Personnel Secretary, South American Mission Society, Allen Gardiner House, Pembury Road, Tunbridge Wells, Kent TN2 3QU

© Tunbridge Wells (01892) 538647

Spain, Portugal and Latin America: Argentina, Bolivia, Chile, Paraguay, Peru, Uruguay

Founded in 1844, the Society exists to encourage and enable the spreading of the Gospel of the Lord Jesus Christ in Latin America and the Iberian Peninsula through partnership with Anglican and other churches, and to initiate and respond to opportunities by mutual sharing of prayer, personnel and resources, with the purpose of being a servant, partner and communication bridge in response to Christ's commission to live out the Gospel among all people

A variety of placements are available, including working with street children and orphanages in Brazil; practical involvement with local churches in Argentina; teaching at a Church school in Paraguay or Chile; and working with local Christian groups on evangelical outreach programmes in Spain. Approx 10 volunteers recruited each year.

Ages 18+. Applicants must be committed Christians with the support and backing of their home church in Britain. They must also have a desire to extend their own personal experience in serving the national Church. Knowledge of Spanish or Portuguese very useful.

6-12 months minimum

Volunteers are expected to contribute towards the cost of accommodation, which will be with other missionaries or with a host family. They must also raise their own return airfare, medical and travel insurance and living expenses.

Orientation not compulsory, but advised. Debriefing meeting and continued follow-up provided on return.

Recruitment all year; apply 4-6 months in advance

THE TIME FOR GOD SCHEME

The Director, Time For God Scheme, 2 Chester House, Pages Lane, London N10 1PR

℡ 0181-883 1504   📠 0181-365 2471

Throughout the UK

A charity sponsored by the Baptist Union, United Reformed Church, Congregational Federation, Methodist Association of Youth Clubs, Baptist Missionary Society, National Council of YMCAs, the Church Army, the Catholic Church, the Scottish Council of YMCAs and the Church of England. Offers young people the chance to explore their Christian discipleship in voluntary service.

Volunteers work in community centres, residential care homes, churches, hostels for the homeless, YMCAs and outdoor pursuits centres. Work can involve arranging activities for youth groups or residents; being good listeners at a community drop-in or at a lunch club for elderly people; visiting people and building up relationships; helping care for physically and mentally disabled children; and helping with typing and administration. Recruits 150+ volunteers annually.

Ages 17-25; overseas volunteers 18+. Applicants should be committed Christians or genuinely searching for a Christian faith, with a concern for others, willing to accept the challenge of Christian service and to be involved in God's work in the world; normally recommended by a local church of any denomination. Those with voluntary work experience can be placed in appropriately challenging placements.

9-12 months (10-12 months if from overseas)

Full board and lodging in private house, staff quarters or self-catering flat, plus £22 per week pocket money. Fare home paid for initial visit and every 3 months of service. 40 hour week; 1 week's leave after 3 months. For UK volunteers the home church contributes £500 towards training costs (help given where backing not available). Overseas volunteers pay £635 to cover training costs, plus travel and insurance.

3-4 day Preparation for Service Course; Mid-Service Course after 4 months; 2 day End of Service Gathering. The training programme is seen as an essential part of the voluntary service, encouraging reflection on the experience and the linking of faith and action. Volunteers receive support and supervision, and one or more visits during the year.

UK volunteers should apply 2-8 months in advance; overseas volunteers should apply before 31 January for September start

THE UNITED SOCIETY FOR THE PROPAGATION OF THE GOSPEL

United Society for the Propagation of the Gospel, Partnership House, 157 Waterloo Road, London SE1 8XA

© 0171-928 8681   ▭ 0171-928 2371

The Methodist Church, 25 Marylebone Road, London NW1 5JR

© 0171-486 5502

Countries in Africa, Asia, Latin America, Caribbean and the Middle East, and Britain, Ireland

Founded in 1701, the Society supports the work of overseas churches by offering them personnel, funding and bursaries. The programme is run jointly by the Society and the Methodist Church.

Volunteers required to work alongside local people in church-based projects such as schools, development projects or hostels. Participants learn to see the world through other people's eyes and understand better the issues facing people of the South. Participants are strongly encouraged to share what they have learned from their experiences with church groups on their return. Also, in Britain and Ireland, Root Groups; applicants should be those who are looking for a challenge as to how Christianity should affect their lifestyle and attitudes. Includes elements of youth work, befriending the lonely and the disadvantaged, leading worship and Bible study, and volunteering at community centres. Groups consist of 3/4 people living together, supporting one another.

Ages 18+. No specific skills required but applicants should be flexible, adaptable, resourceful and open to new ideas.

6-12 months, usually starting in autumn; limited number of January starts. Grant available but participants will also need to raise approx £1,500-£2,000. Advice given on fundraising and obtaining sponsorship. Root Group placements last 10-11 months, September-July/August.

Volunteers pay their fares and insurance, and contribute to board and lodging costs

Compulsory orientation course together with in-service training, pastoral support and debriefing

Apply by 12 May for autumn departure overseas and Root Groups; by 8 September for January departure

WYCLIFFE BIBLE TRANSLATORS

Wycliffe Bible Translators, Horsleys Green, High Wycombe, Buckinghamshire HP14 3XL

© Radnage (01494) 482521   (01494) 483297
short_termers_uk@sil.org   http://www.wycliffe.org.uk

Africa, South Africa and Asia; occasional UK placements

Established in 1942, growing out of a conviction that God wishes to communicate with people in the language they understand best. Workers are currently involved in Bible translation, literacy and linguistic research in over 900 languages.

One-To-One mission programme is an overseas placement based on individual skills in areas like finance, computing, wordprocessing, library work, tutoring, teaching, bible translation and general practical tasks. The Graduate International Programme (GRIP) places graduates in Bible translation teams, working on language analysis, dictionary building, literacy programmes, running computer workshops or cultural studies. Applicants are selected for their skills and are sent to countries where these skills are needed. Most opportunities are in the developing world, though help is sometimes needed in the UK. 20 placements per year.

Ages 18+. GRIP applicants must be under 30 and recent graduates or undergraduates on track for a good honours degree in any discipline, but especially mathematics, science, engineering, computer science, languages, linguistics or anthropology. Must be committed Christians and physically fit, with a skill to offer. Knowledge of French, Spanish or Portuguese useful. Participants should have a willingness to learn and serve in a cross-cultural setting; previous experience useful but not essential. UK nationals only; other nationalities should apply through Wycliffe offices in their home countries. **B D PH W** if work allows

2-12 months (One-To-One); 9-12 months (GRIP). Various start dates.

Approx 40-45 hour week. Participants must fund themselves throughout their stay, including accommodation, food, travel, insurance, vaccinations and possibly special clothing.

One-To-One participants attend a simulator weekend to familiarise with some of the situations overseas. GRIP participants attend a 15 week linguistic training programme at the Wycliffe Centre in early September.

Apply at least 3 months in advance

YOUTH FOR CHRIST

Youth for Christ, National Ministries, PO Box 5254, Halesowen, Birmingham B63 3DG

℡ 0121-550 8055   📠 0121-550 9979
📧 100434.3535@compuserve.com

Throughout the UK

Established in 1947 and specialises in communicating the Christian faith to young people

Runs a series of programmes: Operation Gideon is discipleship training in youth work and evangelism, working in teams with churches and YFC centres with involvement in schools work, street work and with all aspects of church youth work. TVB is a training opportunity for those with musical ability to use contemporary music in schools, in the street and in churches. The Apprenticeship Scheme is an opportunity to pursue a vocational training course in Christian youth work. Activate is a scheme giving hands-on experience in music, theatre and dance, touring the UK with a show dealing with relevant youth issues. Approx 100 placements annually.

Ages 17-28 (Operation Gideon); 18-28 (TVB); 23+ (Apprenticeship Scheme); 18-29 (Activate). Experience and qualifications required depend on the programme. Some youth work experience, however limited, is an asset. Applicants must be committed Christians who want to make a difference. Mainly UK nationals, although overseas applicants may be accepted. **B**

11 months, 1 September-31 July

Approx 40 hours per week. Costs vary according to programme. Operation Gideon: £2,500, which includes training, accommodation, holiday travel expenses and £15 per week pocket money. TVB: £3,500 includes training, accommodation and £20 per week pocket money. Apprenticeship Scheme: £800-£2,700 includes transport, training, study (including residential and accredited courses), some project costs. Activate: £3,500 includes training, expenses and £20 per week pocket money.

Early application advised

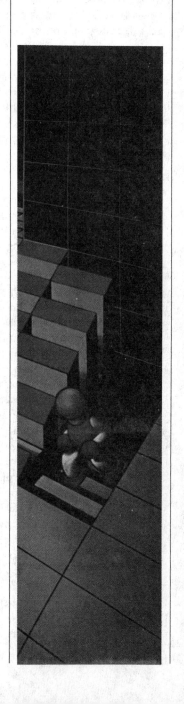

A year between offers an excellent opportunity to broaden academic experience beyond the subjects you have studied or will be studying. You could even acquire some practical skills relevant to a future career. This section outlires some of the available opportunities, including foreign language learning and attending school/college in another country.

Short courses You may be considering the option of taking a course of study for part or all of your year between. If your examination results are disappointing you may be undertaking a revision course before re-takes. Or perhaps you would like the chance that a course will give you to devote time to a hobby or interest. If you are unsure of what degree course to take or what career to pursue, a short course may help you to make a decision by giving you insight into a specific subject or type of work. It could give you experience and qualifications which will widen the choices available to you. You may wish to gain a recognised qualification in a certain field, or some vocational training before taking up employment. Or you may decide to gain marketable assets such as computer experience or office skills, which you can put to immediate use earning money to finance the rest of your year between.

An introduction to wordprocessing is extremely useful. Keyboarding skills are invariably an asset if you want to get a job to earn money during your year out (or during vacations later on), and it is becoming increasingly common for universities to require essays and dissertations to be typed rather than handwritten. A course which can teach you to touch-type, and give you some idea of what wordprocessing is all about, is definitely a good idea.

There is an enormous variety of short courses suitable for school leavers or postgraduates; some examples are:

Accounting	Librarianship
Administration	Marketing/advertising
Alternative medicine	Martial arts
Archaeology	Mechanics
Art & design	Media studies
Business studies	Music
Car maintenance	Personnel management
Circus skills	Performing arts
Communications	Photography
Computer studies	Pottery
Cookery	Secretarial skills
Dance	Self-defence
Fashion	Social work
Film-making	Sports instruction
First aid	Translating/interpreting
Health & beauty	Travel & tourism
History of art	Teaching
Information technology	TEFL
Interior design	Women's studies
Journalism	Yoga
Juggling	Youth/community work
Languages	

The Open University offers over 150 courses in a wide range of areas, including arts, science, social science, computing, technology, modern languages and business management. Courses are open to EU residents aged 18+; no previous qualifications required. Students work at home on specially written texts and other materials and receive regular tuition from a personal tutor. Whilst most courses lead to BA or BSc, it is possible to take a single course with no commitment to gaining a full degree. For a prospectus write to The Open University, PO Box 625, Milton Keynes MK1 1TY or ℂ Northampton (01604) 673803 (24 hours).

Your school, careers office or local library will be able to provide more detailed information on where to apply to do a particular course. In London, the *Floodlight* guide, issued at the end of July each year, lists thousands of part-time and evening courses. There is also a number of annual directories listing courses offered throughout the country, including *Time To Learn* £4.95, published by the National Institute for Adult & Continuing Education, 21 De Montfort Street, Leicester LE1 7GE ✆ 0116-204 4200.

You may choose to combine travel and study by doing a course abroad. In addition to language courses detailed below there are options to suit most interests. Four Corners School of Outdoor Education specialises in courses with conservation and archaeological themes. For further information contact them at PO Box 1029, Monticello, Utah 84535, United States ✉ fcs@igc.apc.org ✍ http:www. miraclemile.com/ fourcorners.

Unlike first degree and other designated courses, short courses such as these may not qualify for mandatory awards; moreover if you do manage to get a grant it could affect your entitlement later on. Grant and fee-paying entitlements for short courses will vary depending on where you live and where you plan to study. Fees are likely to be higher at privately-run institutions than at public sector ones. If financial arrangements are likely to be a problem, check with your local education authority to find out what you are entitled to, before committing yourself to any course. If there is no possibility of getting a grant you may be able to arrange a bank loan to cover fees and/or living expenses, which you can pay back either during your course if you have the time to take on a job, or afterwards, when you may be able to put your newly-learned skills to use earning money.

Language courses A year out presents an ideal opportunity to learn or brush up on a foreign language, perhaps by spending some time studying in another country. English may well be viewed as a universal language, but over the past few years many areas of business have seen their need for foreign languages expand as European ties have developed and opportunities have opened up in the countries of the former Eastern bloc. Consequently, having fluency in another language can be seen as a great asset for any potential employee. Many university degree courses now involve a language element or a period of work or study abroad; there are also EU programmes such as ERASMUS which offer a chance to study at a university abroad, so it is therefore a good idea to get a head start by learning the relevant language. And anyone going on to do a languages degree would be expected to keep practising and improving their linguistic skills during their gap year.

The cultural section of the relevant embassy or the tourist board will be able to supply details on request of language courses taking place in their country, and useful addresses are given below. Usually, such information will come in the form of a booklet listing courses, plus details of any grants available, so when writing enclose a large, stamped, self-addressed envelope, to be sure of a speedy reply.

If you would rather study in this country there are organisations such as the Alliance Française or the Goethe-Institut, responsible for promoting their country's language and culture, who organise day and evening classes. Your local library will also be able to provide information on language courses available at nearby schools and colleges.

Dutch
Belgian Embassy, Cultural Section, 103-105 Eaton Square, London SW1W 9AB ✆ 0171-470 3700 publishes a leaflet *Dutch and French Courses in Belgium* providing lists of courses organised by universities and language schools.

Royal Netherlands Embassy, Press & Cultural Affairs (Education), 38 Hyde Park Gate, London SW7 5DP ✆ 0171-590 3270 can provide information on learning Dutch in the UK and studying in the Netherlands.

Finnish
Finnish Institute, 35-36 Eagle Street, London WC1R 4AJ ✆ 0171-404 3309 provides information on opportunities for study in Finland.

French
Alliance Française, 1 Dorset Square, London NW1 6PU ✆ 0171-723 6439 and 4 Morwell Street, London WC1 3AN ✆ 0171-636 6054 runs language courses at all levels. Alliance Française, French Chamber of Commerce and French Ministry of Education examinations may be taken.

Belgian Embassy, Cultural Section, 103-105 Eaton Square, London SW1W 9AB ✆ 0171-470 3700 publishes a leaflet *Dutch and French Courses in Belgium* providing lists of courses organised by universities and language schools.

French Embassy, Cultural Service, PO Box 988, 23 Cromwell Road, London SW7 2EL can provide a booklet *Cours de Français Langue Étrangère en France,* giving information on all types of courses in French as a foreign language.

Institut Français, 14 Cromwell Place, London SW7 2JR ✆ 0171-581 2701 offers French courses at all levels in London, and an extensive programme of cultural activities.

German
Anglo-Austrian Society, 46 Queen Anne's Gate, London SW1H 9AU ✆ 0171-222 0366 is a charity promoting Anglo-Austrian relations. Acts as an agent for language courses in Austria and arranges exchange visits.

Austrian Cultural Institute, 28 Rutland Gate, London SW7 1PQ ✆ 0171-584 8653 is the cultural section of the Austrian Embassy; can provide information on grants for study in Austria. They can also supply copies of an annual guidebook giving details of summer courses in Austria, published by the Austrian Committee for International Educational Exchange (ÖKISTA).

German Academic Exchange Service, 34 Belgrave Square, London SW1X 8QB ✆ 0171-253 1736 (09.30-12.30 only) issues a booklet *Scholarships and Funding for Study and Research in Germany* giving details of funding available. Also *Sommerkurse in der Bundesrepublik Deutschland,* an annual booklet listing university language courses, courses run by the Goethe-Institut and summer music courses.

Goethe-Institut, 50 Princes Gate, Exhibition Road, London SW7 2PH ✆ 0171-411 3400 Goethe-Institut, 4th floor, Churchgate House, 56 Oxford Street, Manchester M1 6EU ✆ 0161-237 1077

Goethe-Institut, County House, 32-34
Monkgate, York YO3 7RH
℃ York (01904) 611122
Scottish-German Centre, 3 Park
Circus, Glasgow G3 6AX ℃ 0141-332
3555/6
A German government-funded
organisation aimed at promoting
German language and culture, with
branches in Britain and over 70 other
countries. Runs German courses in
London, Manchester and Glasgow and
at 16 centres in Germany. Offers a
programme of cultural events, library
and information service.

Italian
Dante Alighieri Society, 4 Upper
Tachbrook Street, Victoria, London
SW1V 1SH ℃ 0171-828 9660 is the
London branch of a non-profitmaking
society founded in 1889 to promote
Italian language and culture and act as
a point of contact for Italian
expatriates. Offers evening courses
for adults in Italian at all levels.

Italian Institute, 39 Belgrave Square,
London SW1X 8NX ℃ 0171-235
1461 publishes *Italian Government
Scholarships and Grants*, which gives
details on how to apply for bursaries,
grants and scholarships. Can also
provide current brochures on many of
the language courses in Italy.

Portuguese
Hispanic & Luso Brazilian Council,
Canning House, 2 Belgrave Square,
London SW1X 8PJ ℃ 0171-235 2303
gives information and advice on all
matters relating to Portugal, Spain and
Latin America, including language
courses and other opportunities.
Organises lectures, runs cultural
events and a library of 60,000 books.

Russian
Society for Cooperation in Russian &
Soviet Studies, 320 Brixton Road,

London SW9 6AB ℃ 0171-274 2282
organises evening classes in Russian
and courses in Russia. Also publishes
an annual *Russian Information Guide*
£5.95 providing information on
language courses and services, both in
the UK and the former Soviet Union.

Spanish
Hispanic & Luso Brazilian Council, *see
under* Portuguese, *above.*

Instituto Cervantes, 22 Manchester
Square, London W1M 5AP ℃ 0171-
235 1484/5 arranges language courses,
cultural activities and a library, and
can provide information on courses in
Spain.

Swedish
Swedish Embassy, Cultural Section,
11 Montagu Place, London W1H 2AL
℃ 0171-724 2101 provides an annual
publication, *Svenska Institutets
Internationella Sommarkurser*, which
gives information on summer courses
organised in association with various
Folk High Schools in Sweden.

Miranda Hayman spent part of her
year out doing an intensive Spanish
course in Barcelona:

*I was almost a complete beginner, but
after 3 weeks I saw a definite
improvement. The school was very
friendly and encouraging, and CESA
(Cultural and Educational Services
Abroad) organised everything apart
from transport, which took away the
pressure of having to organise the
accommodation etc, myself. I am now
doing beginner's Spanish at university,
where a high level has to be reached
after one year. The course in
Barcelona has definitely been an
advantage in all aspects, as well as
having learnt something about Spanish
life. It has also given me the*

confidence to participate in class. Overall my gap year has improved my confidence, given me independence and the task of organising things by myself. It is so far the best year of my life and has contributed to my having a fantastic time at university.

Homestays/term stays Another way to improve language skills is to take part in a homestay, where you are welcomed into the home of a foreign family. This provides an excellent opportunity to immerse yourself completely in another lifestyle, language and culture. A term stay involves attending a foreign school for one or two terms or for a full academic year. There are some opportunities to attend boarding schools, but in most cases accommodation is in carefully selected host families, where the participant may be matched with a partner of the same age and interests. Term stays provide the opportunity to become totally immersed not just in family life, but in school and community life as well. In general, term stay opportunities are open only to students who are still attending school, but the organisations listed here are able to cater for those wishing to attend a foreign school after leaving school in this country, as part of their year between. For those interested in a term stay in the United States, however, it should be noted that one of the US visa requirements for this type of stay is that participants must be under 19 years of age on 1 January of the year that they intend to take part in the term stay. The Central Bureau's guidebook **Home From Home** gives details of agencies arranging homestays and term stays, plus full information on travel and preparation. Available from bookshops or direct from the Central Bureau price £8.99.

Academic Year in France, Germany or Spain

Academic Year in the USA

AFS/Intercultural Education Programmes

Art History Abroad Courses Ltd

Cambridge Advisory Service for Language Courses Abroad

Challenge Educational Services

Le Cordon Bleu School

Cultural & Educational Services Abroad

EF International Language Schools

English-Speaking Union

Euro-Academy Ltd

European Educational Opportunities Programme

International Study Programmes

John Hall Pre-University Courses

Queen's Business and Secretarial College

Tante Marie School of Cookery

STUDY / TERM STAYS   3 1 5   STUDY / TERM STAYS

ACADEMIC YEAR IN FRANCE, GERMANY OR SPAIN

Academic Year in France, Germany or Spain, Study Associates International, Gold Peak House, Wilmerhatch Lane, Epsom, Surrey KT18 7EH

© Ashtead (01372) 275005   ☎ (01372) 273976

France, Germany, Spain

Established in 1983, Study Associates International specialises in responsible international student exchange programmes for students wishing to venture overseas to live and study, often for the first time. It is run by British parents and offers year-round support to the students during their time abroad through full-time local staff in each of the countries offered.

Students attend a *lycée*, a *Gymnasium* or Spanish high school, whilst studying alongside young people of their chosen country. They live with a carefully selected host family and have the year-round support of a community representative in addition to the full-time local staff. Total immersion in the foreign culture enables the student to achieve fluency in a comparatively short period of time and to develop a bi-cultural understanding which will enable the student to compete on an equal footing with their European colleagues of the future.

Ages 16-19. Most applicants will be taking a year between school and university. Minimum 5 GCSEs (or equivalent) grade C or above, including the relevant language, required. A level or equivalent desirable, although not essential as study habits, motivation and commitment to the programme are of equal importance. Preparation courses available. British school recommendation required.

3, 5 or 10 months

Programme fees from £1,995 for 3 months, £2,495 for 5 months and £2,995 for 10 months

Student orientation provided

Limited places available. Most applications are processed 8-18 months prior to start of programme, with a limited number accepted up to 4 months prior.

ACADEMIC YEAR IN THE USA

Academic Year in the USA, Study Associates International, Gold Peak House, Wilmerhatch Lane, Epsom, Surrey KT18 7EH

© Ashtead (01372) 275005   (01372) 273976

United States

Established in 1983, Study Associates International specialises in responsible international student exchange programmes for students wishing to study abroad often for the first time. It is run by British parents and offers year-round support prior to departure and during the programme through full-time staff in each of the countries offered.

Academic Year in the USA offers students the opportunity to live and study in the United States. Students attend an American high school and live with a carefully selected host family. The high schools offer an exciting school curriculum with a broad range of subjects often not available in the UK, including excellent sports, music and drama opportunities. Each student has a local community representative and regional manager who are supported by full-time national and regional offices.

Ages 15-19. Students must have at least 5 GCSEs (or equivalent) and are required to provide a British school recommendation.

5 or 10 months

Programme fees from £2,575 for 5 months and £2,990 for 10 months

Student orientation provided

Limited places available. Most applications are processed 8-18 months prior to start of programme, with a limited number accepted up to 4 months prior.

AFS / INTERCULTURAL EDUCATION PROGRAMMES

The National Director, AFS/IEP, Arden House, Wellington Street, Bingley, West Yorkshire BD16 2NB

℗ Bingley (01274) 560677   ✉ (01274) 567675

55 countries in most world regions, including western and eastern Europe, North America, Latin America and Asia

AFS is an international, voluntary non-profitmaking organisation represented in 55 countries. It has operated in the UK since 1947 and is a registered charity. Provides intercultural learning opportunities to help people develop the knowledge, skills and understanding needed to create a more just and peaceful world. The only organisation of its kind to receive a citation from the United Nations in recognition of its work for world youth.

Opportunities to spend a year abroad living with a volunteer host family as a member of that family, whilst attending school, gaining another language and an insider's appreciation of the culture

Ages 15-18 and in full-time education at time of application. Applicants should be flexible, adaptable and interested in other cultures and ways of life. It is not a requirement to speak the language of the intended country before departure.

11 months departing July-September depending on the host country

Cost from £1,000-£3,950. A system of financial assistance is available from AFS, and special scholarships are offered each year. All participants are given advice and support on doing their own fundraising. The fee covers travel to and from the host country, medical insurance, orientation courses and ongoing support from volunteers and staff in the host country and in the UK.

Orientation courses held before departure to help participants prepare for the experience, and at regular intervals during the year. Introductory language course held in some countries.

Applications accepted up to 18 months in advance of departure. Early applications receive priority for choice of countries and financial assistance. Prefer to receive applications at least 6 months before departure, but can occasionally accept late applicants.

ART HISTORY ABROAD
COURSES LTD (AHA)

Art History Abroad Courses Ltd (AHA), Prioryfield House, 20 Canon Street, Taunton, Somerset TA1 1SW

℗ Taunton (01823) 323363   ▱ (01823) 271072

London and Italy: Venice, Rome, Florence, Milan, Siena

Organise educational courses on art and architecture, in groups of no more than eight while accompanied by knowledgeable, experienced tutors, mostly freelance lecturers and historians. The courses are not set in a classroom but involve visits to artistic and historical places of interest, allowing students to put paintings and buildings into a wider historical and social context so that the study of art mingles with history, literature, poetry, classics and theology.

Orientated towards students who are in their gap year prior to attending university, the spring course is a comprehensive overview of Italian art. One week of introductory lectures in London followed by five weeks in Italy where the time is split principally between Florence, Venice and Rome with two shorter stops in Milan and Siena. The London week is made up of a series of seminars and visits to the principal Italian collections. The stay in Venice coincides with the Carnival. As well as the other cities visited, day excursions to Vicenza to study Palladio, to Padua to study Giotto and to Pisa to see the famous tower and cathedral are arranged. Throughout the course participants are encouraged to speak Italian. Maximum 24 students.

Ages 17+. No previous specialised knowledge of art or history required. Applicants must have an interest in European cultural history and/or Italian art. Basic Italian necessary. All nationalities welcome.

2½ months, late January-early March; summer course also available, late July-mid August

36-40 hours of tuition per week. Cost £3,400 includes return flight, accommodation in Italy, travel between cities, travel to and from museums, entrance charges, excursions, all lectures and seminars in Italy and London and travel insurance. Summer course costs £1,500.

Two Italian lessons provided at the start of the course

CAMBRIDGE ADVISORY SERVICE FOR LANGUAGE COURSES ABROAD

Cambridge Advisory Service for Language Courses Abroad, Rectory Lane, Kingston, Cambridge CB3 7NL

℗ Cambridge (01223) 264089 ▭ (01223) 264188

Austria, France, Germany, Italy, Portugal, Spain, Switzerland; Ecuador, Japan, Mexico

Founded in 1988, the Cambridge Advisory Service offers a personal service giving advice and background information for British students wishing to attend language courses abroad. It has links with some 18 schools in Europe running year-round and summer courses; also a school in Japan running courses in spring and summer, and permanent schools in Ecuador and Mexico.

There are opportunities to learn French in Paris, Aix-en-Provence, Amboise, La Rochelle, Lausanne and Tours; German in Berlin, Cologne and Vienna; Spanish in Madrid, El Puerto de Santa Maria, Malaga, Nerja, Salamanca, Valencia, Cuernavaca and Cuenca; Italian in Florence and Siena; Portuguese in Lisbon; and Japanese in Kanazawa. Most schools offer a programme of extra-curricular activities, including excursions, films, sports and social events.

Ages 17+ (18+ for Japan). In most cases there are courses for all language levels from beginner to advanced.

Length varies from 2-4 week short courses to 10-20 week semester courses

Fees vary according to school and length/intensity of course. 4 week summer course, 25 hours of tuition per week, inclusive of accommodation approx £1,581 in Paris; similar course in Cologne approx £1,329; in Japan, £2,053. Accommodation usually arranged on a half-board basis in private homes, but courses also available on a tuition only basis. Students arrange and pay for their own travel and insurance.

Advisable to apply at least 2 months in advance, if possible

CHALLENGE EDUCATIONAL SERVICES

Challenge Educational Services, 101 Lorna Road, Hove, East Sussex BN3 3EL

© Hove (01273) 220261   (01273) 220376

France, United States

Runs a variety of cultural exchange and educational programmes, including French university language and American academic year programmes

In France, students may study for a year or semester at the universities of Angers, Nantes, Poitiers or Paris-Sorbonne; there are also shorter summer courses in Paris, Angers and Poitiers, and year-round courses at Bordeaux, Cap d'Ail and Montpellier. In the United States, students live with an American family while studying for a semester/academic year at an American high school.

France: ages 13+, beginner level upwards
United States: ages 16-18

France: ½ week to 1 academic year
United States: 5 or 10 months

Further details and costs on request; accommodation is included on all programmes

Apply at least 2 months in advance

LE CORDON BLEU SCHOOL

Le Cordon Bleu School, Admission Office, 114 Marylebone Lane, London WIM 6HH

✆ 0171-935 3503   ☎ 0171-935 7621

London, Paris, Tokyo, Sydney and North America

Established in Paris in 1895, Le Cordon Bleu has acquired an international reputation built on excellence in culinary education. With 30 distinguished master chefs, the majority from Michelin-starred restaurants, it has achieved privilege partnerships and articulation agreements with various governments, universities and culinary associations that promote French *Art de Vivre* throughout the world.

Offers a variety of day and evening courses, as well as longer diploma courses, taught by leading master chefs in modern kitchens with state of the art equipment. The 10 week Classic Cycle course, taught at basic, intermediate and superior levels, enables students to obtain a thorough knowledge of the basic principles and techniques of French cuisine and pastry, and the mastery of a wide range of diverse and demanding recipes from classical to contemporary cuisine. The 4 week Essentials Course is suitable for gap year students wishing to improve their menu planning and food preparation, and includes an overnight trip to Paris and the Royal Institute of Public Health and Hygiene certificate course.

Ages 17+. No experience or qualifications required. Participants should have a passion for food and cooking, and should speak English. All nationalities welcome.

Courses run all year round, from one day to nine months

Fees from £65 to £4,020 with discounts for multiple course enrolments. A list of accommodation agencies, hostels and hotels is available. No travel or insurance provided.

Applications can also be made to the following offices:
France: 8 rue Léon Delhomme, 75015 Paris, France
North America: 404 Airport Executive Park, Nanuet, NY 10954, United States ✈ http://www.t-mark.com/cordonbleu

CULTURAL & EDUCATIONAL SERVICES ABROAD

Miss Katherine Brand, Managing Director, Cultural & Educational Services Abroad (CESA), Western House, Malpas, Truro, Cornwall TR1 1SQ

℃ Truro (01872) 225300 ⟳ (01872) 225400
✉ languages@cesa.demon.co.uk

French in France, Switzerland and Belgium; German in Germany, Austria and Switzerland; Spanish in Spain, Mexico and Costa Rica; Portuguese in Portugal; Dutch in the Netherlands; Greek in Greece; Italian in Italy; Mandarin and Taiwanese Chinese in Taiwan; Russian in Russia; and Japanese in Japan

Founded in 1980, CESA is a leading language agent, serving the foreign language needs of the individual student and the business client

Specialises in arranging tuition in the countries in which the language is spoken, offering impartial advice on language programmes. As an independent company offers flexibility, choosing courses from a wide range of language training organisations. Several colleges offer course options, such as Italian and art history courses in Florence, French and sporting activities in Nice or German and skiing in Kitzbühel. Many colleges now offer preparation for state-recognised diplomas.

Courses are open to complete beginners as well as to those studying at degree level and all points in between, although some colleges cater more specifically for certain levels of linguistic ability. A written and oral assessment of each student takes place on the first day, allowing the college to place students in classes of the correct linguistic level.

Average course length 6-12 weeks; minimum duration of 2 weeks for group tuition, 1 week for private tuition

Price varies according to the language required, location of the college and the intensity of the course attended; eg £3,888 for a 12 week small group programme in French at Tours covers 20 lessons per week and half board family accommodation; £537 for a 4 week standard Spanish group programme in Seville covers 20 lessons per week and student apartment accommodation. Students pay own travel and insurance.

For most programmes 4 weeks' notice is sufficient, unless the student has special requirements. Courses do not run during the Christmas fortnight. The busiest time of year is July-August, and 2 months' notice is strongly recommended.

EF INTERNATIONAL LANGUAGE SCHOOLS

EF International Language Schools, Kensington Cloisters, 5 Kensington Church Street, London W8 4LD

© 0171-795 6675   ▭ 0171-795 6635

Nice, Munich, Barcelona, Quito, Florence and Moscow (Language Year Abroad); Reims, Nice, Munich, Florence, Barcelona, Quito, Costa Rica, Moscow and Beijing (Multi-Language Year)

Established in 1965, the world's largest private educational organisation, with offices in 65 countries worldwide. Offers a wide range of full immersion courses, lasting from two weeks to an academic year, at different levels from complete beginner to advanced.

Offers two gap year courses: the Language Year Abroad and the Multi-Language Year. Both enable participants to live abroad and study the language of the host country, allowing them to be completely immersed in the culture and practise language skills with native speakers.
The programmes are combined with cultural visits and excursions.

Both schemes offer Spanish, French, German, Italian and Russian; the Multi-Language Year also offers Chinese. The Language Year Abroad focuses on one language; students on the Multi-Language Year can study 2 or 3 languages and can choose how the 36 weeks of study is divided between the different languages. Successful participants are awarded a Diploma in International Studies and the EF Academic Record.

Ages 16+. Open to anyone wanting to perfect their language skills, from beginner to advanced level.

9 months; September-June for the Language Year Abroad; from any Monday of the year for the Multi-Language Year

Both programmes include 24 language lessons per week; Multi-Language Year also offers an intensive course of 30 lessons per week. Fees start from £5250 and include tuition, international flights, travel to host family/residence, accommodation, most meals, activities and excursions. Insurance is not included, but can be arranged. Enrolment fee £75.

Write for an application form

ENGLISH-SPEAKING UNION

The Director of Education, English-Speaking Union, Dartmouth House, 37 Charles Street, London WIX 8AB

✆ 0171-493 3328   ▭ 0171-495 6108

Canada, United States

A registered charity founded in 1918 with the aim of promoting international understanding. Administers a wide variety of educational programmes including school scholarships to North America.

The object of the scholarships is to enable British school leavers to spend an additional year as senior students at schools in Canada and the United States. Placements are mainly at independent boarding schools in many parts of North America, the majority in the New England states.

Applicants should be British, have taken A levels (or equivalent) and not exceed the age of 19½ before they leave Britain. Their schools are asked to submit full confidential reports; a medical certificate is also required.

Three terms, beginning September, or two terms, beginning January

Students are provided with board and lodging at the school. In the case of day schools, students stay with a host family, for which a weekly contribution is required. Hospitality may be provided during the shorter holidays; students are permitted to travel at the end of the academic year. Students pay their own travel expenses and insurance, plus £1,500-£2,000 to cover incidental expenses. Application fee £3, administration fee £175; refundable deposit £50.

Short-listed candidates must attend an interview at Dartmouth House

Apply by 1 February for September departure; by 1 October for January departure

EURO - ACADEMY LTD

Euro-Academy Ltd, 77a George Street, Croydon CR10 ILD

℃ 0181-686 2363   ☞ 0181-681 8850

Austria, France, Germany, Italy, Portugal, Russia, Spain and Ecuador

A language school, established in 1971, which offers language courses throughout the year. Also organises art courses in Italy, homestays and farmstays.

Range of courses offered at all levels from beginner to advanced, including short-term, long-term, intensive and individual tuition. Previous activities have included long-term courses of up to 12 weeks in Berlin, Madrid, Salamanca and El Peurto; semesters at Caen or Perpignan Universities; and academic semesters at the art institute in Florence where students have studied painting and fine arts or architecture and interior design.

Minimum ages 12, 16 or 18, depending on the course. No qualifications required as courses are offered at all levels. All nationalities welcome.

Courses are offered throughout the year and last from 2 weeks to a semester; specific start dates for beginners

Fees from £265 for homestays and £200-£1,100 for courses. Accommodation, travel and travel insurance is not included but can be arranged at extra cost.

All students undertake an assessment test before commencement of the course or a needs analysis for 1:1 tuition

EUROPEAN EDUCATIONAL OPPORTUNITIES PROGRAMME

Sue Bugden, European Educational Opportunities Programme, 122 Canterbury Road, Lydden, Dover, Kent CT15 7ET

℗ Dover (01304) 830948   ▭ (01304) 831914

France, Germany, Spain, United States

Founded in 1986, an organisation offering homestay and term stay programmes through carefully selected homes, schools and allied agencies

Can place students in French, German and American schools, with accommodation in host families. Students are integrated totally into family life and enter fully into school academic and social programmes.

Ages 16+. Applicants must be recommended by their own school. Reasonable fluency in the language of the country selected is required.

1-3 terms. Both semester and academic year programmes are available.

For stays in France, Germany and Spain, a fee of £440 per month covers accommodation, school fees and administration. For the United States fees are from $3,650 depending on the programme. Participants arrange their own travel.

Private language tuition can be arranged, if necessary

France, Germany and Spain: apply at least 2-3 months in advance; United States: apply at least 6-9 months in advance

INTERNATIONAL STUDY PROGRAMMES

ISP Department, Council on International Educational Exchange, 52 Poland Street, London W1V 4JQ

℗ 0171-478 2004   ☐ 0171-734 7322   ☐ infouk@ciee.org

Australia, Belgium, Canada, China, Costa Rica, Czech Republic, France, Germany, Ghana, Hungary, Indonesia, Italy, Japan, Mexico, Netherlands, Poland, Spain, Taiwan, Thailand, United States, Vietnam

The Council on International Educational Exchange is a non-profit, non-governmental organisation dedicated to helping people gain understanding, acquire knowledge and develop skills for living in a globally independent and culturally diverse world. Founded in 1947, it has a variety of programmes and services for students and teachers at secondary through to university levels.

Provides two enrolment services: students can enrol directly onto a number of courses at certain institutions (eg French Language, Literature & Civilisation at the University of Stendhal, Grenoble) or onto degree modules of mainstream university courses (eg Wollongong University, Australia); alternatively, students can enrol in courses at Council study centres based at universities worldwide. These centres provide courses focusing on topics such as the environment or business, or area studies programmes which examine the culture and history of a region. These courses are predominantly taught in English but also involve a language component.

Ages 16+. Course requirements vary according to programme.

One week to one academic year, depending on course

Costs from £170 per week, tuition only; accommodation options available for all courses. Insurance, orientation materials, visas and emergency support included.

Orientation provided for most programmes

Application deadlines vary according to programme and country

JOHN HALL PRE-UNIVERSITY COURSES

The Secretary, John Hall Pre-University Courses, 12 Gainsborough Road, Ipswich, Suffolk IP4 2UR

Ipswich (01473) 251223 (01473) 288009

Venice, Italy, with an introduction to the course in London, and optional extensions in Florence and Rome

Founded in 1965, the John Hall Pre-University Course provides an introduction to European civilisation, in particular its art, music and styles of living, making clear the continuity of the tradition into the present day. It combines a university style of learning and living with the unique experience of being in three of Europe's most beautiful and historically important cities.

The daily programme varies, but typically includes practical classes and visits in the morning, two lectures in the afternoon, and language classes in the early evening. Weekends are free for excursions to local places of interest. Lectures are conducted by top quality guest speakers. Practical classes cover such topics as life drawing, portraiture and photography. Beginners classes in Italian are arranged as an optional extra.

The course is for students who have just left school; average age 18. It is open to arts and science students alike; no previous knowledge of European art, music or history is required.

Seven weeks, late January-mid March, followed by optional extension of 7 days in Florence and 5 days in Rome

Fees £3,650 include half-board hotel accommodation in shared rooms in Venice; rail travel London-Venice; full programme of lectures and classes (Italian classes approx £105 extra); some art and photographic materials, and visits and excursions. Fees for extension of course are £545 for Florence and £485 for Rome. Return travel from Rome costs approx £140; return travel from Venice and Florence is not included or arranged.

Introduction to course in London includes lectures, classes and visits to art galleries, dealers and artists' studios. It gives advice on how to look at a painting and architecture and puts the art of Italy into the European context. Accommodation and meals are not included.

Registrations are accepted up to 2 years in advance. Early registration advised, as the number of places is limited.

QUEEN'S BUSINESS AND SECRETARIAL COLLEGE

Queen's Business and Secretarial College, 27 Queensbury Place, London SW7 2DS

℗ (24 hours) 0171-823 9915 or 0171-581 8331   ☐ 0171-823 9915

South Kensington, London, and Cambridge, England

Established in 1924, courses combine professional business skills with a knowledge of marketing, business studies and management, providing students with skills which are invaluable for future study, career and personal development

Runs the following courses: marketing and administration; business studies; European business administration; executive secretarial; secretarial certificate and information technology. For overseas students there is a course in English and secretarial. Students may choose to take French, German, Italian and Spanish. Journalism, book keeping and other subjects available on request. Individual subjects are backed by the external examinations of the London Chamber of Commerce and Industry, the Royal of Arts and Teeline Education.

Ages 16+. Applicants must have good GCSEs and 2 A levels or equivalent. The European business administration course is open to post-A level students who are bilingual. Participants should be well-motivated, flexible and committed. All nationalities welcome. **PH D**

6-36 weeks. Courses commence July, September, January and April.

Fees per 12 week term £2,400, London; £1,800, Cambridge, which includes tuition fees, books and stationery. Participants must finance their own accommodation which can be arranged in hostels, self-catering flats or with families. No travel provided.

TANTE MARIE SCHOOL OF COOKERY

Tante Marie School of Cookery, Woodham House, Carlton Road, Woking, Surrey GU21 4HF

© Woking (01483) 726957   (01483) 724173

Woking, Surrey

Cookery day school founded in 1954 by the distinguished cookery writer, Iris Syrett. The name, Tante Marie, is taken from the cook of French legend, the counterpart of Britain's Mrs Beeton.

Offers a range of practical cookery courses. The certificate course is suitable for those wishing to learn to cook for family and friends, and for those hoping to find short-term work in the hotel and hospitality industries. The diploma course is aimed at those pursuing a career in the culinary world and the career-oriented intensive diploma course is targeted at mature students with previous experience; both diploma courses include a four day seminar preparing students for the certificate examination set by the Wine and Spirit Education Trust. Also offers short courses on a range of topics such as cooking for buffets, dinner parties and microwave cookery.

Ages 16+. No prior experience required for the certificate and diploma courses; the intensive diploma course is designed for those with some previous cookery experience who wish to consolidate and expand their practical and theoretical knowledge. All applicants should have an interest in the presentation of good food to a very high standard. Fluency in English essential. All nationalities welcome; visas arranged. **PH D**

The certificate course runs for 12 weeks starting in January, April or September; the diploma course starts in September and consists of three 12 week terms; and the intensive diploma course lasts for two 12 week terms starting in January, April or September.

Course fees £2,700-£3,300; students may qualify for tax relief on the courses and for career development loans. Help provided in finding suitable accommodation, either with local families or on a self-catering basis.

Write for an enrolment form

SECTION XI

ADVICE FOR TRAVELLERS

INDEX & COUNTRIES INDEX

REPORT FORM

ADVICE FOR TRAVELLERS

Some placement organisations are happy to make or advise on travel arrangements, although this service is not always included in the fee. You may wish to sort out your own plans, especially if you are thinking of any independent travel before or after the placement. A number of operators specialise in youth/student fares; details are given below. There is also a wide variety of travel outlets ranging through high street travel agencies, bucket shops and individual airline offices. There are many discount fares on offer, so it is a good idea to compare to see what suits you best, and what constitutes the best deal. For example, you may find that last-minute charter flight bookings are just as cheap as student tickets, but definitely not as flexible. Inter-Rail passes are good value for multiple destinations, but extra charges may be levied, for example on high speed trains. Bucket shops usually supply tickets direct from the airline or from consolidators (agencies responsible for filling seats on scheduled flights). They advertise their bargain fares in the national press, often in the travel pages of Sunday papers. They can offer great discounts on airline tickets, but as they tend not to be covered by travel associations such as ABTA, they are viewed as slightly risky. If you want to be sure that the shop you are dealing with is reliable, check that they are licensed by the International Air Transport Association (IATA), and see if they will accept payment by credit card, as credit card companies are usually pretty careful about whom they deal with. The Air Travel Advisory Bureau (© 0171-636 5000) should be able to refer you to a reputable agency, or an airline may be

able to refer you to their own preferred agent or consolidator. Your local travel agent might be more convenient, but will be limited in their range of destinations. The availability of tickets to many destinations will also vary according to national and regional holidays, religious festivals and specific tourist events. Try to travel off-season if you want a better deal - for many destinations May-September is the peak period to avoid.

Certain countries (for example, those that make up the Former Soviet Union) can have extremely complicated systems for obtaining internal travel tickets, which makes things rather difficult for independent travellers. Some countries also have restrictions on internal travel to certain destinations. On the other hand there may be some good bargains to be had and you should be on the look out for special offers. In many cases national airlines offer free or discounted flights to selected destinations on their domestic network simply to fill internal flights. For some countries, including Australia, Canada and the US, it is possible to buy a pass before you leave which will allow you up to a month's unlimited travel on the internal air, coach or rail network.

Within Europe, perhaps the cheapest way to travel is by coach. This way you can explore the continent at fares that won't hurt your pocket. Eurolines, 4 Cardiff Road, Luton LU1 1PP © Luton (01582) 404511 or © 0171-730 8235 offers a wide range of coach services to over 400 destinations in Europe, including daily services to Paris, Amsterdam, Frankfurt, Cologne and Dublin. Bookings can be made through any National Express agent and most student travel agencies.

If you'd rather travel by train, then Eurotrain offers cheap fares for those under 26 on various European routes. Tickets are valid for 2 months and allow you to plan your own route and stop off anywhere along the way. Eurotrain Explorer tickets take in several cities, for example the Capital Explorer covers Paris, Brussels and Amsterdam, and the Eastern Explorer includes Amsterdam, Berlin and Prague. Tickets can be obtained at most student travel agencies.

Inter-Rail passes allow up to one month's unlimited travel on the national railways of 28 countries in Europe and around the Mediterranean. The cost in 1997 is £279 (ages under 26) or £275 (ages 26+, 19 countries only). Available from major railway stations, student travel agencies and the British Rail International Rail Centre, Victoria Station, London SW1V 1JY ✆ 0171-834 2345. Also issues Euro-Youth low-cost rail tickets to any one of 200 selected destinations in mainland Europe (ages under 26 only) and can provide European timetable information and assistance with journey planning.

For those going further afield, Round-The-World (RTW) air tickets are a popular, good value option. They are usually valid for a year and include at least three stopovers. Prices can range from £650-£1,500 depending on how many flights the ticket covers. You have to decide in advance which countries you wish to visit and for how long, but there is often a certain degree of flexibility allowing you to

change the dates en route, although a fee will probably be charged for each amendment. Remember, though, that you need to keep travelling in one direction to make these tickets worthwhile. So choose your final destination then pick some interesting places to visit on your outward and return journeys. RTW tickets are reassuring to those who like everything planned and paid for in advance, but if you want the freedom to change your mind at the last minute, then this kind of ticket may be too inflexible. Another popular type of air ticket is one with an open jaw facility, which means you can enter a country or continent by one airport and leave by another.

Wherever you travel by air, don't forget to re-confirm your flight booking at least 72 hours before departure. Phone the airline and make sure you're booked onto the flight - there's nothing worse than checking in to find your seat's been given to someone else and the plane's full. If you're only staying a couple of weeks it's worth re-confirming your return flight at the airport as soon as you arrive. Another thing to bear in mind is that many countries charge airport tax, so keep enough currency to pay the tax when you leave.
The following companies specialise in student/youth or long haul travel:

Campus Travel - offices on university campuses throughout Britain, including a student travel centre at 52 Grosvenor Gardens, London SW1W 0AG ✆ 0171-730 3402 (Europe) ✆ 0171-730 2101 (North America) or ✆ 0171-730 8111 (worldwide) ✆ http://www.campustravel.co.uk. Their sister organisation across the Irish Sea is USIT, with main offices at Fountain Centre, Belfast BT1 6ET ✆ Belfast (01232) 324073, and at

Aston Quay, O'Connell Bridge, Dublin 2 ✆ Dublin (1) 778117.

Council Travel, a travel division of the Council on International Educational Exchange, with over 50 offices worldwide, specialises in student, youth and budget travel. Services offered include discounted airfares, budget accommodation, adventure tours and travel insurance. The London office is at 28A Poland Street, London W1V 3DB ✆ 0171-287 3337 for European reservations or ✆ 0171-437 7767 for reservations worldwide.

North-South Travel, Moulsham Mill, Parkway, Chelmsford, Essex CM2 7PX ✆ Chelmsford (01245) 492882 was founded with the aim of combining a personal and efficient travel service with a commitment of profits to charity. It arranges competitively priced, reliably planned flights to many destinations. All profits are given to projects in the developing world.

STA Travel's London branches are at 86 Old Brompton Road, London SW7 3LQ and 117 Euston Road, London NW1 2SX. Also offices in Aberdeen, Bristol, Birmingham, Cambridge, Glasgow, Leeds, Manchester, Newcastle and Oxford and over 100 offices worldwide. ✆ 0171-361 6161 (Europe), ✆ 0171-361 6262 (worldwide), ✆ 0171-361 6160 (accommodation and insurance). 🌐 http://www.futurenet.co.uk/statravel.

Trailfinders have a Travel Centre at 42-50 Earls Court Road, London W8 6FT ✆ 0171-938 3366 and another branch at 194 Kensington High Street, London W8 7RG ✆ 0171-938 3939 which has a travellers' library, bookshop and information centre, a visa service and an immunisation centre for overseas travel

vaccinations. Branches also in Birmingham, Bristol, Manchester and Glasgow.

Customs If you are going to spend some time abroad you should be aware of the Customs regulations governing all the countries you will be visiting and what you may bring back into your home country. Australia, for example, has strict quarantine regulations covering the importation of foodstuffs. A good country guidebook or a brochure from the relevant tourist office will be able to advise on the regulations applying to the country you intend to visit. Full details of UK Customs regulations are given in the *Customs Public Notices* available from Customs & Excise local offices or from Customs at ports and airports in the UK. There are prohibitions and restrictions on the importation of certain goods ranging from drugs and weapons to foodstuffs and plants. Further information may be obtained from local Customs enquiry offices or from HM Customs & Excise Advice Centre, Dorset House, Stamford Street, London SE1 9NG ✆ 0171-202 4227.

Money It's obviously important to work out how much money you'll need. The exact amount will depend on a variety of factors, including the services already covered in any fee levied by the placement organisation, the cost of living in the country you will be visiting, and the total length of time you will be away, including what proportion of this period will be spent travelling rather than on placement. The organisation should be able to advise on how much money to take to cover expenses. If you are going to be in paid employment you will need some money to live on until your first pay day; this need only be pocket money if food and accommodation are being found for you. On the other hand, you may have to pay for your board, lodging and other needs, and you may be paid monthly, not weekly. If you're undertaking voluntary work in a remote location, with food and accommodation provided, a small amount of pocket money may be enough to cover your needs. However, it is advisable to have sufficient funds spare to cover unforeseen circumstances. A good guide is to ensure you have enough spare to pay for one or two nights' accommodation and a few long-distance phone calls. If you do run out of money it is possible to arrange for funds to be transferred from the UK to a bank abroad, but this may take several days and bank charges can be expensive.

The most secure way of taking large amounts of money abroad is to use travellers' cheques. When obtaining these from a bank or travel agency you'll generally need to give a few days' notice and produce your passport. Shop around beforehand to compare commission rates charged. Try and get a variety of small and large denominations - you may not want to cash a £100 cheque if you're only staying in a country for a couple of days. Read carefully any instructions given, particularly with regard to signing cheques and keeping a note of the numbers. Some travellers' cheques can be replaced while you are still abroad, others will be honoured by the issuing bank on your return. If you have a current bank account you will probably be able to obtain a supply of Eurocheques and a cheque card. These can be cashed at most European banks and in many cases are accepted by shops and restaurants.

You'll need to carry some local currency, obtainable at major travel agents and banks - but shop around for the best exchange rates. If you're doing a lot of travelling around different countries it's also a good idea to take a supply of US dollars as this is the most widely accepted currency abroad. And don't forget to take some of your own currency with you for use on the outward and return journeys. Credit cards are very useful items to have when travelling, but may not be accepted everywhere. It's best not to use your card for everyday expenses, otherwise you may come to rely on it, so leave your flexible friend for emergencies or for the occasional luxury. It's worth crediting your account before you go or arranging to pay your monthly bill by standing order or direct debit.

Passports If you intend to travel far or if you plan to do any work abroad, then you will need a full UK passport. This is valid for 10 years and costs £15. Application forms are available at main post offices; completed forms can be sent or taken to your regional passport office (see below). Applications take at least four weeks to process, and can take longer during the summer months and over Christmas; a good guide is to apply at least 3 months in advance.

Passport Office, Clive House, 70-78 Petty France, London SW1H 9HD

Passport Office, 5th Floor, India Buildings, Water Street, Liverpool L2 0QZ

Passport Office, Olympia House, Upper Dock Street, Newport, Gwent NP9 1XA

Passport Office, Aragon Court, Northminster Road, Peterborough, Cambridgeshire PE1 1QG

Passport Office, 3 Northgate, 96 Milton
Street, Cowcaddens, Glasgow G4 0BT
© 0141-332 0271

Passport Office, Hampton House, 47-53
High Street, Belfast BT1 2QS

For further information © 0990
210410. If you plan to travel through
a lot of countries, make sure you have
enough blank pages in your passport
for all the entry and exit stamps. For
£27 you can get a 48 page British
passport instead of the usual 30 page
one. Some countries have entry
regulations that stipulate a minimum
passport validity of six months, so
don't travel on a passport that's
running out.

If your passport is lost or stolen while
abroad, the local police should be
notified immediately, and if necessary
the nearest British embassy or
consulate will issue a substitute. It is
therefore wise to keep a separate
note of your passport number.

Visas For entry into some countries
a visa or visitor's pass is required, and
in many countries a work and/or
residence permit may be necessary
depending on how long you plan to
stay and whether you will be working.
Organisations arranging placements in
such countries will be able to advise,
and details of application procedures
are available from the consular section
of the relevant embassy. Entry and
work regulations vary considerably,
particularly outside the European
Union, and it is advisable to apply
early to the relevant embassy or
consulate as it may take some time to
obtain the proper documentation.
Some countries will issue different
types of visa depending on how much
travelling you will be doing: tourist
visas allow you to enter the country
once only and stay for a certain length
of time; re-entry visas allow you to
make a return visit; and multiple-entry
visas allow you to return more than
once within a specified period. Some
travel companies, such as Trailfinders,
will arrange visas for you for a small
charge. Contact the Trailfinders Visa
Service on © 0171-938 3848.

Identity & concessionary cards
The International Student Identity
Card (ISIC) provides internationally
accepted proof of student status and
consequently ensures many special
facilities including fare reductions,
cheap accommodation, reduced rates
or free entry to museums, art
galleries and historic sites. Obtainable
from official student travel offices,
students' unions and by mail order,
the card is available to all full-time
students, along with a copy of the *ISIC
Handbook*. The card costs £5 and is
valid for up to 15 months:
1 September-31 December of the
following year. For a further £8, a
Travelsave stamp gives card holders
reductions of up to 50% on rail and
coach travel within Ireland and on
certain ferry services to Ireland. To
get an ISIC card you'll need to prove
you're a full-time student, so don't
wait until you've left college/university.

The FIYTO (Federation of
International Youth Travel
Organisations) International Youth
Card is a recognised card offering
concessions to young travellers
including transport, accommodation,
restaurants, excursions, cultural
events and reduced rates or free
entry to many museums, art galleries,
theatres and cinemas. The card costs
£6 and is valid for one year from date
of issue. Available to all those aged
12-26, together with a booklet giving
details of concessions. Available in the
UK from Campus Travel offices
(London office: 52 Grosvenor

Gardens, London SWIW 0AG
© 0171-730 3402).

European Youth Cards are
concessionary cards issued by a
number of youth agencies, entitling
holders to a range of discounts and
special offers on travel, cultural events
and goods in high street shops in 22
European countries. Cards are
renewable annually, and holders
receive a directory of discounters and
a regular magazine informing them of
new discounts and activities. The
cards are obtainable from the
following organisations:

England and Wales: Under 26 Card
available from Under 26, 52
Grosvenor Gardens, London SWIW
0AG © 0171-823 5363. Cost £7.

Scotland: Young Scot Card available
from the Scottish Community
Education Council, Rosebery House,
9 Haymarket Terrace, Edinburgh EH12
5EZ © 0131-313 2488. Cost £7.

Northern Ireland: European Youth
Card available from USIT, Fountain
Centre, Belfast BT1 6ET © Belfast
(01232) 324073, and other USIT
offices. Cost £7.

Ireland: European Youth Card available
from USIT, Aston Quay, O'Connell
Bridge, Dublin 2 © Dublin (1) 778117,
and other USIT offices. Cost IR£6.

Health Changes in food and climate
may cause minor illnesses, and,
especially when visiting the hotter
countries of southern Europe, North
Africa, Latin America and the Far East
it is wise to take extra care in your
hygiene, eating and drinking habits.
Native bacteria, to which local
inhabitants are immune, may cause the
visitor stomach upsets, so it is worth
trying to avoid drinking tap water if

you can help it. In a hot climate you
should never underestimate the
strength of the sun, nor overestimate
your own strength. Drink plenty of
fluids, make sure there is enough salt
in your diet, wear loose-fitting cotton
clothes, even a hat, and guard against
heat exhaustion, heat stroke and
sunburn.

In the UK the Department of Health
issues leaflet *T5 Health Advice for
Travellers*, available from post offices,
travel agents, libraries and doctors'
surgeries or © 0800 555 777. Also
available on Ceefax pages 564-569 and
on Prestel, to which most travel
agents have access. This includes
details of vaccinations, other
measures that can be taken to protect
one's health, information on rabies,
AIDS, malaria and other diseases.
There is also advice on types of food
and on water supplies which may be a
source of infection. Even if you are
not planning to spend time abroad,
you should make sure that you have
an anti-tetanus injection if you are
going to be involved in any type of
manual outdoor work such as
construction work, gardening, an
archaeological dig or a conservation
project. Make sure any cuts or grazes
are covered with a plaster before you
start doing outdoor work, especially if
you will be working in ponds, ditches,
rivers or lakes where cuts may
become infected.

A certificate of vaccination against
certain diseases is an entry
requirement for some countries. The
organisation arranging your placement
should be able to advise you, or you
can consult the relevant embassy, as
such requirements are continually
subject to review. As a general rule it
is wise to make sure that your
protection against typhoid, polio and
tetanus is up-to-date if you are

travelling outside Europe, North America or Australasia. Up-to-the-minute printouts indicating the immunisations and malaria tablets appropriate for any specific journey are available from the Medical Advisory Service to Travellers Abroad (MASTA). By calling them on 0891 224100 you can leave a recorded message listing countries you will be visiting, the month of arrival in each, and the living conditions (rural, towns, cities, business, tourist). The required information will be sent by return; calls are charged at 45p/50p a minute (cheap rate/other times). MASTA printouts are available without charge for those attending British Airways travel clinics; for details of the clinic nearest to you call (01276) 685040. Remember that protection against some diseases takes the form of a course of injections over several weeks, so allow plenty of time.

Whilst abroad it is unwise to have your skin pierced by acupuncture, tattooing or ear piercing, for example, unless you can be sure that the equipment is sterile. A major cause of the spread of viruses, including AIDS and Hepatitis B, is the use of infected needles and equipment. In some countries blood for transfusions is not screened for the presence of the AIDS virus, but there may be arrangements for obtaining screened blood. The doctor treating you, or the nearest British consulate or embassy may be able to offer advice.

If you are concerned about the availability of sterile equipment whilst abroad, emergency travel kits are available through MASTA, see above, and other suppliers, and can be ordered through retail pharmacists. They contain a variety of sterilised and sealed items for use in emergencies. MASTA also has a range of health care items such as mosquito nets and water purifiers; available mail order © 0171-631 4408. Trebova Medical Student and Junior Doctor Supplies, 7 Burton Close, Gustard Wood, Wheathampstead, Hertfordshire AL4 8LU © Kimpton (01438) 832661 ☎ (01582) 831155 also provides a range of medical packs containing sterile equipment that can be given to medically qualified staff in the event of an emergency. The packs contain equipment recommended by doctors who are experienced in travelling to remote locations and by the Department of Health.

Wherever you are planning to travel, don't forget to have a thorough check-up with your doctor and dentist well before you leave. It is also essential to inform the placement organisation (or anyone else who will have responsibility for you) if you are taking medication or if you have a medical condition such as asthma, epilepsy or any particular allergies. If you wear spectacles or contact lenses, it's a good idea to take a prescription with you in case you need to get replacements.

Drugs If you are taking prescribed drugs it is advisable to carry a doctor's letter giving details of the medical condition and the medication, thus avoiding any possibility of confusion. It will also be useful to find out the generic rather than the brand name of the medicine, so that if need arises further supplies can be obtained abroad.

Any prescribed drugs, anti-malaria tablets, painkillers, pills or potions that you feel you need should be packed in a clearly marked first aid box so as to avoid questions from suspicious Customs officials. If you are prescribed any tablets or medicine when overseas it may not be legal to bring them back into Britain; if in doubt, declare the drugs at Customs when you return.

Don't assume you will be let off if you are caught buying or possessing small amounts of controlled or illegal drugs abroad. Penalties can be severe, even for so-called soft drugs, and may also involve lengthy detention before trial without any chance of bail. Keep an eye on your luggage whilst travelling, and don't let anyone tamper with it. Don't agree to carry anyone else's bags or drive someone's car over the border. In some countries possessing or selling alcoholic drinks may also carry a heavy penalty.

Reciprocal health agreements
You are only covered by the NHS whilst in the UK, and may therefore be expected to pay the full costs of any treatment abroad. However, there are health care arrangements between all countries in the European Economic Area (EEA) - Austria, Belgium, Britain, Denmark, Finland, France, Germany, Greece, Iceland, Ireland, Italy, Liechtenstein, Luxembourg, Netherlands, Norway, Portugal, Spain and Sweden.
British citizens resident in the UK will receive free or reduced cost emergency treatment in other EEA countries on production of form *E111,* included inside leaflet *T5 Health Advice for Travellers,* see above.
This leaflet explains who is covered by the arrangements, what treatment is free or at reduced cost, and gives the procedures to be followed to get treatment in countries where form *E111* is not needed (usually Austria, Denmark, Finland, Ireland, Norway and Portugal). Form *E111* must be taken abroad and, if treatment is needed, the correct procedures must be followed.

There are also reciprocal health care arrangements between Britain and Australia, Barbados, Bulgaria, Channel Islands, Czech and Slovak Republics, Gibraltar, Hong Kong, Hungary, Isle of Man, Malta, New Zealand, Poland, Romania, Russia, former republics of the USSR (except Estonia, Latvia and Lithuania), the former Yugoslavia and the British Dependent Territories of Anguilla, British Virgin Islands, Falkland Islands, Montserrat, St Helena, and Turks and Caicos Islands. However, private health insurance may still be needed in these countries; leaflet *T5* gives full details.

Despite reciprocal arrangements it is still essential to take out full medical insurance whenever travelling overseas. The health treatment available in other countries may not be as comprehensive as in the UK, and none of the arrangements listed above cover the cost of repatriation in the event of illness.

Insurance You must find out from the organisation arranging your placement whether they provide insurance cover against risk of accident, illness and possible disability. Many organisations either include insurance cover in the placement fee or can arrange it at additional cost. It is important to ascertain exactly what is included in the cover offered, as frequently it is limited to third party risk and accidents. It is up to you to decide exactly what extent of insurance cover you require. A typical insurance package should cover cancellation and delay, medical and emergency travel expenses, personal accident, loss of luggage and money, and personal liability. If you are planning to work abroad as well as travel it is wise to inform the insurance company of your plans. Some travel insurance policies are for holiday purposes only and will not cover accidents at work. The same applies for some sports such as white water rafting or skiing. However, the company may be prepared to extend the cover for an additional fee if you can inform them in advance what sort of work or activity you will be undertaking.

The International Student Insurance Service (ISIS) policy is a leading policy for young travellers and provides, at competitive rates, a wide range of benefits covering death, disablement, medical and other personal expenses, loss of luggage, personal liability and cancellation, loss of deposits or curtailment. An advantage of this policy is that medical expenses can be settled on the spot in many countries by student organisations cooperating with ISIS. A 24-hour assistance service is provided to handle all medical emergencies. Details in the UK from local Endsleigh Insurance centres.

The Patrick Leigh Travel Insurance Agency, PO Box 984, Lewes, Sussex BN8 6RW © Lewes (01273) 858536 provides insurance cover to pay for an economy round trip air ticket should a family member or person close to you fall very seriously ill in the UK. A 24 hour emergency telephone service can arrange a booking on the next available flight home. Also provides an extremely cheap travel insurance policy, premium £107 (6 months), £215 (12 months). It protects your baggage and money and pays for any medical expenses, amongst many other benefits.

Baggage If you plan to be doing a lot of travelling, then you are likely to be carting your belongings around with you, especially if you're going independently. Most first-time

travellers say they took far too much - a good rule of thumb therefore, is to pack what you think you'll need, and then halve it! Or try walking a mile carrying your pack - you'll soon know if there's too much in it. Use a travel bag or rucksack for most of your belongings, a smaller day pack for hand luggage and a money belt, neck purse or bum bag for smaller, essential items that you want to have on your person at all times. Remember to remove all the old airport stickers from your bags, case or rucksack, as these can cause confusion and may result in your luggage going astray.

Take clothes which are hard wearing and easy to care for, and don't forget to leave space for presents and souvenirs. If you're travelling through various climates think about forwarding heavy, warm clothes to a *poste restante* address to pick up when you arrive, and posting them back home when you no longer need them. Even if you're travelling to a hot country, it's wise to take some warm clothes for cool evenings. Respect local customs: shorts and skimpy tops may not be acceptable in some countries, particularly if you are going to be visiting churches or other sacred monuments. For women, a sarong is a very useful lightweight item that can be used as a long skirt, a beach towel or worn over the shoulders to protect from the sun.

The following items take up little room and are likely to come in useful:

Universal plug for hostel sinks or baths that don't have them.
String, to hang your washing on or do emergency repairs.
Pocket torch and batteries.
Basic first aid kit, eg plasters, cotton wool, antiseptic cream, insect

repellant, sun block, aspirin,
contraceptives.
Alarm clock.
Notebook and pen.
Sunglasses.
Maps.
Light waterproof.
Small towel.
Torch.
Water bottle.
Flip-flops.
Driving licence.
Phrase book.
Little presents such as postcards of
your home town etc.
Photos of your family to show local
people.
Spare passport photos.
Toilet paper/tissues.
Padlock and key, useful in
guesthouses/hostels if you want to
leave belongings in your room.
Small sewing kit.
Swiss army knife.
Sleeping bag, a simple sheet one may
be all you need for hot countries.

Packing everything in individual plastic
bags not only helps keep things dry
but also keeps your rucksack tidy.
Whatever you decide to pack, try to
keep the following items separate and
with you at all times, and let some
one responsible back home have
copies of them in case they need to
send them to you or refer to them:

Copies of the relevant pages of your
passport (number and personal
details).
Travellers' cheque numbers.
Copy of insurance policy.
Copy of your air tickets.
Emergency phone numbers
(insurance, credit cards, etc).
Contact address and phone number of
placement organisation or anyone
with responsibility for you abroad.
Your itinerary (where you're supposed
to be, and when).

Problems Thorough research and
preparation should help minimise the
chances of anything going seriously
wrong during your travels and there
are a number of precautions you can
take once you are abroad to avoid
potentially dangerous situations. For
example, if you know you are going to
be arriving late in a country, it is
advisable to reserve accommodation
in advance and to work out how you
are going to get to it. Plan to spend a
little more on your first night, for
example on decent accommodation
and perhaps a journey from the
airport in a licensed cab; of course,
once you have got to grips with the
locality in the daylight you can get to
work on finding cheaper options.

It's also essential to have adequate
insurance. Shop around and check
what exactly is offered by different
policies; the one that is most suited to
your needs, may not be the cheapest
(see Insurance).

If you are considering an organised
programme or scheme and are
concerned about the credibility of the
organisation running it, ask to be put
in touch with people who have taken
part in previous years so that you can
get a clear idea of what is involved,
how the activity is organised and
whether it is right for you. Any
reputable organisation shouldn't have
any qualms about putting you in touch
with former participants. If, during
your time abroad you encounter
problems or difficulties, or if the
activities or duties don't meet your
expectations, contact the sending
organisation or its local representative
in the host country in the first
instance. As part of the predeparture
briefing you should be provided with
information on what to do in an

emergency and who to contact and many organisations offer a 24-hour helpline for participants.

If you are travelling independently make sure that someone back home knows about your plans, where you are hoping to be and when, and touch base regularly to let them know that you are OK. If you do encounter difficulties, a good insurance policy should cover you for most eventualities and some credit cards offer rescue services or 24-hour helplines for their users.

Many countries, particularly in Europe, offer information and advisory services for young people which can give advice on securing safe accommodation, finding work and getting around. It's also a good idea when you arrive in a country to check how you can contact the emergency services. A good guide book, such as those published by Lonely Planet or Rough Guides, should cover this essential information.

British citizens should note that there are consular offices at British Embassies in foreign capitals and at Consulates in some provincial cities. Consuls maintain a list of English-speaking doctors and will advise or help in cases of serious difficulty or distress. However, embassies and consulates cannot not help in finding work, they cannot provide money (except in certain specific emergencies), telex or telephone facilities, interpreting or legal advice services, or pay bills, whether legal, medical, hotel, travel or any other debts. As a last resort a consul can arrange for a direct return to the UK by the cheapest possible route, providing the person concerned

agrees to have her/his passport withdrawn and gives written confirmation that s/he will pay the travel expenses involved.

The organisation arranging your placement must be your first contact should any problems arise. However, if any dire emergency occurs whilst you are travelling independently then you should contact the British Consul. There are consular offices at British Embassies in foreign capitals and at consulates in some provincial cities. Consuls maintain a list of English-speaking doctors and will advise or help in case of serious difficulty or distress. As a last resort a consul can arrange for a direct return to the UK by the cheapest possible passage, providing the person concerned agrees to have their passport withdrawn and gives written agreement that they will pay the travel expenses involved. The telegraphic address of all British Embassies is *Prodrome* and of all British Consulates *Britain*, followed in each case by the name of the appropriate town.

If you lose your ticket at the last minute, you should contact the airline/shipping company/tour operator immediately to see if a replacement can be issued. If luggage is lost during a flight and does not turn up on arrival, the duty officer of the airline concerned should be informed immediately. If the luggage cannot be traced, a claim form must be completed. Most airlines will immediately provide a small payment to cover necessities, but they are under no obligation to do so, and the amount varies considerably from airline to airline. This payment does not usually have to be repaid if the luggage is traced. If after 3-4 weeks the luggage still has not been found, compensation will be paid by the airline according to the declaration made on the claim form. In any event, and to cover loss on other means of transport, it is advisable to take out a personal insurance policy which covers luggage loss. Any losses should of course be reported to the insurance company concerned.

Culture shock If you're going to be staying in a foreign country, experiencing a totally different lifestyle and culture, then you may well experience culture shock. This is a real phenomenon, can happen to anyone, but if you're prepared you can deal with it and it will pass.

At the beginning of your stay, although you may miss your home environment, you are likely to find everything very new and exciting, and you'll spend perhaps the first month or so on a high. As the excitement fades, you may experience anxiety, tiredness, irritability, depression and homesickness. The stresses of working hard to communicate in another language, trying to decipher a difficult accent, making an effort to be polite and adapt to what may seem an alien culture, will all combine to get you down. You will probably feel that your mood has been brought on by other people: *you've* been making every effort to be flexible and courteous, it's just all these foreigners who are making life difficult for you. You'll wonder why you ever came to the country. You may even want to get on the next plane home.

This low point, which can last up to 3 weeks or more, is all the worse considering the excitement you felt when you first arrived. The best way

of dealing with culture shock is firstly to expect it to happen - if it doesn't, then count yourself lucky.

Try to stand back from your feelings and realise what is happening to you and why. It *is* tiring to communicate in a different language, and coming to terms with another culture can be really difficult, as it challenges beliefs, customs and codes of conduct that you've been absorbing and accepting since birth. So it's only natural for you to feel stressed, but do your best not to give in to negative feelings. View it as a positive experience - at least it means that you are starting to become aware of cultural differences. Relax, learn to accept the ways of life of your new country, without forgetting your own. As you become more attuned to your new environment, so the culture shock will pass.

Prepare yourself If you're travelling to a country where the language is not your own, then make the effort to learn at least a few words of their language. It's only polite after all; people will appreciate the gesture and it can help to break the ice. Find out as much as you can about the culture of the host country. A good way to gain a cultural insight is to read novels written by local authors; guidebooks such as *Rough Guides* and *Lonely Planet* books often have recommended reading lists. Try to talk to natives of the country before you leave; are there any studying at your school or university, or could you get in touch with a local immigrant community or refugee group?

Most people are keen to talk about their home country - they may even be able to put you in touch with people to visit out there.

Do some research into codes of behaviour and dress - in some countries, for example, it is considered offensive to expose too much of the body, and bare arms or legs may be frowned upon. You might be expected to show respect to the national flag, or stand up when the national anthem is played. Be prepared to cover your head and/or remove footwear when entering a place of worship.

Find out more about your own country. You may feel that you know all about it already, but then you might be surprised how many questions you will be asked about your home life and about current affairs - they may be better-informed, no matter how far away their country is. If you have room, pack a few newspapers or current affairs magazines, take postcards of your local area and photographs of your family and friends.

Keep in touch Your parents will be understandably concerned about you travelling, especially if it is the first time you will be spending any real length of time away from home or outside your own country. Be sure and include them in all your plans and preparations; tell them why you want to go and what you know about the placement and the countries you will be visiting.

Before you leave, establish some lines of communication. They should know how to contact the agency placing you, and have at least an initial contact address for you overseas, if not a complete timetable of where you will be and when. Find out how long post will take to reach them from the country you'll be visiting, and whether phone or fax communication is a practical option. If you don't yet have an overseas address, post offices will hold, usually for up to one month, any letters or parcels clearly marked for the receiver's attention and with the words *poste restante*. To claim mail, the receiver has to produce identification.

Do write home. It doesn't have to be pages of purple prose; in fact the odd scribbled postcard every few days might be far more reassuring than a fat letter that takes ages to write and even longer to arrive. Warn your parents about culture shock (see above) as your letters or cards are likely to reflect low points as well as highlights. If you do feel blue, put a bit of humour and balance into your letters, and try to resist phoning home to pour out your woes. In a couple of weeks you'll probably feel more positive, so there's no point worrying people who are thousands of miles away and unable to help! Don't exaggerate or sensationalise things, it will only cause more anxiety at home: two days of the runs is *not* dysentery and a cockroach on your hotel room floor does *not* constitute an infestation! Finally, when you're having a whale of a time with all the new friends you've made, try and find 10 minutes in your fun-packed day to drop your folks (and everybody else who helped you to have, and fund, your year out) a line and let them know.

INDEX

COUNTRIES INDEX

REPORT FORM

Up-to-date reports enable us to improve the accuracy of information in our guides, and monitor the opportunities available. After you have undertaken a year between project or placement, the completion and return of this form to the Publications Unit, Central Bureau for Educational Visits & Exchanges, 10 Spring Gardens, London SW1A 2BN, would be much appreciated. **All reports will be treated in strict confidence.**

Name and address of organisation

How efficient were they in arranging the project/placement?

Type of project/placement

Where were you placed?

How long did the placement last?

Salary/terms of employment (where applicable)

PLEASE TURN OVER

If you paid a placement fee, did you consider it justifiable?

Were food and accommodation provided?

Age range of other participants

Nationality of any other participants

Were your expectations achieved?

In what way do you think the experience was particularly beneficial?

Name
Address

Age   Signed   Date